THE ARMS RACE AT A TIME OF DECISION

THE ARMS RACE AT A TIME OF DECISION

DECISION

Annals of Pugwash 1983

Edited by
Joseph Rotblat and Alessandro Pascolini

Foreword by Dorothy Hodgkin

St. Martin's Press   New York

All rights reserved. For information, write:
St. Martin's Press, Inc., 175 Fifth Avenue, New York, NY 10010
Printed in Great Britain
Published in the United Kingdom by The Macmillan Press Ltd.
First published in the United States of America in 1984

ISBN 0-312-04950-1
Library of Congress Catalog Card Number 84-40288

CONTENTS

Part One. Space Militarisation: Stabilising and Destabilising Aspects

Part Two. Strategic Nuclear Arms Race

Part Three. Security in Europe

Part Four. Problems of Regional Security

Part Five. Security-Related Third World Problems

FOREWORD

Dorothy Hodgkin

Ever since the first atom bomb was dropped on Hiroshima the danger of nuclear war has been growing - not regularly, but continuously; there have been periods of slowing down, often followed by moments of sharp escalation. Today the arsenals of the great powers are larger than ever before, the weapons more rapid and more accurate in action. We also know today far better than we did in 1945 how catastrophic the effects of an all-out nuclear war could be. To the local terrible destruction observed long ago, and magnified as it would be now, we must add world-wide effects from radioactive fall-out and darkness over the surface of the globe produced by clouds of dust which might lead to the disappearance of many kinds of living systems.

Against these dangers we place the growing hope that people everywhere will realise before it is too late that to make the world safe it is necessary not only to abandon nuclear weapons but to abolish war. In an earlier moment of realisation President Eisenhower said 'Some day, the demand for disarmament by hundred of millions will, I hope, become so universal and so insistent that no man, no nation, can withstand it.' At the time these words were spoken, there were already many people taking part in demonstrations in favour of a ban on all testing of nuclear weapons - we used to say hundreds in the United Kingdom, thousands in Germany, hundreds of thousands in Japan. Today the numbers supporting disarmament are much larger, running into millions in the United States, while from the east over a hundred million signatures supported the petition presented by the Soviet Union to the United Nations Special Session on Disarmament of 1978.

All the same, to effect the fundamental changes in the attitudes of the nations to one another, needed to secure peace, is a slow process; still greater efforts need to be made by still more people. We have to be concerned with many different aspects of the world situation: the causes of

ix

conflicts both between and within nations; the contrast between the needs of the very poor in both developing and developed countries and the enormous sums spent on arms; the concentration of scientific manpower on weapons research which hinders the use of science for human well being; arms control and disarmament seen as a means not only to peace but also to plenty.

These are the essential purposes, the essential topics of the Pugwash Conferences on Science and World Affairs which have been held since 1957. They began with a small nucleus of scientists from east and west meeting to discuss ways to reduce nuclear confrontation, and to establish a firm basis of understanding. Over the years the number of participants has increased, other nations have joined the first few and the subjects under discussion have broadened as many experts in related fields have come to the meetings. When we looked back, we found that the recorded discussion at the first Pugwash Conference (there were no prepared papers) was still very relevant today – on the dangers of the use of nuclear weapons, the characteristics and limitations of deterrence, the responsibilities of scientists. This has encouraged us to feel that some of the papers we discuss each year at our meetings would be useful to a wider audience interested in our common aims.

The least that this first volume of the Annals of Pugwash can achieve is to demonstrate the reality of cooperation within our conferences in the search for a safer world between scientists from East, West, North and South.

PREFACE

1983 was the year of vital decisions likely to affect the fate of mankind. In March of that year President Reagan announced a new policy, popularly described as 'Star Wars', which - if implemented - would extend the nuclear arms race into space and create new areas of conflict and confrontation. At the end of the year, NATO began to implement its decision to deploy Pershing II and Cruise missiles in Europe: this has led to the breakdown of negotiations in Geneva to reduce both strategic and intermediate range nuclear forces, and to the start of a new spiral in the arms race. Throughout the year, hostilities in the Middle East drew in more nations, with the threat of even wider escalation of the conflict. All these events have markedly increased the risk of nuclear war.

These various issues have been debated in several meetings organised by Pugwash in 1983, the most notable of which was the 33rd Annual Conference held in Venice at the end of August. The main work of the Conference was carried out in Working Groups, each of which discussed a specific topic, the discussion being generally based on invited and proferred papers by the participants. This volume contains most of the invited and some of the proferred papers of the Venice Conference plus three papers from other meetings as mentioned below. The division of the material into five parts corresponds roughly to the Working Groups at the Conference.

Part One is concerned with the two opposing aspects of space militarisation, stabilising and destabilising. It is supplemented by the report from a Pugwash Symposium held in October 1982, in Versailles, on the role which an International Agency for Satellite Observation could play in stabilising the world situation.

Part Two deals with the central problem of the evolution of the strategic nuclear arms race. It examines its technical and military aspects, and attempts to make a realistic assessment of the likelihood of reaching an agreement which

would reduce the probability of a nuclear war. The last paper
links the global security issues with the specific European
problem which is the theme of the next part of the book.

Part Three is devoted to the various aspects of European
security, nuclear and conventional, military and non-
military. Chapter 14 is a paper discussed at a Pugwash Workshop on Nuclear Forces in Europe, held in June 1983 in
Geneva. The paper of Chapter 16 was presented at a Pugwash
Symposium on a nuclear weapon-free zone in the Balkans, held
in October 1983 in Bucharest.

Part Four continues the debate on security problems but
extends it to several other sensitive regions. Special attention is given to the situation in the Middle East and the
Mediterranean area, and to non-proliferation issues arising
from it. The Tlatelolco Treaty is described in detail to
illustrate what can be achieved.

Part Five - although the security of the Third World is
specifically mentioned in its title - covers in fact wider
ground. It links the problems of the Third World with the
topics raised in the earlier parts by analysing the economics
of the arms race, the means of reducing the burden of military expenditure, and the utilisation of resources on projects of benefit to everybody.

Participants in Pugwash meetings come from different geographical and political areas (see notes on contributors) and
the views they express are their own. As will become evident
to the reader of this book, highly divergent opinions are
presented by individual authors on issues which are of great
concern to us all. Some of these opinions are not shared by
the majority of Pugwash scientists, but it is the main purpose of the Pugwash forum to bring together people with
diverse standpoints, listen to their arguments and then try
to reconcile the different approaches and inferences.

It would be unrealistic to expect a consensus to emerge
on all issues discussed; however, some convergence usually
results. It is the task of the Pugwash Council to gather
together the main drift of the debate, define the areas of
agreement (or disagreement) and to formulate the conclusions
in a statement issued to the public. The text of the Council
Statement after the Venice Conference is given as Appendix A.
Appendix B contains background information on the Pugwash
Conferences by the Secretary-General of Pugwash.

We believe that these independent contributions by expert
scholars will be useful to policy-makers as well as to the
concerned members of the community who at present are strongly affected by security issues but lack adequate information.
We hope that this volume will thus contribute towards the
creation of a more secure and less armed world.

Acknowledgments

Most of the papers were specifically written for the Pugwash meetings, but a few are parts of larger works published elsewhere:

An extended version of the paper by John Polanyi (Chapter 1) will appear in Nuclear Weapons vs. Security (Gwyn Prins ed.) to be published by Chatto and Windus.

The paper by Kosta Tsipis (Chapter 7) has been excerpted from a much larger technical report Technical Uncertainties in Countersilo Attacks, by the author and Matthew Bunn, and published as Technical Report No.9 by the Program in Science and Technology for International Security, MIT, Cambridge, Mass.

A larger version of the paper by Lawrence Freedman (Chapter 13) appeared as a chapter in The European Missile Crisis (H.H. Holm & N. Petersen eds, London: Frances Pinter, 1983).

The paper by Maurizio Cremasco (Chapter 22) is a synthesis of a longer paper The Mediterranean Region: Economic Interdependence and the Future of Security (Giacomo Lucinai ed. London: Croom Helm, 1984).

*   *   *   *

In editing this volume we were greatly helped by Dr John Beckman and Professor Patricia Lindop to whom we express our gratitude. We also wish to give our thanks for technical assistance by Jean Egerton, Maggie Hall, Geraldine Youell and, above all, Edith Salt without whose efforts the preparation of the camera-ready copy would not have been accomplished.

Joseph Rotblat
Alessandro Pascolini

NOTES ON THE CONTRIBUTORS

L. ANSELMO (Italy) space physics. Researcher at the National Centre for Electronic Computation (CNUCE), Pisa.

G. ARYA (Thailand) electrical engineering. Professor at the Chulalongkorn University, Bangkok.

N. BEHAR (Bulgaria) international economics. Head of the Economic Department of the Institute of Contemporary Social Studies at the Bulgarian Academy of Sciences, Sofia.

B. BERTOTTI (Italy) space physics and general relativity. Professor of Theoretical Physics at the University of Pavia.

A. BOSERUP (Denmark) peace and conflict research. Professor at the Institute of Sociology, University of Copenhagen.

H.C. CARS (Sweden) economics of military expenditure. Deputy-Director of Planning and Budget, Ministry of Defence, Stockholm.

M. CREMASCO (Italy) international security. Senior Researcher at the Istituto Affari Internazionali, Rome.

M. DOBROSIELSKI (Poland) international relations. Professor at the University of Warsaw; former Vice-Foreign Minister at the Polish Ministry of Foreign Affairs.

V. EMELYANOV (USSR) metallurgy. Corresponding Member of the Soviet Academy of Sciences; former Chairman of the State Committee for Atomic Energy of USSR.

P. FARINELLA (Italy) space physics. Researcher at the Scuola Normale Superiore and at the Department of Mathematics of the University of Pisa.

L. FREEDMAN (UK) international security. Professor of War Studies at King's College, London; former Head of Policy Studies at the Royal Institute of International Affairs.

D. FREI (Switzerland) international relations. Professor of Political Science at the University of Zurich.

S. FREIER (Israel) nuclear physics. Research Worker at the Weizmann Institute of Science; former Head of the Israel Atomic Energy Commission.

E.E. GALAL (Egypt) medical practice and pharmacology. Advisor to the Academy of Science Research and Technology, Cairo.

A. GARCIA-ROBLES (Mexico) international relations. Peace Nobel Laureate. Head of the Mexican Delegation at the United Nations; former Minister for Foreign Affairs of Mexico.

R.L. GARWIN (USA) physics. IBM Fellow and Adjunct Professor of Physics at Columbia University, New York; former member of the President's Scientific Advisory Committee.

K. GOTTSTEIN (FRG) elementary particle physics. Professor of Physics at the Max-Planck Institut für Physik und Astrophysik, Munich.

W. GUTTERIDGE (UK) international relations. Professor of International Studies at the University of Aston in Birmingham.

DOROTHY HODGKIN (UK) crystallography. Chemistry Nobel Laureate. Emeritus Professor of the University of Oxford; President of Pugwash.

M.M. KAPLAN (USA) microbiology. Secretary-General of Pugwash; former Director Research Promotion and Development, World Health Organisation.

C.M. KHAMALA (Kenya) entomology. Chairman of Kenya National Academy for Advancement of Arts and Sciences.

S. LODGAARD (Norway) peace research. Director of European Studies, SIPRI, Stockholm.

J.K. MIETTINEN (Finland), radiochemistry. Professor of Radiochemistry at the University of Helsinki; Chairman of the Finnish Pugwash Group.

I.L. NEDEV (Bulgaria) international relations. Researcher at the 'Lyudmila Zhivhova' International Foundation, Sofia.

R.R. NEILD (UK) economics. Professor of Economics at the University of Cambridge; former Director of SIPRI.

A. PASCOLINI (Italy) theoretical physics. Professor of Mathematical Methods of Physics at the University of Padua; Secretary of the Italian Pugwash Group.

J.C. POLANYI (Canada) physical chemistry. Professor of Chemistry at the University of Toronto.

J. ROTBLAT (UK) physics. Emeritus Professor of Physics at the University of London; Secretary-General of Pugwash 1957–73; Chairman of the British Pugwash Group.

A. SALAM (Pakistan) physics. Physics Nobel Laureate. Professor of Theoretical Physics at the Imperial College of Science and Technology, London; Director of the International Centre for Theoretical Physics, Trieste.

C. SCHAERF (Italy) nuclear physics. Professor of Nuclear Physics at the University of Rome at Tor Vergata; Director of the International School on Disarmament and Research on Conflicts (ISODARCO).

JANE SHARP (USA) political science. Resident Scholar in the Peace Studies Program at Cornell University in Ithaca.

K.S. SUBRAHMANYAM (India) international security. Director of the Institute for Defence Studies and Analyses, New Delhi.

K. TSIPIS (USA) physics. Associate Director of the Program in Science and Technology for International Security at MIT.

E. VELIKHOV (USSR) physics. Vice-President of the Soviet Academy of Sciences; Director of the Kurchatov Institute for Atomic Energy.

V.F. WEISSKOPF (USA) theoretical physics. Emeritus Professor of Physics at MIT; former Director of CERN, Geneva.

M.S. WIONCZEK (Mexico) energy economics. Senior Research Associate in Economics at the University of Mexico.

ACRONYMS

ABM	anti-ballistic missile
ACDA	Arms Control and Disarmament Agency
ALCM	air-launched cruise missile
ASAT	anti-satellite weapon
ASBM	air-to-surface ballistic missile
ASEAN	Association of South-East Asian Nations
ASW	anti-submarine warfare
BMD	ballistic missile defence
C^3	command, control and communications
CBM	confidence-building measures
CDLN	communications and data link network
CEP	circular error probable
C^3I	command, control, communications, and intelligence
CMP	counter military potential
COSPAR	Committee on Space Research
CSCE	Conference on Security and Cooperation in Europe
CTB	comprehensive test ban
DEW	directed energy weapon
EEZ	exclusive economic zone
EMP	electromagnetic pulse
EMT	equivalent megatonnage
ENF	European nuclear force
ERW	enhanced radiation weapon
ESA	European Space Agency
ESC	European Security Conference
FAC	fast attack craft
FBS	forward-based system
GDP	gross domestic product
GEODSS	ground-based electro-optical deep space surveillance
GLCM	ground-launched cruise missile
GNP	gross national product
GPS	global positioning system

xvii

IAEA	International Atomic Energy Agency
IC	industrialised country
ICBM	intercontinental ballistic missile
ICSU	International Council of Scientific Unions
IISS	International Institute for Strategic Studies
INF	intermediate nuclear forces
IRBM	intermediate range ballistic missile
ISMA	International Satellite Monitoring Agency
ISMO	International Satellite Monitoring Organisation
LDC	less developed country
MAD	mutual assured destruction
MARV	manoeuvrable re-entry vehicle
MBFR	mutual and balanced force reductions (NATO name for MFR)
MEECN	minimum essential emergency communications network
MFR	mutual force reduction
MHV	miniature homing vehicle
MIRV	multiple independently targetable re-entry vehicle
MRV	multiple re-entry vehicle
NASA	National Aeronautics and Space Administration
NATO	North Atlantic Treaty Organisation
NAVSTAR	navigation satellite timing and ranging
NORAD	North American Air Defense
NPT	Non-Proliferation Treaty
NTM	national technical means
NWFZ	nuclear weapon-free zone
OAS	Organisation of American States
OAU	Organisation of African Unity
OCC	operations control centre
OECD	Organisation for Economic Cooperation and Development
PGM	precision-guided munition
PNE	peaceful nuclear explosion
R & D	research and development
RDF	rapid deployment force
RV	re-entry vehicle
SALT	Strategic Arms Limitation Talks
SEATO	South-East Asia Treaty Organisation
SIPRI	Stockholm International Peace Research Institute
SLBM	submarine-launched ballistic missile
SLCM	sea-launched cruise missile
START	Strategic Arms Reduction Talks
UNISPACE	United Nations Conferences on the Exploration and Peaceful Uses of Outer Space
UNSSOD	United Nations Special Session on Disarmament
WTO	Warsaw Treaty Organisation

GLOSSARY

Accuracy

The ability of a warhead to hit near its intended aim point, usually measured in terms of the probability of hitting within a distance (CEP) from that point.

Anti-ballistic missile (ABM) system

Weapon system for intercepting and destroying ballistic missiles.

Anti-satellite (ASAT) system

Weapon system for destroying, damaging or disturbing the normal function of artificial satellites.

Anti-submarine warfare (ASW)

The detection, identification, tracking, and destruction of hostile submarines.

Ballistic missile

Missile which follows a ballistic trajectory when thrust is terminated.

Circular error probable (CEP)

A measure of weapon delivery system accuracy: the radius of a circle, centred on the target, within which 50 per cent of the weapons aimed at the target are expected to fall.

Command control and communications (C^3)

The system for authorising and transmitting to the missile the command to launch.

Counterforce attack

Attack directed against military targets.

Countersilo capability

The ability of a missile warhead to destroy a hardened ballistic missile silo.

Countervalue attack

Attack directed against civilian targets.

Cruise missile

Missile which can fly at very low altitudes along programmed paths. It can be air-, ground- or sea-launched and carry a conventional or a nuclear warhead.

Deterrence

The ability to prevent another nation from acting in a hostile manner.

Directed energy weapon (DEW)

Weapon system based on the delivery on the target of destructive energy in the form of a beam of light or of particles with nearly the speed of light.

Enhanced radiation weapon (ERW)

Nuclear explosive device designed to maximise radiation effects and reduce blast and thermal effects.

First-strike capability

Capability to destroy within a very short period of time all or a very substantial portion of an adversary's strategic forces.

Fission

Process whereby the nucleus of a heavy atom splits into lighter nuclei with the release of substantial amounts of energy.

Flexible response capability

Capability to react to an attack with a full range of military options, including a limited use of nuclear weapons.

Fratricide effect

The destruction or degradation of the accuracy and effectiveness of an attacking nuclear weapon by a nearby explosion of another attacking nuclear weapon.

| Fusion | Process whereby light atoms, especially those of the isotopes of hydrogen- deuterium and tritium - combine to form a heavy atom with the release of very substantial amounts of energy. |

Gross domestic product (GDP) The GNP minus transactions with other countries.

Gross national product (GNP) Annual total value of goods produced and services provided in a country.

Intercontinental ballistic missile (ICBM) Ballistic missile with a range in excess of 5500 km.

Intermediate nuclear forces (INF) US designation for long-range and possibly medium-range theatre nuclear weapons. See also: Theatre nuclear weapons.

Kiloton (kt) Measure of the explosive yield of a nuclear weapon equivalent to 1000 metric tonnes of trinitrotoluene (TNT) high explosive.

Launch-on-warning A strategic doctrine under which a nation's bombers and land-based missiles would be launched on receipt of warning (from satellites and other early-warning systems) that an opponent had launched its missiles.

Manoeuvrable re-entry vehicle (MARV) Re-entry vehicle whose flight can be adjusted so that it may evade ballistic missile defences and/or acquire increased accuracy.

Medium-range nuclear weapons Soviet designation for long-range theatre nuclear weapons. See also: Theatre nuclear weapons.

Megaton (Mt) Measure of the explosive yield of a nuclear weapon equivalent to one thousand kilotons.

Multiple independently targetable re-entry vehicles (MIRV)	Re-entry vehicles, carried by one missile, which can be directed to separate targets.
Mutual assured destruction (MAD)	Concept of reciprocal deterrence which rests on the ability of the nuclear weapon powers to inflict intolerable damage on one another after surviving a nuclear first strike.
Mutual reduction of forces and armaments and associated measures in Central Europe (MFR or MBFR)	Subject of negotiations between NATO and the Warsaw Treaty Organisation, which began in Vienna in 1973. Often referred to as mutual (balanced) force reduction.
National technical means (NTM)	The use of technical intelligence collection means for verifying compliance with negotiated arms control agreements. These means must be consistent with the recognised provisions of international law.
Neutron weapon	See Enhanced radiation weapon.
Nuclear weapon-free zone (NWFZ)	Zone which a group of states may establish by a treaty whereby the state of total absence of nuclear weapons to which the zone shall be subject is defined, and a system of verification and control is set up to guarantee compliance.
Precision-guided munition (PGM)	Non-nuclear weapon system characterised by high accuracy achieved by in-flight remote control, usually accompanied by high explosive effects.
Re-entry vehicle (RV)	Portion of a strategic ballistic missile designed to carry a nuclear warhead and to re-enter the earth's atmosphere in the terminal phase of the trajectory.

Second-strike capability | Ability to survive a nuclear attack and launch a retaliatory blow large enough to inflict intolerable damage on the opponent. See also: Mutual assured destruction.

Silo | A missile shelter including a vertical hole in the ground with facilities for launching the missile.

Strategic Arms Limitation Talks (SALT) | Negotiations between the Soviet Union and the United States, initiated in 1969, which seek to limit the strategic nuclear forces, both offensive and defensive, of both sides.

Strategic Arms Reduction Talks (START) | Negotiations between the Soviet Union and United States initiated in 1983 for reduction of strategic arsenals.

Strategic nuclear forces | ICBMs, SLBMs, ASBMs and bomber aircraft of intercontinental range.

Tactical nuclear weapons | See: Theatre nuclear weapons.

Theatre nuclear weapons | Nuclear weapons of a range less than 5500 km. Often divided into long-range (over 1000 km , for instance, so-called Eurostrategic weapons), medium range, and short-range (up to 200 km, also referred to as tactical or battlefield nuclear weapons).

Transponder | Electronic apparatus which returns a predetermined signal in answer to a calling one.

Triad | Strategic nuclear forces composed of three parts: land-based intercontinental ballistic missiles, submarine-launched ballistic missiles, and long-range bombers.

GLOSSARY

Warhead

The part of a missile, rocket or other munition which contains the explosive or other material intended to inflict damage.

Yield

Released nuclear explosive energy expressed as the equivalent of the energy produced by a given number of metric tonnes of trinitrotoluene (TNT) high explosive. See also: Kiloton and Megaton.

<u>Part One</u>

Space Militarisation : Stabilising and Destabilising Aspects

1. **CAN WE AVOID AN ARMS RACE IN SPACE?**

John Polanyi

Introduction

At the time when Pugwash was founded (1957) those who advocated arms control were thought to be impractical idealists.
Today the situation has changed to the extent that arms control is acknowledged, even by conservative thinkers, to be a
vital ingredient in planning for the future[1]. One may ask,
however, whether the situation has really changed, or whether
the proliferation of armaments will continue unabated, but
with a new rationale – the need to bargain from 'strength'.
If so, the advocates of arms control were indeed impractical
idealists.

The superpowers appear at the present time to be on the
verge of a weapons competition in space. The likelihood that
either can improve its security in an enduring fashion by
these activities is negligible. The dangers of such a competition are real, and are already apparent. Fortunately,
the commitment to space war is, for the moment, slight. The
prospects for an arms control agreement, in terms of need and
practicability seem, therefore, to be exceptionally good.

If, in the face of this, the situation is allowed to
develop into an unfettered arms race in space, then the
prospects for arms control in general would appear to be dim.
Not only is this intrinsically an important case, it is also
– as were its forerunners, the ABM and the Outer Space
Treaties – a test case of the international commitment to
responsible behaviour.

The Militarisation of Space

It hardly needs to be said that outer space provides a unique
new vantage point from which to conduct operations on earth.
It is only 26 years since the launching of the first crude
spacecraft (the Soviet Sputnik – sent into orbit two months
after the USSR tested its first ICBM in August 1957). In

3

the intervening quarter of a century space technology has become intimately interwoven with military technology in general. Four vital military functions - Command, Control, Communications and Intelligence (termed C^3I) - make heavy use today of satellite capabilities.

The full catalogue of space devices employed in C^3I is too extensive to be given here. The total military space budget in the USA is currently about \$10 billion per annum. It cannot be very different in the USSR.

(i) This money goes to buy communication satellites, that relay messages (it is often said that two-thirds of US military communications are carried by satellite).

(ii) A second category of satellite uses infra-red detectors to give early warning of missile launchings.

(iii) Another category, equipped with many types of invisible, infra-red, radar and electronic eavesdropping sensors, collects intelligence regarding military capabilities, weapons disposition and readiness of the opposing nation.

(iv) Navigation satellites permit a soldier or a vehicle in the air, at sea, or on land, to determine their position with an accuracy of approximately 10 m in three dimensions, and velocity to 0.1 ms^{-1} (these numbers look ahead to the full implementation of systems of the level of sophistication represented by the US Global Positioning System, or GPS, to be fully deployed by late 1987).

This list is incomplete since it makes no mention of some well established systems (for example weather satellites, geodesic satellites, nuclear explosion recognition satellites, and so on) and experimental systems (for example systems designed to track shallowly submerged submarines). Special mention should be made of important new types of space vehicles, namely shuttles and manned space stations. Both could be important in improving the sophistication, flexibility and long-term reliability of space-based military activities of the type catalogued above.

It should be stressed that **none** of the activities referred to in this section are banned by any treaty (some are in fact legitimised by treaty as will be shown later). Though all are military, since they support the armed forces, none involve the use of weapons in space, nor weapons directed against objects in space.

'Militarisation' of space is to be distinguished from what has been termed 'weaponisation' of space (the placing of weapons - that is destructive systems - in space). Whereas the militarisation of space is actual, weaponisation is still one to four years in the future. 'Militarisation' arguably increases security and stability by diminishing the danger of accidental or uncontrolled war. It would be difficult to argue that weaponisation contributes to security – quite the reverse.

Space Weapons

Anti-satellite Weapons (ASAT)

In view of their high degree of military utility, satellites have become potential targets. Development of ASAT devices has been under way, off and on, since 1963. Between 1963 and 1975 the USA maintained two ASAT bases dependent on ICBM launchers. This early ASAT would have required a nuclear warhead to be effective. It was abandoned, in part, because of the fact that a nuclear explosion in outer space could threaten satellites belonging to the nation launching the attack, as well as the nation under attack.

Since 1967, the USSR has been making sporadic tests – approximately 20 in all – of an ICBM-launched interceptor satellite (launched by a ground-based SS-9 into an orbit close to that of the target satellite) bearing a conventional warhead that explodes when the interceptor is about 1 km from the target. Reliability is still only moderate (about 50 per cent). Tests have been limited so far to low orbits (less than 1500 km), and have been restricted to a particular inclination to the equator (about 66°).

The USA is expected to make its first tests of a much lighter, more flexible and versatile ASAT device – a Miniature Homing Vehicle (MHV) – in the near future. The MHV will intercept by direct ascent, rather than co-orbit, and be fired from two-stage rockets mounted on F-15 fighter planes. This moveable launch platform will give wide coverage to the US ASAT. The MHVs will steer themselves towards the target satellite using a heat-seeking sensor, and, if successful, will destroy the target by impact (there is no explosive charge).

It is evident that neither the USSR nor the USA ASAT systems are yet operational. Neither nation's system – even if operational – would threaten the high orbit (more than 20 000 km) satellites, currently used for missile early-warning, for navigation (GPS, for example), electronic eavesdropping, nuclear explosion detection, and communications. Nor would they threaten projected deep-space communication and nuclear-weapons-detection satellites (about 100 000 km). The US system could (by adding more stages to the MHV rocket) most readily be developed to the point that it threatened satellites of this type. It would seem to be particularly important to forestall this development.

The ASAT story has been told in some detail here, since

this is currently the space weapon that is closest to being operational.

Directed-Energy Weapons (DEW)

Directed-energy weapons would comprise either particle beams (charged or neutral particles) or photon beams (light-beams, coming from lasers operating anywhere in the spectrum from infra-red to X-rays; at present X-ray lasers must be powered by nuclear explosives). Since none of these technologies appear viable as weapons systems at the present time, it is difficult to say which is the front-runner. Almost certainly most R & D has been directed towards the development of efficient, compact, high-energy lasers in the infra-red or visible region, and their associated optics. Recently there has been speculation that laser development for DEW might shift towards X-ray lasers, in view of the efficient absorption of X-rays by the target.

The cost of employing DEWs in space, particularly from a space-based platform, is so high that these weapon systems are not generally regarded as competitive in the ASAT context, where simpler alternatives exist. The context in which DEWs are most discussed is that of space-based anti-ballistic missile defence (termed ABM or BMD).

What is at stake here is, or appears to be, nuclear deterrence. Where the stakes are this high, research and development will continue in the face of formidable obstacles. The obstacles are indeed formidable since it will be difficult to deliver sufficient energy to numerous small, distant, fast-moving targets, and it will be relatively easy for the attacker to implement counter-measures.

The level of funding for R & D appears until now to have remained modest. This is evidence of good sense on the part of the two major protagonists, since an arms race in DEW ABM systems would raise fears which could prove highly destabilising.

This was recognised in the ABM debate of the 1960s. It is still true today. In the 1960s the ABM systems being proposed were designed for point defence of certain military or civilian targets. In the future, the lure of ABMs will be the possibility of an early defence that substantially attenuates or renders inoperative the opponents' attack force.

It is tempting to suppose that the same technological virtuosity that propelled us into the era of nuclear weapons might give us the means to return to the pre-nuclear age. Precisely this argument was made by President Reagan in his speech of 23 March 1983 calling on US scientists to devote themselves to the cause of 'rendering ... nuclear weapons impotent and obsolete'. Policy statements at this level of government must be expected to stimulate activity in the area of DEWs in both the USA and the USSR.

Electromagnetic Pulse (EMP)

The electromagnetic pulse effect became evident in July 1962 when the USA detonated a 1.4 megaton hydrogen bomb at an altitude of 400 km over the Pacific Ocean. About 1300 km away, in Hawaii, street lights went out, burglar alarms rang and circuit breakers opened in power lines. The diagnosis was that gamma-rays had encountered air in the upper atmosphere and ejected Compton electrons. These were accelerated by the earth's magnetic field, and consequently emitted an EMP which, at ground level, amounted to about 10^5 volts per metre. A single nuclear explosion of this magnitude and altitude in a central location over the USA could cause nationwide chaos. This could provide an incentive for placing nuclear weapons in space.

The incentive is lessened by the fact that the Partial Test Ban Treaty ensures that the EMP weapon is poorly understood, and the Outer Space Treaty bans its emplacement in orbit, or its stationing in space. (Presumably it could be legally sent into space by direct ascent – ICBMs pass through space, and are not banned. Legality would, however, cease to be a prime consideration if nuclear war broke out. Arms control would have failed in its central purpose).

The electromagnetic pulse will also emanate outwards into space, and is regarded as a sufficient threat to satellite communication that some (classified) communications links – such as the Minimum Essential Emergency Communications Network (MEECN) – may include EMP-hardened satellites, now or in the future. Obviously, a satellite cannot be hardened against a determined nuclear attack.

EMP is included here as an indication of the complications that can enter, and are already entering, the strategic picture in space, when space is viewed as a battlefield.

Space Treaties

Just as security based upon weapons provides a point of departure for planning additional (modernised) weapons systems, so also security based on agreements to restrict the competition in armaments can assist in the framing of further agreements.

Nine agreements which are currently in force in varying degrees restrict competition in space weapons – weapons which to some extent were unforeseen at the date the treaties were signed. The new technology of ASATs and (particularly) DEWs will require either that the earlier treaties be abrogated in favour of the new weapons systems, or that the structure of these existing treaties be strengthened to block unambiguously further development of space weapons. It will be evident from the list that follows that the nine agreements differ greatly in scope and effectiveness.

The existing agreements are:

(i)   The 1963 Limited Test Ban Treaty

This multilateral treaty, often referred to as the Partial Test Ban, binds the parties 'not to carry out any nuclear test explosion, or any other nuclear explosion' in the atmosphere or in outer space (or in any environment that could cause the spread of radioactive debris beyond the borders of the state conducting the explosion). Over one hundred nations are parties to this treaty.

This treaty did not render the first US ASAT illegal, since it was never tested with its nuclear warhead. However, it rendered that system still less attractive, since it could not be tested.

(ii)   The 1967 Outer Space Treaty

This treaty goes beyond the partial test ban (item (i)) in forbidding the stationing in outer space of nuclear weapons, or any other weapons of mass destruction. In addition, the treaty bars all military activities on the moon or other celestial bodies.

Neither the 1963 nor the 1967 treaties put a major obstacle in the way of contemporary space weapons, since (with the exception of the X-ray laser) they do not require nuclear explosives. In spirit, the Outer Space Treaty militates against deployment of weapons in space, since it was drafted 'Recognizing the common interest of all mankind in the progress of the exploration and use of outer space for peaceful purposes ...' so that outer space would be 'the province of all mankind'. Such broad generalities have, however, limited value in curbing an arms race in space.

(iii) The International Telecommunications Convention

Over a period of years this expanding body of regulations has attempted to minimise radio-frequency interference with satellite systems. Since such interference could be embodied in ASAT devices, its prior restriction is advantageous. Moreover, it gives evidence of an internationally recognised need to protect satellite links on a global basis.

(iv) The 1971 'Hot Line' Modernisation Agreement

This was an update of the 1963 'Hot Line Agreement'. In the updated treaty the USA and USSR agreed to cooperate in maintaining two satellite-communications systems, so as to increase the reliability of their direct communications at times of emergency.

(v)   The 1971 Agreement to Reduce the Risk of Nuclear War

This agreement, designed to provide safeguards against war through accidental or unauthorised use of nuclear weapons, hinges on the inviolability of ballistic missile early-warning systems - without, however, explicitly guaranteeing that inviolability.   The Parties undertake to notify each other immediately '... in the event of signs of interference with these systems or with related communications facilities...' (Article 3). The treaty serves, at the very least, to acknowledge and to legitimise the mutual dependence of the signatories (USA and USSR) on the unimpeded functioning of satellite systems.

(vi)   The 1972 ABM Treaty

This Treaty places impediments in the way of the acquisition of a major category of space weapons: anti-ballistic missile (ABM) weapons.   Article V, item 1, reads: 'Each Party undertakes not to develop, test or deploy ABM systems or components which are sea-based, air-based, space-based, or mobile land-based.' (Here item 1 ends). This would appear to be sufficiently unambiguous. When, therefore, Mr. Reagan committed the USA to research into viable space-based ABM systems capable of 'nullifying the nuclear threat', he was limiting activity to weapons **research**, since in the same speech he explicitly re-affirmed the US intention of abiding by the 1972 ABM Treaty.   Nonetheless, the encouragement of such activities clearly threatens the treaty and provides grounds for wishing to re-examine and strengthen it.

(vii) The 1972 Interim Agreement on Strategic Arms
        (SALT I)

In common with the ABM Treaty and the SALT II Treaty, this treaty provides for verification of compliance by 'national technical means'. It then goes on to bind each party not to interfere with these means of verification.

(viii) The 1975 Convention on Registration of Objects
       Launched into Outer Space

According to Article 4, states launching objects into space
should notify the Secretary-General of the United Nations of
'the general function of the space object'. Up to the
present, statements of function have been so general as to be
of little value in providing the reassurance that is needed
if an arms race is to be avoided.

(ix) The 1979 Moon Treaty

The treaty outlawed the stationing of weapons of any kind,
the testing of weapons of any kind, the establishment of
military bases or fortifications or military manoeuvres on
the moon or any other celestial body (other than the earth).
In this restricted domain, weapons of **all kinds** - and not
just weapons of mass-destruction - are outlawed.
  This is not a complete list of the conventions governing
the use of space. It omits, for example, the Space Liability
Convention, and also the Agreement on the Rescue of Astronauts, the Return of Astronauts, and the Return of Space
Objects.
  It is evident that there exists, for the present, a degree
of civilisation in space.

Avoiding an Arms Race in Space

In view of the fact that DEW ABM systems lie in the future,
and ASAT weapons have not yet been developed to the point
where they threaten existing satellite systems, it is not too
late for an agreement which would foreclose on an expensive
and hazardous arms race in space.
  There have already been promising discussions on an ASAT
ban: the bilateral USA-USSR negotiations in 1978 and 1979.
During this period the Soviet Union halted its tests of ASAT
weapons. The talks were adjourned following a final meeting
in Vienna in June 1979. At this date Presidents Brezhnev
and Carter signed the SALT II Treaty. With SALT II
ratification as the most urgent topic on the arms control
agenda, considerations of halting an actual arms race took
precedence over measures to halt a potential arms race in
space.
  A prime condition for arms control is the technical one:
there must be a shared perception that the parties to the
proposed agreement have more to gain from agreeing now, than
they have from continuing their competition in an attempt to
achieve military advantage. This would appear to be the only

sensible reading of the present situation in regard to space weaponry. The second requirement is a political one: there must be a strong desire for a gesture of 'conciliation'. This could be the case in the coming period.

The Soviet Union has expressed interest in renewed discussions on this topic on several occasions. President Reagan's speech of 23 March 1983 - though often alluded to as a 'Star Wars' proposal - did not commit the USA to any specific weapons system for rendering nuclear weapons obsolete. It did commit the USA to abiding by the 1972 ABM Treaty. The effect could be to heighten consciousness of the alternatives and to help force a re-examination of priorities in space.

As regards formal proposals for bans on weapons in space, the most recent is the Soviet draft Treaty on the prohibition of the stationing of weapons of any kind in outer space, submitted to the UN in August 1981. Regrettably, the United States has not yet responded in any way to this initiative.

The wording of this Soviet draft will need revision. It lays particular stress on weapons 'in orbit' (Article 1), and could therefore be read as banning the Soviet co-orbiting ASAT, yet permitting the US type of direct-ascent weapon.

Prime Minister Trudeau of Canada proposed a somewhat improved wording in a speech to the UN Second Special Session on Disarmament (UNSSOD II, August 1982), calling for a ban on all weapons 'for use in outer space'. He stressed that verification would be readily achievable for a limited time only, since operational testing of such weapons is at present incomplete - and testing is a conspicuous activity. If we delay until testing is complete, we shall find it vastly more difficult to halt the spread of weapons into space.

More recently, President Yuri Andropov of the USSR, in an interview[2] significantly widened the terms of the proposed ban to include any use of force in outer space, and all space weapons directed at ground targets. It would appear necessary to add, explicitly, earth-based systems directed against space, in order to clarify the intention to halt all destructive activities in outer space.

Fostering Peaceful and Peace-Keeping Uses of Space

It will be evident from an inspection of the nine agreements listed above, that the safeguarding of space for peaceful purposes tends to impose barriers to the concurrent arming of space. The greater the commitment to exploiting space for peaceful purposes (including such dual purposes as communication, observation, and so on) the greater will be the reluctance to forfeit the security which objects and individuals in space presently enjoy.

The costs of major projects in space are sufficiently high that cooperative activities make financial sense. Politically such activities also make sense, if space is to escape becoming a battlefield. The precedents already exist: the Soviet Union has launched a satellite for India and has included French and Indian cosmonauts in space missions; the United States has made NASA 'Landsat' satellite data widely available, and has launched satellites for Britain, Canada and other NATO countries. The European Space Agency is a going concern, with several joint ventures in the areas of meteorological communications and earth resources satellites, as well as an organisational structure that provides for the sharing of costs and benefits.

What are needed, however, are conspicuous joint programmes involving the USA and USSR in some of the many global tasks that can be accomplished from space. One must look hard for initiatives of this kind in the chill international climate that prevails. One such initiative which deserved wider notice was the offer made by the United States at UNISPACE 82 (the Second United Nations Conference on the Exploration and Peaceful Uses of Outer Space, held in Vienna in August 1982) to embark on, and contribute largely to, a cooperative international study from space of the prospects for Global Habitability. The study would be aimed at the year 2000 and beyond; it would concern itself with the changing global environment, and its implications for the habitability of our planet.

A cooperative project, with more profound political implications, which could engage the interest of nations currently establishing themselves as independent users of space, is the International Satellite Monitoring Organization (ISMO) or a corresponding agency of the UN (ISMA), discussed for some years past by Pugwash[3] and at the United Nations. An ISMA would probably centre on a group of industrially advanced nations (such as those presently involved in the European Space Agency, but with wider political and geographic representation) who, in cooperation, could work toward achieving the earth reconnaissance capability that is currently the monopoly of the superpowers. The very large superpower investment in space reconnaissance in recent decades is evidence of conviction that there are major gains to national security from such activities. Now that the technology is becoming more accessible, other nations will wish to move in this same direction for military, political and commercial reasons.

The ISMA concept is intended to provide an organisational framework for these seemingly inevitable developments - a framework that maximises the contribution of secondary powers' space-based intelligence to the preservation of peace, rather than to the achievement of narrow national goals. The ISMA would stress such functions as the verification of arms control agreements, particularly those which have clear relevance to the security interests of secondary powers (for example non-proliferation of nuclear weapons, nuclear-free zones, or regional disengagement). At a somewhat later date, the ISMA could involve itself in the technically more demanding activities of crisis monitoring - such as the provision of early-warning of hostile preparations - and also the support of UN peace-keeping activities.

The performance of these functions requires the solution not only of technical (reconnaissance) problems, but also of difficult political problems; how much information should be released, in what form, and to whom? These problems will not disappear simply because we choose to postpone addressing them. It would seem preferable that they be addressed today in a far-sighted fashion, than a decade from now in a mood of rancour and panic. Not only do we still have, for the present, an opportunity to forge the ISMA into a force for peace, we can also use it as a further instrument to stake a claim to space as a vital haven for activities that foster peace.

Contemporary weaponry has proliferated to the point that it threatens all of us on earth. There is no acceptable reason why we should now permit this contagion to spread into outer space. There is, on the contrary, an urgent need to alert the world to the fact that we have a few years at most to prevent this from occurring.

References

1. General Brent Scowcroft, <u>Report of the President's Commission on Strategic Forces</u>, US Government Printing Office, 11 April 1983.
2. <u>Der Spiegel</u>, 27 April, 1983.
3. <u>Pugwash Newsletter</u>, vol.17, (1980) p.86, and vol.20 (1982) p.90; see also Chapter 5 of this book.

2   DIRECTED ENERGY WEAPONS : TECHNICAL OVERVIEW

Kosta Tsipis

There has been considerable interest in directed energy weapons, both as potential space-borne anti-ballistic missile systems (ABM) and as anti-satellite (ASAT) weapons. This paper attempts to summarise some technical and operational considerations relating to the feasibility of such systems in these two contexts.

Any weapons system needs evaluation according to a set of comprehensive criteria. These may be summarised in a series of related questions: a) does the system answer a specific military or security need or set of needs? b) does it satisfy this need adequately? c) are there alternative systems available within the same time frame which can perform the same function(s) more cost-effectively? d) are there sufficient data available to make an effective evaluation of the system now? e) are there counter-measures which an opponent can use to nullify, or severely degrade the performance of the system at a fraction of its cost?

One can characterise directed energy weapons by two essential features: a) destructive energy is transmitted, at the speed of light, to strike a distant target without the transfer of significant mass; b) destruction can occur only if the beam strikes the target. A corollary of the latter property is that the target must be locatable to within its own length, or the diameter of the beam, whichever is greater.

Translation of these characteristics into operational criteria leads to a set of specifications for the design requirements of beam weapons, whether for ABM or ASAT use. Such a weapons system must be able to accomplish a complete set of tasks, many common to existing systems. The target must be identified among decoys and noise. Having been identified, it must be tracked with suitable sensors, in such a way that the beam can be aimed and held on target. The system must generate a beam and fire it, and the beam itself must be able to propagate through the intervening medium to

14

the target without impedance or deviation. It is then necessary to ascertain whether a hit has been scored and, if so,
to evaluate destruction or damage. If not, the system sensors
must assess the aiming error, re-point, and re-fire. This
capability would also be needed in case of failure to destroy
the target. The aiming and firing cycle must be rapidly
repeated until the target is effectively destroyed. The
system must transmit status information to the command
authority, and be ready for deployment on a fresh target.

The components required for these operations would be as
follows: a) sensors to detect and track a rapidly moving
target; b) controls which couple the sensors to the energy
beam with very tight feedback; c) transmission links for fire
control, and communication if necessary; d) a beam producer,
which would be either a particle accelerator or a laser and
its associated optics, together with a power source, and its
associated cooling system.

There are two fundamentally different types of directed
energy weapons: those using sub-nuclear particles, either
charged or neutral, and those based on lasers.

Charged Particle Beams

These weapons will not work for the following reasons:

a)   The beam will return to the accelerator platform because
     of the 'virtual cathode' effect.
b)   The beam will disperse due to the force on a uniform beam
     of charged particles. The self-repulsion of the particles
     carrying identical charges is always greater than the
     magnetic attractive component, therefore the force is
     always outward. Using relativistic particle dynamics, the
     beam diameter at a given distance from the source can be
     predicted. With an initial beam diameter of 1 cm, an
     energy of 1 GeV, and a current of 1000 amperes, the diam-
     eter of an electron beam will be 15 m at a target 1000 km
     away; for protons the beam diameter will be 18 000 m at
     the target. This means that the beam will not be intense
     enough to destroy the target, because for this purpose
     the beam diameter should not exceed 1 m.
c)   The beam will be bent somewhat unpredictably by the
     geomagnetic field.

In a uniform magnetic field, the radius of curvature of a
singly charged particle can be easily calculated. A 1 GeV
electron will have a radius of curvature 110 km, and a 1 GeV
proton - 190 km in the earth's magnetic field; therefore,
neither beam will reach a target 1000 km away.

The uncertainty in the position of a 1 GeV particle due to the uncertainty of the value of the magnetic field will be 100 metres at a 1000 km range; therefore, the beam could not be aimed.

The geomagnetic field can be suddenly, greatly and unpredictably disturbed by a nuclear explosion in the stratosphere.

Conclusion: Charged particles as beam weapons in space may be ignored.

Neutral Beams

A **gamma-ray beam** generated by an intense electron beam interacting with matter will be 500 m in diameter 1000 km away. This is not intense enough to damage anything.

A **neutron beam** generated by bombarding a hydrogenous material with 1 GeV protons will disperse to a 1 km diameter, 1000 km away from the accelerator. Again, not enough to destroy a target.

A **negative hydrogen beam** steered and then stripped to form a neutral hydrogen beam could be kept in principle to about 7-10 m diameter at 1000 km from the accelerator. The total area of the beam at the target will then be about 4×10^5 cm^2. Since it takes $2\text{-}3 \times 10^3$ J/cm^2 to damage a target assuredly, the energy requirement is about 10^9 joules per pulse. Energy sources for accelerator and magnets of a space-borne BMD have a 50 per cent efficiency of the staging system to beam energy, and a 30 per cent efficiency of the primary power to staging system, giving an overall efficiency of 15 per cent. The required energy would thus be about 10^{10} joules per pulse.

Since high explosives can be used to power the generators and each gramme of high explosives contains 4000 joules, the system would need about 2.5 tonnes of explosives per pulse (several pulses per second would be required in the case of ABM use, and a few tens of pulses in ASAT use). It would need at least six times more coolant, since the efficiency of the power source alone is 15 per cent.

An ABM system operating from an orbit 1000 km above the earth will need 50-100 accelerators in orbit, each able to fire 5000 to 10 000 pulses in a few minutes. The amount of fuel that would have to be carried into outer space would then be 625 thousand tonnes, at a mininum. This is equivalent to 20 000 shuttle loads.

The beam must physically hit the target; but the miss vector cannot be ascertained with any accuracy and, therefore, there is no way to correct the aim if the beam misses.

The counter-measures against a space-borne ABM are:

a) jam the communication link with the command and control centre;
b) jam or blind (or spoof) the sensors on the platform.

Conclusion: Particle beams as ABMs are not effective. As ASATs they are too expensive for a job that can be done trivially by other means, for example, by ASAT missiles that could be easily hardened to withstand satellite defensive measures.

Lasers

Lasers can in principle be used as directed energy weapons based in space for ballistic missile defence. The technological requirements for the achievement of such weapons are:

a)   laser cavities with adequate power and energy outputs;
b)   development of suitable laser mirrors;
c)   stable detection and tracking system;
d)   space transport facilities.

One mode of producing an ABM 'kill' is to melt a hole in the target by continuous laser illumination. Using representative values for the physical properties (specific heat, melting temperature, latent heat of melting, surface thickness, surface reflection, and density) of the target material, we can calculate the time taken and hence the energy delivered to the target in order to achieve such a kill. For example, for a CO_2 laser radiating at 10^{-5} m with a 1-metre mirror, a target at a range of 1000 km could be penetrated given 180 seconds of illumination with a 100 megawatt source laser. The corresponding figure for an HF laser, radiating at 3×10^{-6} m wavelength, and using a 4-metre mirror would be 1.5 seconds at 100 megawatts. The corresponding stores of energy per kill, even assuming perfect efficiency of transposing the energy into laser radiation, come to 4.5 tonnes per kill for the CO_2 laser, and to one tonne per kill for the HF laser. Given the requirement of 1000 kills per satellite, this system would require an optimum fuel store of 30 shuttle loads per satellite in the HF case. For an effective ABM system of several tens of satellites it would require, as a very conservative minimum, 1000 shuttle loads.

An alternative mode of destroying an ABM using a laser is by thermomechanical shattering of the target via very intense light pulses. In this mode, the CO_2 laser with a 1-metre mirror would need 10^{11} joules per pulse, and the HF laser with a 4-metre mirror 10^9 joules per pulse. The fuel requirement for the CO_2 weapon, assuming the high explosives within the generators giving a specific energy of 4000 joules per gramme, is 25 tonnes per pulse. For the HF laser, a highly optimistic calculation, using a theoretical specific energy of 1500 joules per gramme (against achieved values of 500 joules per gramme) shows that the minimal extra coolant requirement is half a tonne of fuel plus coolant per pulse. Assuming five pulses per kill, one needs 2500 tonnes of fuel plus coolant per satellite. If we can postulate a limited system of 50 satellites on station, the total fuel and coolant requirement would be of order of 100 000 tonnes. For a shuttle load of 30 tonnes, and four shuttles each making ten trips per year, it would take 100 years of shuttle flights to put the system in place.

It should be noted that X-ray lasers powered by the detonation of a nuclear warhead, that have been bruted about, are operationally impractical for a number of reasons, even if they were made to work. Furthermore, there exists a variety of counter-measures that can degrade the performance of a laser BMD system very severely at a fraction of the cost of a laser-powered BMD system.

Conclusions

a) Current state of high energy long wavelength, infrared lasers cannot support an operational space-borne ballistic missile defence system.
b) Research into short wavelength lasers may in the future (perhaps 10-20 years) provide prototype lasers with the requisite characteristics for such a weapon system by an increase of beam concentration by two orders of magnitude.
c) Numerous other technical and operational problems have to be solved before one can even begin to imagine how such a system could be made operational.

3.   OUTER SPACE WARFARE

Evgeni Velikhov

When discussing the complex issue of weaponisation of space two main topics have to be considered.

Firstly we have the problem of military surveillance activity in space. Everybody agrees that such activity is a crucially important part of the national means of verification. As such it offers objective investigation of complaints about breaches of negotiated agreements. It is an inherently stabilising activity. Therefore, any anti-satellite weapons, whether launched from space or otherwise, will have a negative influence on future negotiations, and on the stability of the strategic balance.

The second problem is the development, testing and possible use of destructive weapons in space, for which anti-satellite weapons launched from space vehicles might be an early practical step. This is another reason why anti-satellite activity would have a negative influence on the development of arms reduction and negotiations.

After satellite surveillance comes the importance of weapons in space in a more general context. There was a two-day discussion of these topics in the USSR National Academy of Sciences, and I shall pick out two or three salient problems here. First, we should be clear about what kind of space weapons we are discussing. Most attention is given to a 'global' anti-ballistic missile defence. The question here is whether such a defence is really feasible. The second question, which would arise if such a system in space were shown to be feasible, is of course the military and political consequence of such a defence, given that earth-based systems are clearly not feasible. I shall give you my personal views on these matters.

The Technical Problems

Two aspects of the technical possibilities need to be looked into.

19

One is whether it is possible to build a system which can destroy ballistic missiles in the active, fuel-burning part of their trajectory, and whether such a system could be designed with the near 100 per cent efficiency required to make it worth deploying. The technical requirements for a system based on conventional projectiles which could destroy ballistic missiles in the active part of their trajectory have been discussed in the open literature. Although many details of such systems remain secret, there is enough published material to draw useful general conclusions.

However, another possibility is that of directed energy beam weapons. In his paper (Chapter 2), Professor Tsipis considers different types of such weapons. I will make a comment on one type, the chemical laser, which seems to me to be the best candidate for a space-borne system. The requirement for an anti-ballistic missile defence is basically to destroy 2000 missiles, with close to 100 per cent efficiency, in a relatively short period, as little as 100 seconds. How can this be done with a laser beam? Neglecting the very real problem of beam propagation, I will deal here with the delivery of sufficient energy per unit area of missile surface. To effect a kill would – with present missiles – require some 500 to 1000 joules per cm^2, but missiles designed to withstand laser attack could raise these requirements by an order of magnitude.

To show how demanding are the design requirements for such a system let us follow, as an example, a system published in an aerospace journal in 1982. This comprised 20 stations, in a relatively low orbit of altitude 1700 km, so that at any one time at least two such stations were covering the territory from which the missiles were being launched. Each station would then need to destroy 1000 missiles in 100 seconds. This gives one-tenth of a second per kill operation, assuming that each firing is a success. A station of this kind, with a 15 metre diameter mirror, which can be pointed with an accuracy comparable to its diffraction limit, that is of the order 10^{-7} radians, would require an average power consumption approaching 100 megawatts. This figure is optimistic, bearing in mind the possibilities of hardening the surface defence of the missiles, and that it is not easy to make in space a large telescope with a mirror diameter greater than some 4 metres. Probably one gigawatt would be a more realistic figure for the required power. Delivery of one gigawatt in a tenth of a second would require a chemical laser with a fuel efficiency of 100 joules per gramme and consumption of 1 tonne of fuel in a tenth of a second; in other words, a rate of 10 tonnes per second. Although there is no fundamental reason why such a system could not operate, and why the pointing accuracy of 10^{-7} radians could not be maintained during this flow rate, one can see the immense problems entailed. The total system, even to be capable of destroying only 2000 missiles would require 1000 tons of fuel for each of the 20 stations. The problem of maintaining such a system is not one of numbers but of orders of magnitude.

Attempting to cost such a system is not straightforward, but we agree essentially with the American calculations which put the figure at around a trillion dollars. This works out at a cost of half a billion dollars to destroy a single missile, which is at least an order of magnitude more expensive than the cost of present missiles. Clearly, such a system does not offer a great attraction as a weapon, but of course one must never underestimate peoples' ingenuity, and one may envisage some improvements in the situation if one were prepared to spend a billion dollars.

The situation looks even worse when you take whole systems into consideration. Defensive systems have always lagged behind offensive systems, and if you start to develop such a system this would inevitably give an impetus to the development of offensive systems. Since the latter cost is at least one order of magnitude less, the position is altogether a bad one.

Let us consider as an example the current United States proposals. We have proposals not only for space defence but the Scowcroft proposals for a single warhead missile, to be based in a very non-uniform distribution over the land area of the United States. This poses many problems, because for such a non-uniform distribution one would need many more than two space stations for the defensive role.

Another consideration is the cost of destroying such a system. This question is complicated by the fact that it entails, first of all, the location of a target whose position varies with time. Having located a potential target in space, it is then necessary to identify it, to send the information to a decision centre, to issue the command to fire, to await the result of firing, which for missiles can take a considerable time and, having evaluated the effect on the space-borne system, to be ready to fire again if necessary. All of this requires considerable signal time, particularly if the distances involved are quite long, say 3000 to 5000 km. The time delay is not due to the time of flight at the speed of light, but rather to the time taken to process the signals. As an example, there is a TV link between Moscow and California. I can see myself again on a large screen in California with a time delay of 2 seconds. Of course, a military system would be much faster, but the amount of information to process is much greater.

Since the offensive system is, in this case, a series system attacking a parallel system, the series system will be able to destroy it partially, thus making it extremely vulnerable. In theory, it is possible to envisage a self-defence for the space-borne system, but the system designed to attack it could be relatively simple. As an example of extremely resistant systems we can take the Jupiter probes, presently under development, for which the requirement is about 100 megajoules per cm^2. Although such probes are themselves very sophisticated, it is possible to construct even stronger monolithic metal systems relatively simply. It seems to me that exact conclusions are not dependent on the details of the offensive system used to attack the space station, but that one can confidently predict that the latter would be very vulnerable.

The Political Problems

After this technical discussion, we must consider the political aspect. What would be the consequence if such a system were found to be technically possible? It is most probable that in the first instance this would be a system which could deal not with thousands of ICBMs but rather with hundreds, say 500. This type of system could only be considered to form a part of a first strike capability, because it is both very provocative, and very vulnerable. You will have no chance to use it if you are in a defensive posture, because before you can use it it will have been destroyed by the enemy. Furthermore, if you possess such a system, it is much simpler to synchronise it with an offensive plan involving a first strike capability. I do not believe, however, that these considerations are very practical, because the technical question is clearly more important. Maybe the most important practical consequence is simply that even an illusion of the possibility of realising such a system can divert our attention from disarmament. This is the main conclusion that we can reach about any system which is really based in space. There may be many differing views, but I believe that everyone, including Edward Teller, thinks that such a system is impractical if based on a satellite or orbiting system. This is a very important conclusion, and I hope that all the scientific community will concur with it, because if we do not speak with one voice, the situation may be turning in the wrong direction.

There is, of course, a further possibility which has not received such wide treatment and about which there is not much information in the open literature. I refer to the use of X-ray lasers. We need more discussion of this matter; I am not familiar with the detailed mechanisms involved but I believe that they will not be easy to build.

What is the conclusion we can draw from the above discussion? More important, what will be the consequence in terms of practical measures to be taken by our governments? We are living today in very difficult times because the American administration not only has no will to negotiate - no political will - but has a very practical reason to stop any negotiation. It is a widely publicised view today that if you wish to increase public support for rearmament you need to bring any negotiations to a halt by adopting an impractical negotiating position. Under these circumstances we cannot be very optimistic about any negotiation. But negotiation on outer space is very important and urgent, because if hundreds of millions of dollars have already been spent, this will have generated a very large momentum, especially in the United States, and it will be very difficult to reverse or even to stop it.

At present, there is one ground-based and one air-based system, even though neither is very effective. The ground-based system was tested by the United States but testing stopped in 1975. After that, on our part, we made preparations for a more effective air-based system. A very important step proposed by our government would entail a stop to any development, and subsequently would lead to the elimination of any anti-satellite system. A first measure must be our pledge not to put into orbit any anti-satellite orbiting system. It is a unilateral pledge, and therefore not connected with any problems of negotiation. It is a very important unilateral pledge, because in many publications in the US literature, administration officials put forward the following argument: the Soviet Union is ahead of us, and will put anti-satellite weapons into orbit within a short time. We say, no, we will never be the first to put any anti-satellite weapons into orbit. This is very important.

A second measure is the proposal for an agreement not only not to put anti-satellite weapons into space, but to eliminate any ground-based or air-based anti-satellite weapons.

A third part of the plan is our proposal to ban any weapons in space which are directed against space vehicles, or against any system in the air or on the earth's surface. This part is a reflection of the wish of our government to stop the development of any arms race in space.

The first draft of the agreement was proposed one year ago. The second draft was to some degree influenced not only by our military defence department, and the foreign ministry of the USSR but by discussions with the Soviet scientific community.

Professors Garwin and Sagan sent a letter on this subject to President Andropov and he answered to the effect that this discussion should be not only with us but with the American scientists. I believe that the second draft is an improvement; this does not mean that it is free from difficulties, but at least it is on the table for negotiation. It is very important to put forward negotiations in the United Nations forum, but at the same time our government is not against any bilateral negotiation with the United States. All channels of negotiation to stop the arms race are open.

At present this important issue is more technical than military or political. We are open-minded and our government feels that this is an appropriate question for scientists. Let the scientists discuss it and afterwards come forward with scientific proposals. This is why Soviet scientists are interested in as deep a discussion as possible about this matter with their US counterparts. That is why we drafted the second part of the agreement but we are open to parallel discussions with any organisation or group. I believe that the matter is well suited for the Pugwash Movement, which is an appropriate forum for a profound scientific discussion.

4   SECURITY IN SPACE

Luciano Anselmo, Bruno Bertotti and Paolo Farinella

Weapons in Space

The different kinds of space weapons which are being developed and tested by the superpowers, or can be conceived in principle, have been described and discussed in several recent papers[1]. As a background for the following discussion, Table 1 contains a classification of all weapon systems in terms of the site (earth's surface, air or outer space) where they can be deployed, and where their targets are located. It is clear that two main types of weapons have a possible location in space: anti-satellite (ASAT) weapons and anti-ballistic missile (ABM) systems. The latter could conceivably be targetable also against objects on the ground.

Table 1. Classification of Weapon Systems

Target / Weapon site	Earth (land, sea)	Air (aircraft missiles)	Outer space (orbiting vehicles)
Earth	Guns etc.	Missiles, ABM systems	Beams from ground?
Air	Bombs etc.	Air-to-Air missiles	ASAT from aircraft
Outer Space	Beams to ground?	ABM beam systems?	Space-based ASAT beam systems?

The present technical limitations and problems of both these categories have been discussed in detail in recent literature[1]. In this section we shall discuss briefly some general arguments which, in our opinion, should make it politically and militarily advantageous for all parties to sign a treaty banning explicitly **all** types of space weapons, without the limitation to the 'means of mass destruction' forbidden by the Outer Space Treaty of 1967.

We shall start with ASAT systems and their implications, both as regards the weaponry already developed, that is the killer satellites tested since 1968 by the USSR and the aircraft-launched missiles developed by the USA, and the projected beam weapons widely discussed in recent times. Apart from 'technical' objections, like the fact that ASAT attacks would be easily recognised and that damaged satellites could be quickly replaced, two arguments need to be pointed out: (a) the development of ASAT weapons will unavoidably trigger a new arms race between aggressive and defensive systems; the need to protect unarmed military satellites, by hardening armours and/or increasing mobility, will greatly increase the weight and cost of these spacecraft; (b) the establishment of any international surveillance activity from space for security purposes will become more and more difficult and hazardous as space becomes 'weaponised' (see next section).

The present attitude of the superpowers to the banning of ASAT weapons is in some ways paradoxical. The Soviet Union has recently submitted to the United Nations a draft treaty on the prohibition of the stationing of weapons in space[2]. This is certainly a positive step; however, in our opinion, the treaty should define more precisely what is meant by 'weapon'. The USSR draft states that the destruction of any spacecraft is forbidden unless it carries some weapon on board, but without a precise definition of 'weapon' ASAT attacks cannot be excluded. (This point has been made somewhat clearer in the later version of the treaty proposal presented on 22 August 1983). Moreover, oddly the draft does not forbid the development of aircraft-launched sub-orbital ASATs, which are no less dangerous than orbital systems. The United States, on the other hand, after the breakdown of previous negotiations on this issue in 1979, have not proposed any new specific arms-control measures related to space activities. This is strange considering that the US technology involved in unarmed military satellites is more advanced and more vulnerable than that of the USSR, so that a treaty banning ASATs would be advantageous to the defence of US spacecraft, by decreasing both dangers and costs. Other countries (for instance France) have often

requested such a treaty, but a world-wide campaign is needed
to convince the superpowers that ASATs are dangerous and not
useful even from the military point of view[3].

Turning now to space-based ABM systems, much discussion
has recently followed President Reagan's proposal to build
by the end of the century an ABM shield consisting of space-
based laser or particle beam weapons. Apart from the formidable scientific and technical problems involved in this
project[4] it needs to be emphasised that the 'defensive'
character of these weapons is not justified. On the contrary,
behind an illusory defensive potential new risks of war will
be generated for several reasons. (a) At the time of the ABM
treaty the superpowers agreed that: 'Each party undertakes
not to develop, test or deploy ABM systems or components
which are sea-based, air-based, space-based or mobile-land-
based'. Thus, Reagan's proposal implies the abrogation of
the ABM treaty, one of the most significant and valuable
achievements obtained in 20 years of arms-control efforts.
(b) A really **safe** ABM system should have more than a
99 per cent efficiency in preventing penetration by ICBMs
in an all-out nuclear attack by the other party. Since
such efficiency seems out of reach, space-based ABMs would
more probably be developed, at least in a first phase, as an
anti-retaliatory defence to be used after a first strike,
thus undermining the basic assumptions of the MAD strategy.
On the other hand, should fail-proof ABMs become possible
in the future, this would encourage first strike strategies,
both by the nation possessing the capacity and by its
enemies as a pre-emptive measure. (c) The military uses
and consequences of this ABM system have a wider scope than
defence. For example, it might be used to attack targets
on the ground or in the low atmosphere, and serve as a
counterforce weapon. However, even though it may provide
some defence against ICBMs, it will not protect against
other weapons, such as strategic bombers and cruise missiles whose further development will thus be strongly encouraged.

There are other consequences which require careful and difficult assessment. A space arms race between the superpowers
(and possibly other nations) would be initiated, creating a
highly unstable equilibrium and demanding ever increasing
expenses; the estimated cost of an **efficient** ABM system
in space runs into hundreds billions dollars. Moreover, even
more than in the case of ASATs, the deployment of space
ABMs could jeopardise, and perhaps make impossible, all
civilian exploitation of space for scientific, economic and
security purposes.

These considerations lead us to believe that space-based

ABM systems (as well as ASATs) will have dangerous negative consequences, namely, increase international tension and the risk of nuclear war, as well as positively endangering peaceful space activities. These consequences should be understood by all nations, particularly those that are not actively engaged in the militarisation of space. They should be the first to press for immediate negotiations by the superpowers for a treaty to ban weapons of any kind from space.

Surveillance Satellites

The fundamental importance of surveillance satellites in the strategic balance between the superpowers is well known and obvious; we want to stress that it is a very positive factor for the preservation of peace, the verification of disarmament agreements and the control of arms-race activities[5].

It is important to note that the dividing line between civilian and military programmes is becoming more and more blurred. As well known examples we quote the NAVSTAR global positioning system[6] and the remote sensing French programme SPOT, capable of reaching in one of its modes of operation a resolution of 10 m, which is certainly sufficient to identify military installations[7]. Thus, the resolution, coverage and organisation of civilian satellite programmes will soon become of military interest and the monopoly of the USA and USSR in this field will disappear. One can easily envisage cases in which a third nation (for example France) will be able to sell to another party (Iraq) photographs of military operations by its enemy (Iran); or even to monitor missile deployments in the territory of the two superpowers. The dangers and the international complications which may arise from this state of affairs have prompted the General Assembly of the UN to propose the establishment of an 'International Satellite Monitoring Agency' to provide remote sensing data of military interest for monitoring local crises and verifying disarmament treaties[8]. This topic has been discussed extensively at two recent Pugwash Symposia, in Avignon, 14-17 April 1980, and Versailles, 25-29 October 1982 (see Chapter 5). It is obvious that this kind of activity, as well as any space surveillance by third countries (that is other than USA and USSR), would be seriously jeopardised by the possibility of hostilities in space, especially if some surveillance activities are regarded as potentially hostile. The space programmes of an increasing number of nations are developing at a very fast rate and are serving vital purposes not only in surveying the earth, but also in telecommunications, manufacturing in space, scientific research, and so on. All these activities can be conducted in a reasonable and effective way only if outer space is a safe environment, acknowledged as a common property of mankind.

Outer Space as Common Property of Mankind

The legitimacy of surveillance activities in space has been questioned by some developing countries; the most extreme position is the one taken by Brazil and Argentina who, in their draft of a UN treaty of remote sensing, have proposed that[9] 'a state acquiring information relating to the national resources of another state by remote sensing shall not divulge such information without the express authorisation of the party to which the natural resources belong'. In our opinion, it is in the interest of all countries, including the developing ones, to adopt a different juridical and political point of view, in exchange for guarantees by the superpowers of security in space.

For a possible juridical set-up of activities in outer space it should be noted that according to international law, the world space is usually divided into three different categories: a) national territory, under the sovereignty of a state; b) territories, like the high seas, which cannot, by law or by fact, be a part of a state ('territorium extra commercium'); c) territories which are not now part of a state, but may become so in the future ('territorium nullius')[10]. It is clear that outer space should belong to the second category; as far as the moon and the other celestial bodies are concerned, this principle has been officially recognised by the 1979 Moon Treaty.

There is indeed a widespread opinion among international lawyers that any activity by anybody in a 'territorium extra commercium' should be regarded as legitimate, as long as it does not bring physical damage to property or to the environment. The United States has supported this view in the case of space and have advocated the concept of 'open sky', that is opening the whole world for inspection.

It is interesting to recall that on 1st May 1960, the Soviet Union shot down a US U-2 plane while it was flying in USSR air space. The USA accepted this action and the subsequent trial of the pilot. However, when two months later a second US reconnaissance aircraft was shot down by the Soviet Union while it was over high seas, the USA protested and took the matter to the United Nations. The Soviet Union implicitly recognised the validity of this protest and returned the crew to the USA without trying them in court[10]. This makes it clear that the two superpowers have 'de facto' accepted the legitimacy of remote sensing from a 'territorium extra commercium', and, therefore, do not wish to interfere with alien military satellite systems. This point of view has been recently accepted in an explicit way by the USSR, whose proposal for a ban of weapons from space was already mentioned. Apart from the comments made in the first section, it is clear that this proposal combines the two principles we have enunciated, namely the prohibition of all weapons in space and the pledge that all spacecraft belonging to nations abiding by the treaty will not be subjected to hostilities.

Finally, we wish to point out that hostile activities in space can be carried out not only from spacecraft, but also from aircraft and from the ground. We, therefore, submit that real and complete security in space can be achieved only if all forms of hostilities against spacecraft are explicitly banned. Such a comprehensive treaty would be acceptable by all parties and significantly foster the cause of disarmament and peace.

In the 1981 proposal for a draft treaty to ban weapons in space[2], the USSR has considered only national means of verification (Article 4). This provision may be sufficient to assure success of the treaty as far as the USA and USSR are concerned, and to prevent gross violations. However, it clearly privileges the most advanced countries which have already developed the necessary technology, but it could prevent a general acceptance of the treaty by the majority of nations. International means of verification, although not necessarily required, could be an essential complement of the treaty, without infringing any national sovereignty (the latter was a strong objection to international verification in the case of other disarmament treaties).

Monitoring Alien Spacecraft: USA and USSR Activities

At present, the superpowers have effective monitoring and reconnaissance capabilities, based upon radar and optical tracking techniques developed early in the Space Age. In the USA NORAD (North American Air Defense Command) manages a world-wide radar network created several years ago, with which it is possible to pick-up a space object only ten centimetres in size and thousands of kilometres away[11]. Recently, the GEODSS (Ground-based Electro-Optical Deep Space Surveillance) has reached the operational phase; it represents a crucial improvement over the existing systems. In fact, the five stations of this new network, located at White Sands (New Mexico), Taegu (South Korea), Diego Garcia (Indian

Ocean), Mount Haleakala (Hawaii Islands) and in Portugal, can
detect an object as small as a football in a geosynchronous
orbit by using a couple of 100 cm aperture telescopes equipped with photomultiplier devices[12].

Radars and electro-optical systems allow the USA to determine the orbit of, and to monitor, a rapidly growing number
of space objects, in part satellites and in part exhausted
upper stages or fragments[11]. Moreover, the received
radar-echo signal and/or the observed optical magnitude of a
space object enables NORAD to determine roughly its size. In
order to gather more precise information on alien spacecraft,
the United States Air Force can rely at least upon two telescopic cameras able to provide a close-up at very high resolution of artificial satellites by means of computer image
processing[12]. It has been reported that these cameras
were used on the occasion of the first flight of the space
shuttle Columbia to investigate the conditions of the thermal
tiles in critical areas of the spaceship[13].

We do not know the details of the corresponding capabilities in the USSR, but presumably they are similar. While this
shows that national means of verification of a new space-
disarmament treaty can be regarded as satisfactory for
internal use by the USA and USSR, problems may arise when a
claimed violation is exploited politically, or when a third
country wishes to have an independent verification of the
treaty.

Monitoring Alien Spacecraft: Third Country Activities

The knowledge of the orbit and some coarse information about
the shape and size is often sufficient to identify the
mission goal of a satellite with reasonable confidence, and
is accessible to any country with a developed space activity.
The essential problem that has to be faced is the large
number of flying objects; at present NORAD is tracking more
than 5000 objects and, if past trends will continue, the
number of tracked objects can increase by a factor of two to
eight within the next 20 years[11]. Of course, the most
important objects from the point of view of security are
those in low orbit, but their number is still large. In order
to monitor an alien spacecraft one cannot, in general, use
the same facilities aimed at tracking one's own spacecraft,
which have on board transponders or radio-beacons carrying
identifiable signals[14]. When this is not the case, radar
and optical systems are the most appropriate instruments;
moreover, a modified version of the minitrack system may be
used to obtain tracking information by radio-interferometric
techniques[15].

The mere recording of satellite transmissions (telemetry in particular) also allows spacecraft classification through the carrier frequency, the signal modulation, the codification employed, and so on. This latter activity has been carried out with success by several radio-amateur groups scattered throughout the world. In the UK the activity of these groups has achieved remarkable results[16]. As an example of what can be achieved by these methods (even though at present they are not pursued in a coordinated way) we can quote publications like the NASA Spacewarn Bulletin, issued in the framework of the COSPAR (Committee on Space Research) activities, and the Satellite Digest, regularly appearing in 'Space flight'.

A Monitoring Agency

By their very nature and global political significance, space monitoring and verification activities can achieve a real juridical and technical validity only if they are carried out by an international body capable of overcoming the limitations of single nations. One can envisage the activity of such a body at two different levels. Outside the framework of a treaty for security in space it would provide the international community with unbiased technical data about all flying spacecraft. It should be recalled that the UN 'Convention on Registration of Objects Launched into Outer Space' (of November 1974) requires that each launching state provide a register held by the UN Secretary-General with the date and location of launch, four orbital parameters (nodal period, inclination, apogee and perigee) and the general function of each space object (but note that the quoted orbital parameters only give the shape of the orbit; they do not enable one to predict where the spacecraft is). At present little use is made of this register, and no further statistical elaborations on checks are made. In addition the delay with which information is sometimes transmitted makes it of very little use. For our purposes the required technical data would be a complete set of orbital parameters, the types of emitted signals and possibly the size and shape of the satellite. The activity of the Agency could, therefore, be seen within, and as an extension of, this Convention and would be one means for its verification.

On a second level, the proposed Agency could work under an authority established by the new space disarmament treaty to monitor particular spacecraft in order to verify their compatibility with the treaty itself.

At the first level, the described activity is already carried out to some degree by several nations (see previous sections), but this is often done by military organisations and instruments and, therefore, the results are kept confidential. In our view the sharing of these observations and their international organisation would not jeopardise, but on the contrary protect the interest of the countries involved. It is to be noted that a systematic tracking of all spacecraft is very useful in a more general framework; for instance, it will help in predicting the time and the place of re-entry of uncontrolled objects (like the recent case of COSMOS 1402). Any member nation of the Agency may utilise these data to draw conclusions about military space activities by any other country.

An international Agency of this kind would need three different components:

1. The tracking stations, equipped with radar, large-field telescopic cameras, radio-interferometric apparatus and radio-receivers for listening to spacecraft transmissions. It can be shown that   three nearly-equatorial stations, placed at about 120° of longitude distance, are sufficient to monitor all the space objects higher than about 7000 km. Because of the ground-track repetition pattern of the earth satellites, the same three stations, if suitably phased, could also pick-up the lower spacecraft at least once every day. However, more stations would be required if the speed of the orbit determination process were to be improved.
2. An Operations Control Centre (OCC), which collects and processes the data, as well as providing the pointing co-ordinates and the observation schedule in advance.
3. A reliable Communications and Data Link Network (CDLN), connecting the OCC with the stations.

The operational costs are mainly those of the OCC;   the stations can be largely automatised and should need little personnel. The control centre requires, of course, big computers and a competent interdisciplinary staff, comparable to that of the control centre of a space agency; with a staff of a hundred people, it would need a budget of about $40 million.   Capital expenses for the stations, computers and infrastructures are not easy to estimate; depending on the network complexity, the costs could range from tens to hundreds million dollars.

The establishment of such an International Agency would be best carried out as a UN body, which would ensure political globality and impartiality, and juridical validity of the activity itself. Alternatively, it is possible to consider a consortium of nations - like those supporting ESA - which would establish, finance and operate such a centre for their own use, with the ultimate aim, however, of extending the membership to all nations under the UN. An International Agency of this kind would provide an accurate and up-to-date picture of all space activities, and at the same time it would show experimentally to what degree it is possible to verify the peaceful intentions of the space nations.

The above should pave the way for an activity at the second level whenever necessary. Then, in the frame of a space-disarmament treaty, the Agency could be charged, under the political control of the adhering nations, with particular and more extended verification operations applied to 'suspect' satellites. It should be pointed out, however, that hostile activities against spacecraft using ground-based or aircraft-based missiles or beams would not be recognisable by this Agency before the actual offence, which may destroy the target spacecraft, has occurred. Activities of this kind could be monitored and prevented only by satellite or air reconnaissance; but this is outside the scope of the Agency discussed here, and much more expensive.

We conclude that it is high time that all third nations interested in space activities should aver loud and clear that outer space is not a property of the superpowers, but a common heritage of all mankind, and that any hostile activity or equipment which may damage anybody's spacecraft or property should be forbidden; any violation of this law should be verifiable and eventually made public by an international technical body.

References

1. B. Jasani (ed.), Outer Space - A New Dimension of the Arms Race, (London: SIPRI, Taylor & Francis, 1982); K. Tsipis, 'Hostilities in space', Pugwash symposium on An International Agency for the use of Satellite observation data for security purposes, (Versailles, 1982); R.M. Bowman, 'The case against space weapons', Report of the Defense Sciences Institute, (Potomac, 1982); A. Dupas, 'Les programme spatiaux militaires', La Recherche 130, (1982) 259; A.M. Din, 'Stopping the arms race in outer space', J. Peace Research 20, (1983) 221.

2. United Nations General Assembly, 'Draft treaty on the prohibition of the stationing of weapons of any kind in outer space', A/36/192, (1981); V.V. Bogdanov, 'Banning all weapons in outer space', in Outer Space - A New Dimension to the Arms Race, (London: SIPRI, Taylor & Francis, 1982) p.325.

3. Union of Concerned Scientists, 'Anti Satellite Weapons:

Arms Control or Arms Race?', (June 30, 1983).
4. J. Parmentola and K. Tsipis, 'Particle-beam weapons',
   Sci.Am.240, (1979) 54; K. Tsipis, 'Laser Weapons',
   Sci.Am.245, (1982) 35; W.D. Henderson, 'Space-based
   lasers; Ultimate ABM system?', Astronautics and Aero-
   nautics, (May 1982) p.44.
5. K. Tsipis, 'Des satellites pour la paix?', La Recherche
   130, (1982) 267.
6. B.W. Parkinson, 'The global positioning system',
   Bull.Geod.53, (1979) 89; K.D. McDonald, 'Navigation
   satellite systems: their characteristics, potential and
   military applications', in Outer Space - A New Dimension
   of the Arms Race, op.cit. p.155.
7. J. Redfearn, 'French plans for SPOT satellites', Nature
   298, (1982) 698.
8. United Nations General Assembly, 'Study on the implications of establishing an international satellite
   monitoring agency', A/AC 206/14, (1981).
9. B. Cheng, 'Legal implications of remote sensing from
   space', in Earth Observation from Space and Management of
   Planetary Resources ESA SP-134, (1978) p.597.
10. B. Cheng, 'Air and outer space law', Thesaurus Acroasium
    10, (1981) 51.
11. A. Thomson, 'Space debris - A growing hazard', Space-
    flight 25, 1, (1983).
12. J.W. Powell, 'Photography of orbiting satellites',
    Spaceflight 25, 2, (1983).
13. J.A. Pfannerstill, 'The maiden voyage of Columbia: Part
    one', Spaceflight 24, 5, (1982); A. Kenden, 'The shuttle
    and the spy satellites', Spaceflight 25, 3, (1983).
14. W.E. Wagner, 'GTDS - Orbit Determination Subsystem -
    Mathematical Specifications', CSC Report, 1972; W.E.
    Wagner et al, 'Mathematical theory of the GTDS', CSC
    Report, (1975); J.R. Wertz (ed.) Spacecraft Attitude
    Determination and Control (Data Transmission and
    Preprocessing), (Dordrecht: Reidel, 1978).
15. D.G. King-Hele, J.A. Pilkington, H. Hiller, and D.M.C.
    Walker, The RAE Table of Earth Satellites 1957-1980,
    (London: Macmillan Reference Books, 1982).
16. B. Jasani (ed.), Outer Space - Battlefield of the
    Future?, (London: SIPRI, Taylor & Francis, 1978).

5   AN INTERNATIONAL AGENCY FOR THE USE OF SATELLITE
     OBSERVATION DATA FOR SECURITY PURPOSES.

     Report from Pugwash Symposium held in
     Versailles October 1982.

Introduction

The international community in general, and Pugwash in particular, have been interested in the use of satellite observation data for security purposes for a number of years.
Because it was felt to be important to continue progress
towards the definition of an up-to-date and realistic system,
a second Symposium on an International Satellite Monitoring
System was held at Versailles, France, 25 - 29 October 1982.
The first Symposium, held in Avignon, France, 14 - 17 April
1980, resulted from the interest generated a few years earlier in a discussion at a 1977 Pugwash meeting, the report of
a group of the Massachusetts Institute of Technology, and a
specific proposal presented by the President of France to the
First UN Special Session on Disarmament in 1978.
    The report of the first Symposium provided an assessment of
the role and function of this kind of satellite system, of
several constitutional, political and legal considerations,
and of the major technical aspects of its design, development, testing, and execution, including a cost estimate. The
findings of the 1980 Pugwash Symposium were used as a working
input for the experts who prepared a report, on behalf of the
UN Secretary-General, to the Preparatory Committee for the
Second Special Session of the General Assembly devoted to
Disarmament (UNSSOD II). Although this report was a detailed
study of the implications of establishing an international
satellite monitoring agency, it was neither discussed nor
acted on at UNSSOD II.

Purposes and Functions

The continuing interest in many circles, in particular by the
French Government, in the potential of a satellite system,
encouraged the convening of the second Pugwash Symposium. The
potential benefits of a fully operational satellite system

are substantial and would accrue from the following missions
or functions:

reassurance and confidence-building as an inducement to
enter into agreements;
verification of compliance with international agreements,
especially arms limitation and disarmament agreements;
surveillance as a deterrent to violation of agreements;
conflict anticipation for preventive diplomacy;
early warning of preparation for possible attack;
evidence of aggression (border violations, and so on) for
adjudication;
monitoring of ceasefires and demilitarised zones;
monitoring of UN peacekeeping and observation operations
and the provision of up-to-date information to the
Secretary-General and the Security Council.

In the course of reviewing and updating developments since
the first report, it was considered that the most useful
approach would be to focus on a central function of the system that would provide impetus for an early start to the
undertaking. This function would be **the avoidance of armed
conflict and the promotion of the arms control process
through information uniquely recoverable and made available
by satellite technology.**
In this connection it was generally felt to be important
that the verification measures should correspond closely to
the subject matter of any agreement on arms control and disarmament, and that their deployment should take place simultaneously with the concrete steps towards disarmament.
Some doubts were expressed about the utility of a satellite
system in the avoidance of local conflicts, as it was felt
that the gathering and dissemination of data of such degree
of delicacy carried the risk of its use for undesirable purposes, before a resolution or prevention of the conflict had
been achieved. It is even conceivable that conflict could be
provoked rather than prevented by such data availability.
Most of the Group, however, felt that on balance the
potential benefits far outweighed these risks. Even the
anticipation of the establishment of such a satellite system
would promote new arms control and disarmament agreements; in
addition, the system would facilitate the negotiation of
verification measures.
The Group considered strategies for the implementation of
the system. While there were different views about the system's eventual relation to the UN, most agreed that the UN
would be a major beneficiary, that specific steps should be
taken at the earliest opportunity to initiate the process,
and that the UN General Assembly should endorse the principle

of a satellite monitoring system.

The entities to be served by the system would consist of at least two categories:

   a) all states members of the UN system;

   b) international/multinational/regional organisations and such non-governmental organisations that have responsibilities with regard to security or emergency problems (for example, the United Nations and its specialised agencies, regional commissions, affiliated organisations, such as UNDRO and other regional and/or specialised inter-governmental organisations and agencies, and non-governmental organisations, such as the International Red Cross).

Modalities

The Group considered three modalities (A, B, C below) for the implementation of the system. In the first, the sponsor would be the UN itself; in the second, there would be a consortium of nations; and in the third, some form of single governmental or non-governmental entity. The Group felt that further studies should be carried out, to include a more detailed assessment of these and possibly other options. The studies should assess, in the time-frame within which each of the modalities could be implemented, the technological characteristics of the systems involved, their operational and financial implications, and their political acceptability and accountability to all nations. The study should also address itself to long-term developments needed to ensure continuity of system operation, and the updating of the system to incorporate new technologies.

Modality A. There are two ways in which the monitoring system could be set up under UN sponsorship. In the first, the system would constitute an organ of the UN established by a resolution of the General Assembly. In the second, it would be created as a Specialised Agency, requiring the negotiation of a treaty which, among other things, would define its relationship to the UN and to its member states.

Modality B. Scheduling and financial considerations may favour initiating the monitoring system via a consortium of interested countries. If this approach is chosen, it would be highly desirable that the initial membership should include members of the following overlapping categories: a) technologically advanced countries; b) non-aligned and neutral countries; and c) developing countries. Membership would be open to all countries wishing to participate. The monitoring services would be available to non-members according to practices established by the consortium, in accordance with the principles of the UN.

The convention under which the consortium is established should preferably follow a resolution of the UN General Assembly endorsing the basic concept. Most participants felt that the consortium should include provision for its eventual inclusion in the UN.

Modality C. A modality not previously considered, which may offer some interesting opportunities, focuses on the establishment of a centralised, user-orientated data service managed on a not-for-profit but business-like basis. Such an institution, publicly chartered under the legal system of a neutral host nation in conformity with UN principles, would be independently capitalised, and would then be able to become self-sustaining through provision of data services to users. The key difference from options A and B is that the operational service would be a technically 'transparent' one, responsive to user requirements and essentially managed as a regulated entity with an international clientele in a contractual relationship. Enforcement of service obligations would then be initially through normal host-nation legal processes, and only ultimately through recourse to international political bodies.

A majority of participants felt that option C had many interesting elements, which could be successfully considered for options A and B as well; it merited further study. Nevertheless, they had grave reservations about some aspects of option C, in particular about the governance of the system.

Rules and Guidelines

A minimum set of rules and guidelines governing the delivery of data services from the system - under any modality - were suggested by the Symposium for further consideration by all interested parties. These are couched in terms of interlocking **rights** and **obligations** of the system participants (users and managers).

1. All participants (states and organisations) should have the right to receive data sets of their own specification and selection (that is, time, location, and format) that fall within the technical and priority constraints of the system, and without discrimination among participants.

2. Anyone exercising a right of access to the system's data

should at the same time have the **obligation** to inform
the international community through the Secretary-General
of the UN, of the terms (but not necessarily the rationale) of such a data request.

3. The system operator should have the **obligation** to make
available to the sensed party an identical data set under
identical conditions (of time, price and quality) as any
set ordered under the rights noted above.

4. Either the receiving or sensed (but not the system operat-
or) party should have the right to use the data set in any
form or forum as determined by their own self-interest.

5. The system operator should have the **obligation** to make
public, through reports to the Secretary-General of the
UN, any incidents of interference with the operation of
the system from external sources, since this would be
analogous to interference with a national technical means
of verification.

Three important issues that will have to be addressed are
a) means for capitalising and funding; b) methods for ensuring that terms for data access do not place any particular
participant at a financial disadvantage; and c) means for
assuring that analytical services are equitably available to
all users.

In describing these guidelines, the existence of a satellite system was presupposed; an example of such a system is
outlined in the Appendix.

Concluding Remarks

The danger of allowing the arms race on earth to extend into
space, and to threaten the operation of delicate satellite
systems stationed there, was recognised by the Symposium.
The proposal for a satellite system in any of the modalities
suggested above has a bearing on the current development of
various anti-satellite systems. A monitoring system which is
clearly dedicated to the further exploitation of space for
promoting peace (consistent with the 1967 Treaty on the Uses
of Space) may provide a useful counter to the dangerous drift
towards war in space and assist in inhibiting the deployment
of space weapons.

The Group approved the proposals at UNISPACE '82 in Vienna
for international cooperative research efforts, based on
space, to improve global habitability, with particular reference to problems of the environment. It is to be hoped that
any satellite monitoring system that emerges will provide
additional services such as assisting in the management of
natural disasters.

Appendix

A TECHNICAL MODEL FOR STARTING A SYSTEM TO PROVIDE SATELLITE OBSERVATIONAL DATA FOR SECURITY PURPOSES

The following technical approach for the rapid implementation of a minimum system is applicable to each of the three modalities referred to in the main report. The essential consideration has been to maintain momentum in fulfilling the central function of the system, thereby enabling an early start.

The model is predicated on the requirement to implement a system for data acquisition, global in scope but with only selective area cover and based on the use of high technology, including satellites, which could become operational as early as 1986.

It is to be understood that the present proposal will not be adequate to cover immediately all functions listed in the main text, since this would require more time and more means to build up a sufficient capacity. The initial system envisaged here would be mainly suited for reducing the probability of conflicts, and for contributing, to a certain extent, to the monitoring of area-limited arms agreements (within the limits of sensor capabilities, non-ambiguity of data obtained and features observable).

Technical and operational aspects

The implications of the constraints thus defined are:

that efficient use be made of 'industrial capabilities' by a 'manager' to prepare calls for proposals and final specifications;

that procurement be through one prime contractor and sub-contractors, private or state owned, with adequate experience and expertise in this type of 'turn-key' project implementation;

that a call for proposals be open to industrialised and industrialising nations, and be based on existing and proven technology;

It is considered that an early system for data acquisition for security purposes, global in scope but limited in area capability, could be based on a joint and combined operation of two satellites in orbits, for example, of about 98° and 60° retrograde. One satellite would be equipped with

imaging sensors in the visual and near infra-red, a microwave
profiler, 'blob-detector' for gross detection of capital
vessels at sea, and the other with imaging radar, a microwave
profiler and a 'blob detector'. Both satellites would rely
upon sensors, either mechanically or electronically steerable
(pointable) in order to expand coverage capability in terms
of geography and timeliness. It will not be possible, nor in
fact necessary, to implement an early, low-cost system which
has both high resolution and full, indiscriminate global
coverage. Close-look being probably most often required under
the stated constraints, it seems reasonable to accept as
design parameters an option for 3-5 metre resolution in
close-look mode for small areas for the optical infra-red
sensors, and 1-3 metres for the imaging radar, to be operated
to 'spot' or 'sampling' types of observations or surveys.

Further studies will have to indicate the definitions for
area coverage and systems limitations, for example in terms
of precision positioning for such an early system.

An essential design criterion is that the initial system
should have a growth potential, for example in terms of increased area coverage by simply adding elements, including
satellites, in a modular fashion.

Operations

The conditions for the technical operations of the system
are:

    that they be 'transparent';
    that system integrity be guaranteed;
    that the neutrality of the operational entity be
    guaranteed;
    that management be responsive and efficient;
    that services be cost-effective.

These conditions can probably be met best by assigning full
operational responsibility to a single responsive neutral
manager.

Services to be provided

As a basic policy, the data-gathering entity would provide
data without interpretation, evaluation, or judgment, in
formats defined by the client/user (digital data, hard copy,
or, as an alternative, simply data limited to sites/times
where something has changed) and so on. In many cases data
will be required in near real-time; a turn-around time of
1-1.5 days is assumed for design purposes. The data-gathering
entity would not establish data banks; therefore, the opera-

tions would consist of transmitting only requested and relevant data, and discarding and destroying all other data as
part of the processing approach. Priorities within the
limited resources available should be based on judgments of
the criticality of the situation.

Financial Aspects (as of 1982)

Initial cost estimates (in million US dollars):
    1 satellite (visual and infra-red)   100 - 200
    1 satellite (imaging radar)   200 - 300
    Launch costs   50 - 75
    Ground facilities (including all
    hardware/software for parallel pro-
    cessing of large data streams)   50 - 75

Project initiation and implementation (until the start of
the operational stage): a management team of about 50 persons
is foreseen ($5 million per annum).

Recurring cost estimates: multiple parallel processing of
large data streams requiring three shifts of highly qualified
technical experts plus ancillary operational and maintenance
costs for hardware, software, and expendables. Provisional
estimate is $75-100 million per annum.

Data transmission to user/client may vary, depending upon
the method of delivery defined by the user's requirements.
Funding of initial costs and recurrent costs can reflect
different policy options; these will, in turn, dictate the
pricing policy:
- direct funding by member countries;
- bank loan (for example World Bank) plus billing to users/
  clients for services provided, at fixed rates per product
  delivered;
- taxation of users/clients (following whatever norm may be
  acceptable);
- soft loans and/or grants for covering some or all of the
  initial and/or recurrent costs in order to reduce costs to
  users, especially for poor nations, with corresponding
  reduction of rates applicable to product delivered.

Part Two

Strategic Nuclear Arms Race

DOCTRINES AND THINKING ON NUCLEAR WAR
          (Is There Wisdom Without Experience?)

          Richard Garwin

Introduction

This paper provides a point of view on the topic 'Doctrines
and Thinking on Nuclear War'. The evolution of technology,
the growth in numbers of nuclear weapons, and the advent of
new leaders on the political scene impels us once again to
discuss these topics, no matter how distasteful and
unsatisfactory it may be. The subtitle 'Is There Wisdom
Without Experience?' reflects the discrepancy between this
field and those of experimental science, where fantastic
theories can be put to the test and rejected (or accepted)
according to experience. But none among us even hopes for a
nuclear war in order to improve the quality of our theories
in this field!
  'Thinking About Nuclear War' is in fact too narrow a topic.
We are concerned with nuclear **weapons,** and their acquisition as well as use. Nuclear war is an event of such magnitude that it cannot be considered in an existing environment
– it changes the environment, and even the thinking in preparation for nuclear war has a major impact on the environment
and on the likelihood of occurrence of that war.
  So we might talk about **doctrine** for the use of nuclear
weapons, **declaratory policy** for the use of nuclear
weapons, and the **capability** to support this doctrine and
policy. We must also talk about the nature of nuclear war. In
a rational world of nations, doctrine and declaratory policy
should at any time be consistent with capability, although
one's aim should be that the three evolve together towards a
more satisfactory and more secure posture. In a world of
nation states, other nations are affected strongly by the
nuclear weapon regime of a nation state, as is the entire
international political and security environment.
  My discussion owes much to the book, **Nuclear Weapons and
World Politics**[1]. I do not believe that we can or should
attempt to eliminate nuclear weapons so long as there is the

possibility of war between nations. With the advance of technology over the last 40 years, and especially with the
accumulation of stocks of fissile material from nuclear
weapons programmes and from the civilian nuclear power
programmes, even if all nuclear weapons were destroyed and
their fissile material transferred to safeguarded stockpiles,
it would be a matter of months, not years, before a nation
locked in conventional combat would obtain nuclear weapons
crude by today's standards, but very much better than those
used in 1945. Thus, the question is to find a regime to
provide international security in the presence of nuclear
weapons, and preferably one in which the existence of nuclear
weapons provides greater security than would be the case in a
world in which nuclear weapons could not exist.

History

Serious effort on the development of nuclear weapons began in
Great Britain and the United States early in World War II,
culminating in the use of two 20 kiloton fission bombs on
Hiroshima and Nagasaki in August 1945. The work was motivated
initially by fear that Nazi Germany would develop such a
weapon, but in view of the tens of millions of people already
killed in World War II the bomb would surely have been used
in 1945 against Germany as soon as it was available. Perhaps
the opportunity for surrender would have preceded use, but
there was hardly the opportunity to develop doctrine or
policy.

  After 1945 the United States had a monopoly on nuclear
weapons until 1949, and effectively for some time thereafter.
Nuclear weapons were produced at a modest pace, but delivery
by aircraft was not guaranteed of success. A monopoly on
nuclear weapons (with some means of delivery) provides a
nation not only deterrence of hostile acts by other nations,
but also compellence – the ability to force another nation to
accede to demands. The USA did not take advantage of this
power, but it was latent and unacceptable to other nations,
especially the Soviet Union. Logically, the unacceptability
of sole possession of nuclear weapons could have been
countered by supranational possession, but international
cooperation in the nuclear age was not yet developed to that
state, and the opportunity was lost.

  Nuclear monopoly allowed a strategy of 'massive retaliation' by which conventional attack of the other side against
the nuclear power or its allies could be countered by devastating response against the homeland of the attacker. Even
the first two nuclear weapons used in war had killed about
100 000 persons each[2], so that relatively few fission

bombs would suffice to render any potential gain from conventional aggression minimal by comparison, and so to deter conventional attack.

As fission bombs became more numerous, and as thermonuclear
weapons of multi-megaton yield were established as feasible
by the 'Mike' explosion of November 1952, one could conceive
of defeating conventional armies in the field. Nuclear
weapons were also deployed as warheads of otherwise common-
place anti-aircraft missile systems, and became available as
nuclear-armed torpedoes, land mines, and the like. The potential effectiveness of such weapons against traditional operation of conventional armies forced a rethinking of military
tactics, so as to reduce the vulnerability of military forces
to these nuclear weapons. Even though the armies thus adapted
were considerably less vulnerable to nuclear weapons, the
additional constraint made them less capable in their conventional role. Thus, the threat of nuclear attack against conventional armies diminished the effectiveness of the other
side. So long as one had a monopoly on nuclear weapons (in
this case tactical nuclear weapons), the mere possession of
nuclear weapons improved one's (relative) conventional capability. However, it was the threat of **use** of the nuclear
weapons which conveyed these benefits. With the potential
tactical use of nuclear weapons by the other side, and the
advent of tactical nuclear weapons delivered by short-range
rockets, one's own forces lost conventional effectiveness
because of **their** need to adapt to the nuclear threat.

In fact, in the period of nuclear monopoly, the threat of
use of nuclear weapons against the **society** would have
served just as well to deter conventional attack. The capability to use nuclear weapons against military forces in the
field was sought and achieved at great expense, in large part
because the use of weapons against civilians is forbidden by
the rules of war and is especially repugnant to professional
military officers. The experience of World War II, however,
shows that in large-scale conflict one side or the other is
likely to ignore these restrictions on the use of effective
weapons, under which circumstances any codification of the
rules of war appears to allow retaliation in kind.

It was evident from the first, however, that the enormous
effectiveness of nuclear weapons against human beings in
cities limited the degree to which a nation armed with
nuclear weapons could use those nuclear weapons in combat
against the military forces of the other side. The other side
could, if the stakes were high enough, use or threaten to use
a nuclear weapon against a city, thereby destroying about one
million people with a single megaton weapon. Individuals on
the battlefield are far more resistant to nuclear weapons

than are houses and normal buildings (and the people within),
but a more important factor is population density over the
100 square kilometres or so of the kill area of a megaton
burst. Thus began a race between strategic defence and the
evolution of the strategic offensive forces, in order to prevent the emergence of an invulnerable homeland which would
permit once again the use of raw force on the battlefield -
this time including nuclear weapons.

Of course, a primary target of one's own military force
(including nuclear weapons) is the effective military force
of the other side - especially strategic nuclear weapons.
Over the years these strategic offensive forces have evolved
so that they are not readily destroyed and so that they can
penetrate existing defences on the other side. They have
evolved differently on the two sides - the USA having most of
its warheads on strategic submarines and an increasing number
as cruise missiles on bombers, while the Soviet Union has
concentrated 75 per cent of its warheads on ICBMs. These disparities reflect differences in the geographical situation of
the two nations and in the state of their technology.

Recent Influences

Four problems continue to afflict 'deterrence by threat of
retaliation':
- the moral quandary of holding innocent people hostage for
  the decisions of their leaders;
- the concern that if war does start accidentally or through
  misjudgment, one does not preserve one's own country by
  actually destroying the other's;
- that if war does start, one may have vastly more nuclear
  weapons and delivery systems than are required to destroy
  the other side, and would like to use some of them to
  reduce the damage to one's own country;
- that the threat of total destruction may not be deemed
  credible for 'just a little aggression', or even for an
  attack on one's ally.

These various problems have been addressed in policies
known as 'limited response', 'flexible response', 'extended
deterrence', and the like. In fact, official statements indicate that the United States does not explicitly target
weapons on civilians, but on military forces and military-
related industry. The fact that people are located close to
such industry, however, means that there is very little difference in outcome between this policy and one that targets
civilians specifically.

The Pastoral Letter of the American Catholic Bishops[3]
wrestles with the apparent effectiveness of deterrence (of

nuclear attack) by threat of retaliation against the society of the attacker, which would clearly result in the slaughter of innocent people. The Bishops are led to a 'strictly conditioned moral acceptance of nuclear deterrence', but assert that 'sufficiency to deter is an adequate strategy; the quest for superiority must be rejected'.

Another recent influence is the modernisation and expansion of the Soviet intermediate-range nuclear force threat to Europe, with the deployment of the SS-20 mobile, MIRVed missile, and the planned response by NATO of deploying 464 ground-launched cruise missiles and 108 Pershing IIs beginning December 1983, unless an agreement is reached which would persuade NATO that this deployment was unnecessary.

A third major influence is the announcement on 23 March 1983 of the adoption by the United States of a new goal of absolute defence against nuclear weapons, '... rendering these nuclear weapons impotent and obsolete'. The President has directed a comprehensive 'effort to define a long-term research and development program to begin to achieve our ultimate goal of eliminating the threat posed by strategic nuclear missiles. This could pave the way for arms control measures to eliminate the weapons themselves'. He notes: 'And as we proceed we must remain constant in preserving the nuclear deterrent and in maintaining a solid capability for flexible response'.

A fourth major influence is the report of the Scowcroft Commission on strategic forces[4] which made the very sensible observations that vulnerability of the land-based ICBM component **alone** of the strategic forces was unimportant in the context of overall force survivability; that the United States would be more secure by developing a small single-warhead ICBM as the future direction of the ICBM force; that small submarines should ultimately be available to augment or replace the large submarines in the SLBM force; and that the currency of arms control should be numbers of **warheads** rather than launchers, in order to control the threat directly. But contrary to its explicit rationale, the Scowcroft Commission unanimously recommended the deployment of 100 MX missiles in Minuteman silos, claiming that the small ICBM (Midgetman) would be available only in the 1990s. I believe that the Midgetman could be available by 1989 if it were not artificially delayed, as was the Trident-I (C-4) missile.

Politics of the MX

'I can call spirits from the vasty deep' boasted Glendower in Shakespeare's Henry IV, Part I. '...so can any man; But will they come when you call for them?' retorted Hotspur.

Just so - doctrine must make some contact with capability, and proclaimed goals with feasibility. Furthermore, although uncertainty, deception, and even pretence have their place in human affairs and international relations (including in deterring attack), self-delusion can hardly be beneficial.

Unfortunately, even technical alternatives towards the same strategic goals are often not considered with an open mind; how much more difficult it is to compare alternative strategies and doctrines! This seems the nature of human beings - exhibited in the USA and USSR alike; it is one of the personal deficiencies that good government solves and bad government exaggerates. The MX deployment proposed by the Scowcroft Commission[4] is a case in point. The members of the Commission quite frankly acknowledge that the MX in Minuteman silos will be just as vulnerable as Minuteman, and a more attractive target, but they maintain (as does President Reagan) that the deployment of MX is essential in order to advance the cause of arms control. Individual members of the Commission are more explicit in their testimony and statements and say that it is the threat of deploying far more than 100 MX (and so getting an apparent first-strike capability against Soviet ICBM silos) which will increase Soviet motivation to reduce numbers of large landbased missiles. Whatever the validity of the argument, the MX development and deployment comes at great cost - at least $15 billion, and the **same** silo-killing capability can be obtained sooner by improvement of accuracy of the existing Minuteman missiles at a cost substantially less than $6 billion. A greater (and earlier) first-strike capability against silos can be obtained by fitting Trident-I missiles with guidance systems which make use of NAVSTAR satellite navigation signals, thereby providing almost 5000 warheads of shorter flight time than ICBMs with a silo-killing capability.

But it is not at all clear that the Soviet Union can be induced by threats to incur vast costs of uncertain benefit. Of course, it was quite unnecessary for purposes of deterrence for the Soviet Union to build such large numbers of accurate MIRVs, and whatever US analysts think of the validity of a model of the arms race in which the Soviet Union responds to US initiatives, the administration maintains quite frankly that it is building weapons and modernising its forces in response to Soviet weapons.

Strategic Defence

So the MX is unnecessary and excessively costly whatever US demands for a strategic posture! How about the desire for perfect defences against nuclear weapons, presumably to be teamed with extensive civil defence, while still maintaining an offensive strategic capability?

The feasibility of a defence is conditional upon the requirements. If one side with 3000 warheads sets itself the demand to destroy at least 1400 of 1500 hardened silos, it is quite easy to frustrate such an attack, since with reasonable missile reliabilities the defence need destroy or defend successfully against no more than one re-entry vehicle at each silo. However, if the purpose of the defence is to **ensure** that fewer than twenty re-entry vehicles of an initial force of 10 000 strike their **city** targets, the defence has a vastly more complicated task, even if it is not attacked, confused, or bypassed.

If there is any basis for President Reagan's initiative of 23 March 1983, it must lie in a ballistic missile defence (BMD) capable of destroying ICBMs and SLBMs during the boost phase, which for ICBMs is a long distance inside the Soviet Union and far from bases of BMD. Furthermore, the boost phase for the MX lasts only 155 seconds, and even for beam weapons whose effects are carried with the speed of light, the time for assessment and command is critically short. But there are fundamental problems with such systems, independent of the weapon technology.

It seems to me that there is essentially no chance of preserving the US society against a large nuclear strike by the Soviet Union, or vice versa, no matter how hard we work on defences which have been discussed thus far either openly or in government circles. Nor do such (imperfect) defences significantly add to deterrence, already accomplished if one has the capability, the doctrine, and the will to use large numbers of nuclear weapons in retaliation for attack. At a level of a few nuclear weapons exchanged between the superpowers, defences might be effective even in preventing nuclear detonations on cities, but 100 nuclear weapons could certainly be made available to destroy a city, making a grisly point without disarming the attacker.

Between the superpowers, imperfect defences will simply lead to more rapid escalation if nuclear war begins. However, massive defences might have some effectiveness against the strategic nuclear forces of a lesser power, especially if that power has no effective warning system to launch its vulnerable weapons before they are destroyed in their bases, so that only a fraction of the force need be handled by the defences.

However, in addition to weighing the potential benefits of defences if war comes, or of assessing the reduction in likelihood of war, one must consider the disadvantages – that destruction if war comes might be **increased** because of

augmentation of the strategic offensive force; because of
such augmentation and greater application to counter-value
targets, together with attacks on the defence which totally
defeat it; or because defences on both sides make one side
(perhaps rashly) confident that damage will be reduced, but
worried that the other side will be able to improve its
defence in a while so that it will be effective.

If one side believes large-scale nuclear war to be truly
inevitable, then it is only the time when war begins which
must be fixed, and that side is likely to fix it at a time of
its own least disadvantage. It is unconditionally suicidal to
persuade one's opponent that nuclear war is inevitable.

But if nuclear war comes, must we not have planned for the
actual use of nuclear weapons - else they will be totally
unusable and not serve to deter that war? Yes, but there are
limits to the effort and the detail of that planning, just as
there are limits to the numbers of nuclear weapons which need
be available for retaliation. Indeed, those upon whom the
society depends to launch those nuclear weapons must think
about how they will do it, must find targets, must practice
procedures; but the quality of deterrence does not depend in
detail on the targeting of such vast numbers of nuclear
weapons, at least judging by the values held by any human
being I know, whether citizen or leader of the USA, the
USSR, or any other technologically advanced nation.

Conclusion

Political and military leaders of the United States and the
Soviet Union tell us of the expected unparalleled devas-
tation of large-scale nuclear war. General David C. Jones[5],
Chairman of the Joint Chiefs of Staff of the United States
(Retired 1982), expresses grave doubts that any nuclear war
could be limited or protracted. In the United States at
least, expansion of strategic nuclear weapons is supported by
arguments that such expansion improved the 'quality of
deterrence' - that is, that they affect the decisions on the
other side. Would an American President be more deterred from
initiating all-out nuclear war against the Soviet Union by
the thought that accurate Soviet MIRVs could destroy inaccurate US ICBMs (as was the argument in the late 1970s),
or by the thought that inaccurate Soviet warheads would land
on some US cities, and on **all** US cities if there were a
response?

Would a Soviet leader be more 'deterred' from nuclear war
by the thought that accurate US ICBMs could destroy half of
the empty Soviet ICBM silos and thus prevent their being
reloaded with spare missiles, or would he be just as deterred

by inaccurate US ICBM warheads causing sufficient fall-out at those silos to prevent reload? Or by the certainty that nuclear weapons will destroy Soviet society if Soviet weapons are used to destroy another's?

My own view is that the United States and the Soviet Union would both be considerably more secure if they renounced the intention of destroying the opponent's strategic offensive force and began to improve the survivability of their own strategic offensive force by arms control agreements and by unilateral action, such as a move to smaller submarines, to somewhat fewer warheads in Midgetman silos, and in understanding the 'prisoner's dilemma' in which each side finds it in its short-term interest not to cooperate or to reduce the threat to the other side, thereby ensuring an increasing long-term peril to itself.

References

1. R.L. Garwin, 'A second Nuclear Regime' in Nuclear Weapons and World Politics - Alternatives for the Future, D.C. Gompert, M. Mandelbaum, R.L. Garwin and J.H. Barton, (New York: McGraw-Hill, 1977).
2. Committee for the Compilation of Materials on Damage caused by the Atomic Bombs in Hiroshima and Nagasaki, Hiroshima and Nagasaki: the physical, medical and social effects of the atomic bombings, (London: Hutchinson, 1981).
3. 'The Challenge of Peace :God's Promise and our Response', United States Catholic Conference, 1983.
4. General Brent Scowcroft, Report of the President's Commission on Strategic Forces, US Government Printing Office, 11 April 1983.
6. General D.C. Jones, New York Times Magazine, 7 November 1982.

7 VULNERABILITY OF STRATEGIC LAND-BASED WEAPONS

Kosta Tsipis

Introduction

In the fall of 1977, the Soviet Union began a series of tests
of a new guidance system with greatly improved accuracy.
Simplified calculations indicated that once the Soviet
Union had deployed an adequate number of these more accurate
MIRVs, they would have the capability to destroy the bulk of
the US land-based missile force in a first strike. Thus was
born what has come to be referred to as the 'window of
vulnerability'. This concept has dominated American strategic
thinking for several years, providing the primary justification for the development of a new generation of US
strategic weapons, including the MX and Trident II missiles.
The comparable accuracy of US land-based missiles does not
represent a symmetrical threat to the ICBMs of the USSR
because of the insufficient number of US re-entry vehicles
(RV). At any rate, there are considerable uncertainties in
any assessment of the results of a counter-silo attack, which
are not taken into consideration in publicly presented
simplified calculations. Intelligence information is rarely
absolute; faced with uncertainty as to the actual value of
such parameters as the accuracy of Soviet ICBMs, US planners
must make assumptions which are conservative from the US
point of view, and vice versa. Unfortunately, this process
often obscures the fact that any attack would also involve
substantial uncertainty from the **attacker's** point of
view. Due to the limitations of peace-time testing, it is
possible that the performance of a given weapon under the
operational conditions of an attack will be significantly
different from that predicted by the best available estimates
derived from such testing.
Because of the immense destructive power of modern nuclear
arsenals, any nuclear attack on the USA or the USSR would
represent a gamble on a scale absolutely unprecedented in
human history; the future of entire civilisations would hang

in the balance. As a result of the magnitude of the stakes involved, any uncertainty as to the outcome of such an attack will probably act as a powerful deterrent; such gambles are not made without extremely high confidence in the outcome. The question for a planner of such an attack must always be not only 'what is the **expected** outcome but what is the **worst plausible** outcome?'. Thus, in assessing the desirability of an attack, it is crucially important to assess quantitatively the uncertainties involved, in order to develop an assessment which is 'attack-conservative'. This is rarely done in public assessments of the strategic balance; in general, the results of an idealised, flawless attack are presented to the public, while the uncertainties inherent in any such attack are ignored. This paper discusses, albeit briefly, these uncertainties in order to cast the current vulnerability of ICBMs in a more realistic frame.

Probability of Destroying a Target

ICBM silos are generally most vulnerable to the shock wave of the nuclear blast. Thus, the 'hardness' of a given silo is usually expressed in terms of the shock wave overpressure required to destroy it, measured in pounds per square inch (psi). Current US silos housing the 1000 Minuteman ICBMs are generally estimated to be capable of withstanding overpressures up to 2000 psi. The detonation of a half-megaton weapon, such as those carried by the most accurate Soviet MIRVs, would create such overpressures at ranges of roughly 300 metres; therefore, to destroy a US Minuteman ICBM, a half-megaton weapon would have to detonate within 300 metres of its silo. Thus, the accuracy with which the weapon is delivered, while not particularly important in an attack on a city, would be of decisive importance in any attack on hardened targets such as ICBM silos.

To deliver the RVs within several hundred metres of their targets over ranges of 10 000 kilometres requires an extremely sophisticated guidance system. Current strategic weapons utilise a technique known as inertial guidance, in which accelerometers and gyroscopes are used to measure the specific forces acting on the missile[1]. These inertial instruments cannot measure the force of gravity, however, because of the equivalence of gravitation and acceleration described by Einstein. In order to account for the effects of the earth's gravitational pull on the motion of the missile, a mathematical model of the gravity field, as a function of position, must be programmed into the missile's guidance system prior to launch. By combining this gravity model with the measurements of the specific forces made by the accelerometers, the guidance computer can use Newton's laws of inertia to calculate the three-dimensional motion of the missile and direct it to the appropriate trajectory to reach its intended target.

There is a wide range of sources of error which can affect the accuracy of such a weapon. The two largest sources of error are those arising from measurement and alignment errors of the inertial instruments, and those arising from re-entry, each of which accounts for more than 100 metres of error in some current ICBMs. In addition to these errors arising from inertial measurement and re-entry, there are several smaller sources of error which can have some effect on the overall accuracy of the weapon; these include errors in the gravitational model used by the guidance system, errors in warhead fusing, and errors in the determination of the position of the target.

The bulk of the error sources of a ballistic missile will be random from one missile to the next. As a result, if a large number of such weapons were fired at a single target, they would tend to fall in a random scatter, in the vicinity of the intended target. The spread of this scatter is measured by a parameter known as the circular error probable, (CEP); the CEP is the radius of a circle centred on the average point of impact within which 50 per cent of the RVs would fall. Thus, the CEP is a measure of the precision with which a given missile delivers its payload.

Using estimates of the CEP, explosive yield, and reliability of a given weapon, its probability of destroying a target of given hardness can be calculated. As an example, the Soviet SS-19 Mod-3 is estimated to have a CEP of 250 metres; each of its six warheads has a yield of approximately 550 kilotons. The SS-18 Mod-4 has similar accuracy and yield, but carries 10 independently-targetable warheads. Assuming perfect reliability, as many popular sources do, warheads of these types would have a 63 per cent probability of destroying a Minuteman silo hardened to 2000 psi. Assuming statistical independence, two such weapons would have an 86 per cent 'kill probability' against the same silo. Thus, this simplified calculation would indicate that with 2000 warheads, the Soviet Union could destroy nearly 90 per cent of the 1000 US Minuteman missile silos; this is the alarming theoretical result which has been given wide circulation. It should be noted, however, that it is unreasonable to expect that a system as complex as a modern ICBM will have a reliability close to 100 per cent; 75 per cent is a more reasonable estimate for the reliability of current Soviet ICBMs. Such a reliability would reduce the two-warhead kill probability to 72 per cent, which agrees well with the 70-75 per cent figure currently being cited by the US Joint Chiefs of Staff.

Sources of Error

However, this simple figure does not take into account the broad range of uncertainties that must be considered in calculating the possible outcome of any counter-silo attack. The first significant source of uncertainty is the accuracy of the attacking weapons. The bulk of the error sources in an ICBM system will be statistically uncorrelated from one missile to another, contributing to the random distribution described by the CEP. ICBMs, however, experience systematic errors as well as random errors. Thus, while the standard calculations of ICBM vulnerability assume that the centre of the impact distribution will be directly on the target, in fact the distribution will often be offset somewhat; the distance between the target and average point of impact is referred to as the **bias**. For example, if the estimated location of a given target is 20 metres south of its actual position, it is likely that the location of other targets in the same general area, such as other silos within the same missile field, will be similarly mis-estimated; thus, on the average, the RVs attacking that field would detonate 20 metres south of their intended targets. Similarly, the gravitational errors for ICBMs launched from nearby silos will be strongly correlated, as will the errors due to prevailing winds and atmospheric density variations encountered by RVs re-entering the atmosphere in the same area.

Against targets hardened to 2000 psi, any bias smaller than roughly 100 metres has essentially no effect. This is because any weapon falling within three times this distance of the target will destroy it. Because of the nature of bias, it is very difficult to place limits on the magnitudes of bias that might be encountered in an actual attack, because of the statistical properties of large numbers. If an error is simply random from one warhead to the next, then an attack involving 2000 warheads would provide 2000 independent trials for that variable; as with 2000 rolls of a dice, the probability of any significant variation from the average outcome is quite small. By contrast, if an error is completely correlated over some fraction of the force, as in our targeting example above, then for that portion of the force, the attack provides only a single trial; just as a roll of two dice might very well turn up a two or a twelve, rather than the most likely value of seven, so in a single attack, a bias significantly larger than 100 metres cannot realistically be discounted.

There is also some uncertainty associated with the estimate of the CEP of any given ICBM. A variety of sources of information are available concerning the accuracy of a given weapon. Non-destructive ground tests of subsystems, for example, can provide detailed performance specifications for every component of the guidance system. However, many of the significant sources of error, such as those attributable to re-entry, cannot be realistically tested on the ground; in addition, the interaction between the various components of the guidance system in the demanding acceleration, vibration and shock environment of rocket boost is extremely complex. Thus, only statistically significant numbers of realistic full-system flight tests can provide accurate estimates of the CEP of a new ballistic missile. A variation of 10 per cent between the CEP estimated from shots over test ranges and the actual CEP in a large-scale counter-silo strike could not by any means be ruled out; it is, as a matter of fact, a conservative estimate. For the Soviet warheads mentioned earlier, an unfavourable variation of 10 per cent in the CEP alone would reduce the double-shot kill probability against a Minuteman silo from 72 per cent to 66 per cent.

Similarly, there is some uncertainty in estimates of the reliability of any given weapon system. As with any sensitive and complex electromechanical system, high confidence in estimates of overall reliability can only be obtained through full-system tests; the number of such ICBM tests is quite limited. In addition, estimates of the overall operational reliability of ICBMs must take into consideration a broad range of human factors that would be involved in an attack; any large-scale counter-silo strike would require the timely cooperation of several hundreds of people, whose behaviour under such circumstances is unpredictable. Thus, 10 per cent is probably a conservative estimate of the uncertainty in estimates of overall reliability. An unfavourable variation of 10 per cent in the reliability usually assumed for an SS-19 Mod-3 would reduce the number of Minuteman silos destroyed, in a hypothetical two-on-one attack, from 72 per cent to 67 per cent.

Another important source of uncertainty arises from estimates of the explosive power of the thermonuclear warheads. This uncertainty is of two interrelated kinds: first, uncertainty as to the precise effects of warheads of given yield, and second, uncertainty in the estimates of the yield of a given class of warheads. The US Defense Intelligence Agency estimates an uncertainty of 20 per cent in estimates of peak overpressure at a given range; this is quite conservative. Although less is known concerning the Soviet nuclear weapons test programme, it should be noted that when the Partial Test Ban Treaty put an end to atmospheric testing, the Soviet Union had conducted only half as many nuclear tests as had the United States.

In addition to these uncertainties in the prediction of the overpressure at given ranges from a nuclear detonation, there remains some uncertainty in the estimate of the average yield of a given class of thermonuclear warheads. While some estimates can be derived from theoretical considerations, a recent example of the pitfalls of this approach was provided by the case of the warhead developed for the Mark 12A reentry vehicle recently deployed on the US Minuteman III missiles. The first three tests of this weapon revealed that its explosive yield was considerably below that which had been predicted. A modification of the original design was required before the weapon achieved its full yield in a fourth test. While this is perhaps an extreme case, the uncertainty in the average yield of a given class of warheads will be at least 10 per cent.

Since the peak overpressure at a given range from a detonation is proportional to the yield of the detonation, a 20 per cent variation in overpressure at a given range would be caused by a 20 per cent variation in yield; a conservative estimate of the total uncertainty in the effective yield of a given weapon might then be of the order of 25 per cent. An unfavourable variation of 25 per cent in the yield of the weapons involved would reduce the effectiveness of the hypothetical attack already described from 72 per cent to 66 per cent.

The overpressure at which a silo will fail depends primarily on the technical characteristics of the reinforced concrete door covering the top of the silo, and it is extremely difficult to acquire reliable intelligence on these parameters. Thus, the uncertainty in this parameter, from the attacker's point of view, is possibly the largest uncertainty of all. Indeed, even US estimates of the hardness of US silos include significant uncertainties; the fact is that no silo has ever been exposed to a nuclear weapon in any test. Estimates of silo hardness are based entirely on theoretical structural considerations and tests of scale models with conventional explosives. Thus, from the attacker's point of view, the uncertainty in the hardness of the silos to be attacked is likely to be at least 20 per cent, if not considerably more. If the silos under attack were capable of withstanding overpressures 20 per cent higher than expected, the effectiveness of the hypothetical attack we have been describing would be reduced from 72 per cent to 68 per cent.

The Fratricide Effect

So far it has been assumed that the warheads involved in a counter-silo attack would be statistically independent of each other; that is to say, that the detonation of one warhead would have no effect whatsoever on other warheads involved in the attack. In   fact, this is not at all the case; thermonuclear detonations can have extremely destructive effects on other re-entry vehicles, a phenomenon rather ironically referred to as 'fratricide'.

In the first milliseconds after the initiation of a thermonuclear detonation, the weapon gives off an intense burst of radiation, including neutrons, X-rays, and gamma-rays, which in turn cause a powerful eletromagnetic pulse. This short-lived burst of radiation is followed by the rapid expansion of a fireball of hot, compressed gases, generated by the explosion. This fireball expands outwards faster than the speed of sound, reaching a radius of several hundred metres in less than a second. Within the fireball temperatures are several tens of thousands of degrees centigrade, and the winds reach a speed of more than a thousand kilometres per hour. Since the superheated gases at the interior of this fireball are orders of magnitude less dense than the surrounding air, the fireball begins to rise quite rapidly, much like a hot-air balloon. This creates vertical winds of several hundred km/hr; indeed, the drag created by these winds is sufficient to hold aloft a two-tonne boulder. In the case of a weapon burst at the optimum height for an attack on a silo hardened to 2000 psi, the fireball will be in contact with the earth over a wide area for several seconds; as a result the powerful updraft winds will suck thousands of tonnes of dust and debris up from the ground, creating the characteristic mushroom cloud.

This cloud of dust continues to rise quite rapidly; within one minute it reaches an altitude of several kilometres. It then slows considerably, reaching its maximum height approximately ten minutes after the detonation. In the case of a half-megaton weapon, such as those we have been considering, the top of the cloud will stabilise at an altitude of some 18 kilometres, with the cloud bottom roughly 8 kilometres below. By ten minutes after the detonation, the cloud will cover an area of some 100 square kilometres.

The significance of the particles and dust raised by the detonation arises from the fact that re-entry vehicles traverse the atmosphere at extremely high speed. When an RV re-entering the atmosphere in the area of a previous detonation encounters the cloud, it will be travelling with a speed of some 6000 metres per second. Thus, if the RV collided with a particle weighing several grammes, it would probably be destroyed outright, for such a collision would take place at several times the speed of a bullet. The smaller particles and dust in the cloud could have catastrophic abrasive effects on an RV. The resulting unpredictable ablation of the RV's nose-tip would severely degrade its accuracy; in extreme cases it could cause the RV to burn up in the atmosphere. In addition, it should be remembered that the detonation will have completely changed the density and wind profiles throughout the surrounding area, in ways that are essentially completely unpredictable, and would have drastic effects on the accuracy of a re-entering RV.

Since fratricide has never been tested, it is not possible to make a precise assessment of its effect on incoming RVs; only the roughest order-of-magnitude estimates are possible. Suppose, for example, in the case of a second wave re- entering ten minutes after the first, that the passage through the dust cloud and encounters with residual large particles destroyed only 5 per cent of the RVs, and that, on the average, the effect of the dust and atmospheric disturbances increased the portion of the CEP attributable to re-entry by a factor of two. This is a quite conservative estimate of the fratricide such a wave would experience. These effects alone would reduce the kill probability of a two-wave attack by SS-19 Mod-3 warheads on US Minuteman silos from 72 per cent to approximately 65 per cent.

There is another, perhaps more significant uncertainty that arises from the problem of fratricide: if the attacker must allow several minutes to pass between the first and second waves of his attack, then it is quite possible that the ICBMs which survived the first wave will have left their silos before the second wave arrives. However, since the vulnerability of an ICBM increases drastically when it leaves its protective silo, it is possible that the attacker could prevent these weapons from launching by detonating additional weapons over the silo field at regular intervals between the two waves; this is referred to as 'pindown'.

Conclusions

In any real counter-silo attack, all of these uncertainties would be present, making the final outcome of the attack even more difficult to predict. Consider, for example, an 'attack-conservative' calculation of the outcome, in which light fratricide is combined with unfavourable variations of all of the parameters. The destructive power of the weapons involved is 25 per cent less than predicted; the accuracy and reliability 10 per cent less and the silos under attack turn out to be 25 per cent harder than estimated. In this case, only 45 per cent of the US Minuteman silos would be destroyed, even in the absence of significant bias.

While it is perhaps unlikely that an attack would experience large unfavourable variations in all four of the basic parameters of the attack simultaneously, it should be noted that an unfavourable variation of any two of the parameters, when combined with fratricide, would reduce the effectiveness of the attack to less than 55 per cent, even ignoring the possibilities of bias and of ICBMs escaping between the two waves.

However, this comparatively comforting conclusion may not remain valid indefinitely. The state of strategic weapons technology is almost never in stasis, and foreseeable improvements in weapons delivery technology could drastically alter the situation we have described. In the past the accuracy of US and Soviet ICBMs has generally improved by roughly a factor of two every seven years; while the improvement of strategic weapons technology may slow somewhat as the room for improvement narrows, there is little reason to expect that the pattern in coming years will be fundamentally different.

Thus, while the current situation is more stable than is commonly believed, the progress of weapons technology bodes ill for the future. It is still possible, however, that severe limitations on the testing and deployment of ballistic missiles could prevent the development of many of these undesirable technological improvements. Far from locking either the United States or the USSR into a position of vulnerability, such limits, if effective, could prevent the rapid erosion of their security which will otherwise occur in the years to come. Such limitations could be an important component of arms control efforts, and deserve more careful study than they have received to date.

Reference

1. K. Tsipis, 'The Accuracy of Strategic Missiles', Scientific American, (July 1975) 14-24.

REDUCING THE PROBABILITY OF A NUCLEAR WAR

Carlo Schaerf

On August 6 1945 a nuclear bomb exploded over Hiroshima. The consequences of that event are summarised in Table 1. On August 9 a second nuclear bomb exploded over Nagasaki. The nuclear era had begun.

Table 1. Consequences of the Explosion in Hiroshima

Explosive power	:	about 12.5 kilotons
Total population	:	320 000
Killed	:	118 661
Seriously wounded	:	30 524
Slightly wounded	:	48 606
Missing	:	3 667

Source: Committee for the Compilation of Materials on Damage caused by the Atomic Bombs in Hiroshima and Nagasaki. Hiroshima and Nagasaki: the physical, medical and social effects of the atomic bombings. (London: Hutchinson, 1981).

The Nuclear Arms Race

After a few years of American monopoly, a continuous quantitative and qualitative race ensued between the two superpowers aiming at reaching either parity or security through a stable and credible deterrent.

The introduction of the H-bomb in 1952 signified an increase in explosive power by three orders of magnitude. It was not followed by further macroscopic steps in the technology of nuclear bombs, but there was a slow and gradual improvement in the efficiency, reliability and the physical dimensions of the weapons, permitting a diversity in application of nuclear weapons to specific tasks. The introduction of the enhanced radiation weapon, popularly known as the neutron bomb, is only one aspect of this slow process.

The most significant technological race has involved the means of delivery of nuclear bombs and their guidance systems. Strategic bombers have been followed by intercontinental ballistic missiles (ICBM), then by multiple reentry vehicles (MRV), multiple independently-targetable reentry vehicles (MIRV), and now by the cruise missiles. Inertial guidance systems have progressively advanced, reducing the circular error probable (CEP) from kilometres to hundreds of metres. Recently a CEP of several tens of metres was reached with terminal guidance.

The perception of insecurity produced by the technological advances achieved by the opponent, in combination with domestic and international factors, has pushed the two superpowers (and even the other three recognised nuclear weapon states: Great Britain, France and China) into a race aiming at the acquisition of an increasing number of nuclear warheads targeted on the other side. The terrible risk posed to mankind by this race becomes obvious when we remember the casualties produced by the two nuclear blasts on Japan, and considering the 50 000 nuclear warheads now existing, some of them with a yield a thousand times greater than the bombs which destroyed Hiroshima and Nagasaki. Civilisation, as we know it today, will be completely destroyed in the event of a nuclear war.

Currently, the nuclear arms race is advancing even further by two important steps:
- the USSR deploying the more modern and precise SS-20 to replace the obsolete SS-4 and SS-5;
- NATO's decision to install on European soil the ground-launched cruise missile (GLCM) and the Pershing II missile, both of which have a CEP of 40-50 metres. The Pershing II can reach, in less than 10 minutes, the command, control and communication centres of the USSR located near Moscow.

We cannot predict the day when a nuclear war will break out nor can we be sure that it will not break out before a certain date. Our civilisation is like a radioactive nucleus. It is destined to disintegrate but no theory can foresee the exact moment of its disintegration. Science can only calculate the probability of the disintegration per unit of time and derive a mean life. Whereas the probability for the decay of a radioactive nucleus is constant, the probability of destruction of the human civilisation depends on the international climate. It rises in periods of tension and falls at peaceful times. The clock of 'The Bulletin of the Atomic Scientists' provides a reasonable guess to this probability. The closer the minute hand is to midnight, the greater is the risk of a nuclear holocaust (as of January 1984 it was moved to three minutes to midnight).

The most important religious assemblies have recently denounced the intrinsic immorality of nuclear arms. As scientists we must emphasise that the larger the number of nuclear weapons, the higher the risk of a nuclear war. We must insist on the simple formula: more nuclear arms equals greater probability of a nuclear war.

Thirty years of strategic nuclear thinking have led to a situation fraught with terrible danger:
- more than 50 000 nuclear warheads in the arsenals of the nuclear powers;
- 3959 intercontinental missiles and 466 strategic bombers ready to be used;
- more than the equivalent of three tonnes of high explosives for each human being on the face of the earth.

It is now twenty-eight years since the Russell-Einstein Manifesto initiated the Pugwash Movement. At the start of the 33rd Conference we must concentrate our efforts on a re-examination of the basic concepts behind the nuclear strategic thinking over these years.

Nuclear Parity

In my opinion, the most important concept to be re-examined is that of nuclear parity.

In the field of nuclear armaments, the need to recover parity, allegedly jeopardised by the initiatives of one's opponent, has been the main argument used to justify the acquisition of new weapons. There are at least four different indices to measure the current nuclear potential of the superpowers at the strategic level. These are shown in Table 2.

The numbers in Table 2 have been obtained from the 1981/2 **Military Balance** of the International Institute for Strategic Studies (IISS) with the addition of some reasonable hypotheses. Although the numbers are subject to large uncertainties, they clearly indicate the arbitrariness in the measure of parity. Moreover, it is always possible to demonstrate that one party is superior or inferior to the other by an appropriate choice of the index, as is clearly evident in the last two columns.

Even more arbitrary is a similar comparison of the intermediate nuclear forces (INF) assigned to the European

theatre, where many other factors have to be taken into
account.
- In Europe, the geographic position of the two superpowers
is quite different.
- The distinction between tactical and strategic nuclear
weapons is highly subjective. Tactical nuclear weapons are
mainly intended for counterforce use; they are assumed to

Table 2. Indices of the Nuclear Strategic Potential

	USA	USSR	USA/USSR	Superiority
1) Number of missiles and strategic bombers:				
ICBM	1052	1398		
SLBM	520	989		
All BM's	1572	2387	0.66	USSR
Aircraft	316	150	2.11	USA
2) Number of strategic nuclear warheads:				
TOTAL	9268	7300	1.27	USA
3) Equivalent megatonnage (EMT)				
TOTAL	3752	6100	0.62	USSR
4) Counter military potential (CMP)				
ICBM	15 869	32 436		
SLBM	3 877	1 782		
All BM's	19 746	34 218	0.58	USSR
Aircraft	33 261	7 500	4.43	USA
Total	53 007	41 718	1.27	USA

Notes: The equivalent megatonnage (EMT) is given by the
number of warheads multiplied by their explosive yield (in
megatons) to the power of two-thirds.
The counter military potential (CMP) is defined by the
formula: $CMP = EMT/(CEP)^2$.
For gravity bombs a CEP of 200 m was assumed.

be targeted on military installations, have high precision,
a limited yield, and a short or intermediate range. On the
other hand, strategic nuclear weapons are countervalue,
that is for targeting on cities, have a low precision, high
yield and a long range. In Europe, military targets and
cities are so closely spaced that many nuclear weapons can
be used against either and one single bomb could destroy
both.
- Traditionally, NATO refuses to include the British and
French nuclear forces in the evaluation of the Western
deterrent.
However, there is little contention that the Warsaw Treaty
Organisation (WTO) is superior in the field of conventional
forces; NATO has superiority in the field of tactical nuclear
weapons; the USSR has had for a long time superiority in the
field of Eurostrategic nuclear weapons, which has notably
increased with the introduction of the SS-20.

The Risk of Accidental Nuclear War

In this situation, if we harbour no illusions about achieving
parity in a short time by general and complete disarmament,
it is obvious that the search for an undefinable parity will
only result in further driving the arms race, with the mounting risk of an accidental war, initiated perhaps by a trivial
human error or by instrumental malfunctioning.

Both the USA and the USSR have been the victims of surprise
attacks at the beginning of World War II. Today, due to the
advent of nuclear bombs and intercontinental missiles, a
surprise attack can be launched within twenty minutes and
have devastating effects. This historical memory leads both
superpowers to consider a nuclear surprise attack as a threat
to be exorcised. Strategic thinking has concentrated on how
to avoid this danger.

In order to carry out a surprise attack with a reasonable
chance of success, it is necessary to have an appreciable
military superiority and, therefore, only the strongest power
can consider it. With a similar worry by the other side, the
obvious solution is a search for 'parity'. Since increasing
one's own level of armaments is the only response to a true
or supposed perception of inferiority, the world has been
plunged into a continuous arms race.

This argument does not take into account the different
factors inside each alliance, the domestic problems of the
two superpowers, or the role played by other nations, such as
Afghanistan or Iran. It is, therefore, only a first approximation.

I submit that the main factor, neglected so far, is the

danger of an accidental nuclear war. The term 'accidental war' includes a series of possibilities, ranging from a misleading signal received by radar, to the malfunctioning of a computer, to a soldier going insane, to a failure of brinkmanship, and generally any event which can lead to a nuclear war without a clear intention. Of course, all nuclear powers have made immense efforts to minimise this risk by improving command, control and communication (C^3) systems and setting up a special selection procedure for the staff responsible for launching nuclear arms. Notwithstanding all efforts which have been made, this risk can neither be neglected nor calculated. Proper models can estimate the probability of errors in an electronic and electro-mechanical system, but it is impossible to evaluate the much greater risk arising from the man-machine interaction. To neglect this probability is the same as to make a model of car accidents on the supposition that they are all due to mechanical troubles, neglecting the errors of drivers.

The danger of an accidental war, when it is included in strategic thinking, leads to a change in hypotheses, with obvious consequences to the conclusions.

Reducing the Probability of Nuclear War

The simplest way to introduce this new parameter into the calculation is to assume that the probability of an accidental nuclear war is proportional to the total quantity of existing arms. Consequently, if one power increases its military potential, its security is increased by reducing the probability that it may be subject to a surprise attack. But, at the same time, its security is reduced due to the increase in the total quantity of arms with the attendant risk of an accidental war. It follows from this that the condition of minimum war risk is not by achieving parity but by unilaterally choosing a slight inferiority.

This concept can be expressed in simple mathematical formulae. The probability of an aggressive war depends on the military superiority of a potential aggressor and is a rapidly increasing function of this superiority. Suppose that X and Y represent the military potential of the two adversaries. The simplest way to write this probability is:

$$\text{probability of war by aggression} = a\,(X-Y)^2$$

where a is a positive constant. The quadratic expression was chosen to indicate that superiority of either of the two powers rapidly increases the danger of war. The above function becomes equal to zero for X=Y, that is in the case of parity.

As already postulated, the probability of an accidental war depends on the total quantity of existing arms and can be expressed as:

$$\text{probability of accidental war} = b \, (X + Y)$$

where b is a positive constant.

Therefore, the total probability of nuclear war, by aggression or by accident, is given by:

$$\text{total probability of war} = a \, (X - Y)^2 + b \, (X + Y).$$

This expression can have a zero value only for X=Y=0, that is when there are no arms on either side. More realistically, assuming a constant level of arms on one side, Y = constant, the best choice for X is no longer X = Y, but

$$X = Y - b/2a.$$

X is thus smaller than Y, that is the level of armaments of X should be slightly inferior to that of Y, in order to minimise the risk of accidental war.

Since these formulae are symmetrical in X and Y, the same result is obtained for Y, if the value of X is fixed.

Obviously, this model can be criticised for its extreme simplicity. Nevertheless, it focuses on the fact that the danger of a nuclear war comes not only from the opponent's arms but also from its own, since all arms increase the risk of an accidental war. Therefore, when strategic choices are made, and the reduction of the risks of a nuclear attack is contemplated by introducing more sophisticated systems of command, control and communication, the reduction of the risk of accidental war should also be taken into consideration.

The explicit acceptance of a slight strategic inferiority on the part of one superpower is likely to have repercussions on the politics of its opponent. In both political systems there are internal pressures which drive the arms race, as well as groups which would prefer a more sensible policy.

A step in the right direction would be more constructive than to succumb to the general pessimism prevailing today. The Carter administration appeared at certain times sincerely worried about the level of the arms race and was ready to make concessions in order to reverse the tendency. Unfortunately, this happened towards the end of the Brezhnev era and the only result was the SALT II Treaty. Today, the new Soviet leadership appears to be willing to take the first significant steps, to the point of dismantling some bases of SS-20 missiles, but the overall outlook is not very encouraging.

Conclusion

With the theory of relativity and quantum mechanics, the physics community succeeded in overcoming the contradictions of classical physics by accepting new conceptual approaches. A similar open mindedness on the part of the world community is now required in the nuclear arms field.

The first attempts to give up traditional wisdom are not always the right ones, but at the present level of the arms race it is necessary to try new roads.

9.   THE POSSIBILITY OF AN ACCIDENTAL NUCLEAR WAR

Vasily Emelyanov

Militarism and wars have always led to extremely dangerous
situations, but the advent of thermonuclear weapons has
created an especially serious situation for the whole of mankind because of the threat of global annihilation. There has
been an accumulation of such an enormous amount of nuclear
weaponry of monstrous destructive power that the consequences
of their use may lead to the disappearance of all forms of
life on the earth, turning it into a lifeless cosmic body
like the Moon or Mars. The explosive power of nuclear weapons
is so great that even an accidental or unintentional use may
result in huge human losses and serious damage to the
environment.

Already in 1961 President Kennedy, in a speech to the
United Nations, warned us - 'Today every inhabitant of this
planet must contemplate the day when this planet may no
longer be habitable. Every man, woman and child lives under a
nuclear sword of Damocles, hanging by the slenderest of
threads, capable of being cut at any moment by accident or
miscalculation or by madness'.

Causes of Accidental Nuclear War

Members of the scientific community have often debated the
question of the possibility of an accidental nuclear war.
The huge accumulation of nuclear weapons of a large variety
of types and destructive power in different areas of the
globe has created conditions for unanticipated explosions to
occur during the transportation of weapons or their storage
at bases. Many causes of such 'accidental' or 'unpremedi-
tated' nuclear explosions can be envisaged.

One cause may be deficient construction. Another, inadequate action by those who have control of the weapons due to
failure of communications. A third is a state of psychological imbalance among aircraft crews or missile personnel
who have the authority to drop the bomb, or launch a missile

73

with a nuclear warhead. In this connection it should be noted that in our extremely troubled times psychological disturbances, as well as addiction to alcohol and drugs, are on the increase.

A research team led by J. B. Phelps of Ohio State University[1], reporting on the chances of accidental nuclear war, identified five possible causes: accidents to defence systems; human aberrations; spread of limited war; catalytic war; and diplomatic or military miscalculation. The majority of the distinguished and militarily knowledgeable experts agreed that the spread of limited war and diplomatic miscalculation were the two most important possibilities, in that order. One senior military analyst rated the joint probability of war from these two causes at 50 per cent in the next ten years.

Accidents Involving Aircraft

Robin Clarke[2] describes various accidents involving American aircraft with nuclear weapons that took place in the sixties. Most of the accidents occurred over the territory of the United States, but aircraft with nuclear weapons also crash-landed in Spain and in Greenland.

A more detailed study of accidents with nuclear weapons over the period 1950-75 was carried out by R.A. Farmazyan[3], who lists 95 accidents that have occurred in the US armed forces. One of the most serious incidents with nuclear weapons was a land crash of a strategic B-52 bomber which took place in January 1964; just before crashing the pilot dropped two nuclear bombs in the vicinity of Goldsboro, in North Carolina. The shock of the impact of one of these bombs, with an explosive yield of 24 megatons, set off five of the six explosion-proof devices. It was only because the last mechanism did not fail that a nuclear explosion was avoided which could have been a thousand times more powerful than the explosions of the atom bombs dropped in 1945 on Hiroshima and Nagasaki. Only a lucky chance prevented a nuclear explosion at an American base in Great Britain when a fire began there. Three catastrophes happened in the USA in 1980 which could have led to disastrous consequences. At the Grand Fork air base in North Dakota, a fire burned down a B-52 bomber prepared for a flight and loaded with 30 nuclear bombs. Near Little Rock in Arkansas, as a result of fuel explosion in the tank of a Titan-2 intercontinental ballistic missile, its nuclear warhead was thrown out a great distance from the launching pad and was damaged. A F-111 fighter-bomber with nuclear weapons aboard crash-landed near the US eastern coast.

Accidents due to Computer Failure

The strategic changes in the sixties, with bombers giving way to missiles, rapidly accelerated the opportunities of an accidental war. While the bomber can be called back if a mistake is detected or for any other reason, a missile cannot. Once the button has been pushed nothing can be done to prevent nuclear war.

On two occasions early in June 1980, a computer in the headquarters of the North American Air Defense Command (NORAD) sent out false signals about a Soviet missile attack which was reported to have started. As a result, strategic bombers with nuclear weapons aboard were launched into a high state of readiness, their engines were started and the members of the crews took to their seats.

Farmazyan also quotes a leading British politician, T. Dalyell: 'The fact that within four days a computer mistake twice led to the launching of the American military machine should become a number one problem in the agenda of every government and political party of the world[4].

In the report of the US Senate Committee on Armed Forces of October 1980, it was stated that over a period of only one year and a half, due to a variety of technical malfunctioning, NORAD gave 151 false signals that nuclear attacks against the USA had started. A similar mistake happened on 9 November 1979 when 10 interceptor-fighters started to destroy 'intruding Soviet bombers'.

The book by Daniel Frei and Christian Catrina[5] is mainly concerned with unintentional nuclear war - which is distinguished from accidental war - but the latter is also discussed. The authors mention some 130 accidents involving nuclear weapons but they note that the information about accidents is very restrictive; they are not usually fully disclosed to the public.

While the major reason for nuclear accidents is an airplane crash, there are also other causes. No mechanical system, however carefully constructed and monitored, can be presumed to be infallible. At a time of a serious crisis, the likelihood of an accident in transportation of nuclear weapons intensifies because missiles are loaded on a larger scale; emphasis is placed on quick responses rather than on verifications and authorisations. It should also be borne in mind that should there be nuclear proliferation, countries with vulnerable weapons would feel forced to take risky command and control measures typical of an unstable strategic environment.

In the well-known book 'The Fate of the Earth', Jonathan Schell[6] considers possible causes which may lead to a nuclear war and dwells in detail upon mistakes or mechanical failures in the construction of nuclear devices or in the complicated system of information and control:

On three occasions in the last couple of years, American nuclear forces were placed on the early stages of alert: twice because of the malfunctioning of a computer chip in the North American Air Defense Command's warning system, and one when a test tape depicting a missile attack was inadvertently inserted into the system. The greatest danger in computer-generated misinformation and other mechanical errors may be that one error might start a chain reaction of escalating responses between command centers leading, eventually, to an attack.

The Human Factor

The probability of accidental war discussed so far was concerned only with mechanical failure and breakdown of communications; it did not take into account the likelihood of human error.

While the risk originating in technical failure could, in principle, be made quite small – if investments are made in highly sophisticated safeguard systems – the situation is different with regard to the human factor. Officers responsible for guarding, maintaining and possibly firing nuclear weapons are much less infallible than technical systems. The afore-mentioned Phelps Report[1] raised important questions about the mental stability of those entrusted with nuclear responsibilities. It pointed out that since World War II, no less than 43 per cent of all discharges from the United States forces were made for neuropsychiatric reasons. There was no special psychiatric or psychological screening for bomber crews or missile personnel. Even among people in responsible positions, including leaders, the probability of losing self-control in times of crisis is quite high according to the Report. In recognition of these risks, the best technical methods to prevent accidents resulting from them were introduced but it is doubtful whether they would be effective.

Professor John Raser[7], who has also concerned himself with this problem, states that the two basic assumptions on which the fate of the world rests are: that carefully selected men will retain cool judgement at a time of crisis; and that even if one man fails, others will act as a 'fail-safe' device. However, behavioural science research has shown that both assumptions are almost certainly false. Professor Raser has analysed man's relations with his weapons through-

out history and concluded that the advent of nuclear stockpiles has created an entirely new situation.

It may be argued that the ultimate decision to press the
button still rests with the President of the United States or
the leaders of the other nuclear powers. Is this not a
sufficient guarantee that an act of madness will not send
mankind to its doom?

The British psychiatrist Anthony Storr is not so sure[8]:
'Even countries such as our own have not solved the problem
of getting rid of leaders who become senile or mentally ill.
One of the most disastrous political decisions of recent
years was made by a prime minister who was under such tension
that he was taking amphetamine, a drug which notoriously
impairs judgment.'

According to Dr N. Tinbergen[9] the point can be made even
more simply: 'If only one of the major nations were led now
by a man like Hitler, life on earth would be wiped out.'

Miscalculation

A further risk of an unintentional nuclear war - which in the
opinion of many may be the most serious cause - is a misjudgment of the response of an opponent or a miscalculation
of odds.

In their book, Frei and Catrina[5] testify to the general
concern about these issues:

> Larger sectors of the public are increasingly alarmed by
> the traumatic prospect of a system of strategic deterrence
> getting out of control and suddenly confronting mankind
> with a doomsday nightmare ... although the dangers of
> possible nuclear accidents and incidents must certainly not
> be underestimated, the conclusion cannot be avoided that
> the focus on the risk of nuclear war by accident may mis-
> represent the problem and draw attention away from more
> serious risks ... What is being envisaged here is not
> accidental nuclear war, but rather nuclear war based on
> false assumptions, that is, on misjudgment or miscalcu-
> lation by the persons legitimately authorized to decide on
> the use of nuclear weapons.

Frei and Catrina conclude:

- due to technical failure or malfunctioning, nuclear
  weapons may be accidentally detonated or launched;
  technical malfunctioning may also lead to false
  alarms;
- nuclear accidents and incidents may also be caused by

-    unauthorised action, human error or sheer madness;
-    such accidents or incidents with nuclear weapons may
     be misinterpreted by an adversary nuclear power and
     lead it to retaliate immediately;
-    the risks are particularly serious in countries which
     have a newly acquired nuclear capability but are not
     yet able or willing to invest in sophisticated safe-
     guard systems.

This last point cannot be stressed too strongly. Even if we
were to brush aside all the risks of an accidental nuclear
war as long as there are only five nuclear powers, we could
not afford this with ten or fifteen such powers, some of whom
being ready to reinforce their local quarrels with even a
primitive nuclear capability.

The risk of an accidental nuclear war is said to be
proportional to the total number of nuclear weapons in the
arsenals; it is also proportional to the number of countries
possessing nuclear weapons. But this can only be a first
approximation. An important weighting factor is the amount of
effort and expense a country is prepared to put into prevention of an accident, either of a technical or psychological
nature. Another important factor is the experience of the
leaders in handling near-crisis situations. It is not easy
to express these factors in a mathematical formula but simple
logic leads us to conclude that if nuclear weapons are held
by many countries, particularly those which frequently
experience political upheavals, there is a greater likelihood
of a nuclear 'accident' into which other nuclear powers may
be drawn inadvertently, thus leading to a nuclear holocaust.

Conclusion

After the existence of nuclear weapons became known,
thoughtful people everywhere in the world realised that if
the great powers entered into a nuclear arms race, the human
species would sooner or later face the possibility of
extinction. J.Schell writes[6] 'They also realized that in
the absence of international agreements preventing it, an
arms race would probably occur. They knew that the path of
nuclear armament was a dead end for mankind. In the shadow of
this power, the earth became small and the life of the human
species doubtful.'

A leading article in the 'Za Rubezhom' newspaper[10]
convincingly showed the dangerous situation which faces
mankind nowadays:

There is worry in the world. In a number of areas of the

globe the fire of war either starts anew or abates, but does not extinguish itself completely. In other areas hidden tensions create unending threats for the security of peoples. And hysterical speeches heard from Washington confirm that there are forces which want to push mankind even closer to the danger of a new world catastrophe.

The concern of people is expressed in the powerful growth of the anti-nuclear movement which embraces all the continents. Its universal character is confirmed by its composition, with representatives of various political parties, trade unions, youth organisations, religious groups, and so on. The desire to save the world from a nuclear disaster is the platform around which they unite their efforts.

References

1. J. B. Phelps, Accidental War: Some dangers in the 1960s, (Ohio State University, 1960).
2. R. Clarke, The Science of War and Peace, (London: Jonathan Cape, 1971).
3. R. A. Farmazyan, Militarism: facts and figures, (Moscow: Politicheskaya Literatura, 1983).
4. T. Dalyell in Farmazyan op. cit, p. 49.
5. D. Frei and C. Catrina, Risks of Unintentional Nuclear War, (Geneva: Palais de Nations, 1982).
6. J. Schell, The Fate of the Earth,(New York: Knopf, 1982).
7. J. R. Raser, 'The Failure of Fail-Safe', Transactions (1969).
8. A. Storr, Human Aggression,(London: Penguin Press, 1968).
9. N. Tinbergen, 'On War and Peace in Animals and Man', Science (28 June 1968).
10. 'To answer The Wish of Mankind' in Za Rubezhom, no. 19, 1983, p. 1.

10   FREEZES AND DEEP REDUCTIONS; TECHNICAL POSSI-
      BILITIES, PUBLIC SENTIMENT, POLITICAL WILL

Jorma Miettinen

The nuclear freeze movement has spectacularly grown in popu-
larity in the United States in the past two years. It has
become a political force influencing the behaviour of the US
Congress and the Reagan administration. It also is a simple
and straightforward arms control measure promising to halt
effectively the nuclear arms race between the USA and USSR.

The Idea behind the Freeze

The idea behind the freeze is simple: most Americans have the
feeling that a new spiral in the nuclear arms race would not
improve their security. A comprehensive freeze which would
stop all development, testing and deployment of nuclear warheads and their delivery vehicles would effectively stop the
arms race and form a starting point for negotiations on
reductions. The advocates of freeze are convinced that if all
factors are considered, there now exists a relatively stable
strategic balance; a new round of modernisations would mainly
increase warfighting capabilities and would be destabilising.
It would further degrade USA-Soviet relations, create bitter-
ness and increased mistrust, and catalyse attempts to acquire
strategic advantages, thus increasing the risk of nuclear
war.

What would a Comprehensive Freeze contain?

It would contain a mutual and verifiable halt of production,
testing and deployment of nuclear weapons and their delivery
vehicles. Freeze is not a brand new idea. Various freeze
proposals were made in the sixties and seventies, and the
proposed Comprehensive Test Ban contains one element of the
freeze: the testing of nuclear explosives. But there are two
new features in the comprehensive freeze advocated in the
USA: prohibition of the modernisation of nuclear forces and
a ban on production of nuclear warheads and fissile material

for weapons. While other arms control treaties and proposals
mainly set limits on numbers - as for example, the SALT I and
SALT II Treaties, the Reagan START proposal, and the Moscow
SALT/START proposal of July 1983 - the freeze would effectively stop modernisation, except for some limited operations
needed to maintain deterrence, such as replacement of aging
systems, particularly submarines of the same type, on a one-
to-one basis.

The bans on the production of new warheads and of fissionable materials are quite far reaching arms control measures.
This is perhaps the most effective but, at the same time, the
most controversial feature of the freeze. Its critics con-
tend that these bans could not be verified. However, many
knowledgeable experts maintain that any major violation
would be detected and that - in any case - weapon numbers are
now so high that small violations would not jeopardise the
strategic balance.

Critics of the Freeze

The Reagan administration and many arms control experts are
opposed to the freeze, advancing several key arguments.
First, that the Soviet Union has just modernised its ICBMs
and its INFs, while the USA has much older ICBMs which have
only been refurbished but do not have a comparable accuracy/
yield combination (hard target capability). Also, that the
INF forces of the USA (Pershing II and GLCMs) are only just
beginning to arrive; thus the freeze would perpetuate this
imbalance. Furthermore, the ICBMs of the USA would remain
much more vulnerable than the Soviet ones. This would remove
any incentives the Soviet Union might otherwise have for
agreeing to a reduction of nuclear weapons.

A second argument is that the freeze is not fully verifiable.

A third argument is that the Reagan START proposal and the
Moscow July 1983 proposal go much further than the freeze:
they entail deep reductions, not freezing at the present high
levels.

The freeze proponents have, of course, answers to these
arguments. First, they assert that the vulnerability of ICBMs
of either side is not as great as the worst case calculations
suggest. The fact that the Reagan administration is planning
to place the new MX missiles in old, albeit hardened, Minuteman silos, is proof of this. Furthermore, the Soviet ICBM
vulnerability is much greater, since the USSR has a much
higher percentage of its strategic warheads in ICBMs than the
USA. The two other legs of the USA triad - SLBMs and bombers
- are far superior to their Soviet equivalents. In reply to

the second argument, they say that most elements of the freeze are sufficiently verifiable (see below). As for the third argument, that START would go further in reductions, the proponents point out that freeze is only an early prelude to later reductions, and that the freeze would go much further than START, or the Moscow July 1983 proposal, by preventing modernisations.

In short, the opponents of freeze believe that the USA is now strategically inferior, nuclear parity is fragile, and this situation must be corrected by 'rearmament'; while the proponents claim that the nuclear balance prevails and is quite stable.

The false perception of US nuclear inferiority is probably the result of the weakness of the American foreign policy management during the 1970s, when the Soviet Union exploited the stability of the nuclear balance and the impotence of the foreign policy of the United States to project its conventional military power in Africa and Asia. In reality, the freeze opponents want military superiority to counter Soviet projections of power, while the freeze proponents would be satisfied with a stable nuclear balance. The latter believe that conflicts of superpower interests in peripheral areas ought to be solved by means other than nuclear threats.

Partial Freezes and European Freeze Concepts

While the main freeze movement in the USA, organised by Randall Forsberg[1] and supported by Senators Kennedy and Hatfield[2], calls for a comprehensive, mutual, and verifiable freeze, as described above, there are various other proposals of partial freezes in the USA and in Europe.

Many of the proponents of partial freezes argue that a comprehensive freeze is too ambitious and far-reaching in trying to prevent completely any modernisation. A partial freeze, as a first step, could be reached more easily and quickly.

One partial freeze scheme - a freeze on the testing and deployment of all long-range nuclear weapon systems (say over 1000 km) - was proposed by Hans Bethe and Frank Long[3] as a first stage; the second stage would comprise a ban on the production of weapon-grade fissile materials and new warheads, and the testing of any nuclear devices. The USA and the Soviet Union have both about the same number of systems with a range of over 1000 km; thus, there would be rough parity.

Another variant is to freeze the number of warheads on delivery vehicles with a range exceeding 1000 km. This would freeze the strategic and theatre nuclear forces to 11 000 warheads, but would allow for modernisation and replacement. Yet another partial freeze proposal is a freeze of all ballistic missiles plus a comprehensive test ban. Other combinations of some elements of a comprehensive freeze are of course possible.

In Europe, attention has been focused on Euromissiles. Many peace movement factions in western Europe, and all in eastern Europe, demand a freeze on Euromissiles before the deployment of any Pershing II or GLCMs.

The recent massive modernisation and increase of Soviet INF forces - to 1050 SS-20 warheads, with more than 200 of the older SS-4 and SS-5 missiles still operational - are probably the reason for the support by the bulk of the west European electorates of NATO policy to press for an INF treaty and, failing that, the deployment of the new missiles. It is clear that if no treaty is agreed before December 1983, the deployment of Pershing II will take place. There will be massive demonstrations in the FRG, UK and elsewhere, but these would not be able to prevent the deployment process.

The American freeze movement does not consider a freeze limited to Europe acceptable. A regional nuclear 'balance' - if it is at all reasonable to speak in these terms - is much less important than a global balance. Since a partial freeze would not halt completely the modernisation and production of warheads - the two most important novel features of the comprehensive freeze - it would be a much less effective arms control measure than the latter.

The Verifiability of a Comprehensive Freeze

As mentioned above, one of the key arguments against the freeze has been that it is not verifiable. The way this is presented varies from the blunt assertions by Richard Perle[4] that 'the total ban on testing and production called for in freeze resolutions would be unverifiable', to the more cautious State Department statement of 4 November, 1982: 'Many aspects of a freeze on testing, production and deployment could not now be effectively verified. Verification measures would, in fact, require extensive prior negotiation and even then, several aspects of the proposed freeze might not be effectively verifiable.' The freeze proponents argue that verification is not an insurmountable obstacle to the ban, since 'major parts of the freeze are verifiable by national means and those that are not are at least partially verifiable through the addition of cooperative measures and on-site inspections'[5].

Many of the elements of the comprehensive freeze have 'requirements similar to those of earlier treaties (SALT I or

II) or the proposed ones (START, CTB). Thus, the ban on testing and deployment of ballistic missiles and the limit on
numbers of warheads and delivery systems are generally considered to be verifiable. So is the CTB, if an international
network of some 50 seismic stations worldwide is agreed upon.
But some of the aspects of the comprehensive freeze are evi-
dently difficult to monitor by national means only. Such
aspects include bans on the production of new fissionable
materials, warheads, delivery systems, and constraints on
some dual-capable systems.

Verifying a freeze on warheads and fissile materials is
analysed in some depth by Jane Sharp[6]. Christopher
Paine[5] maintains that the incentives to fulfil the treaty
obligations would be great for the Soviet Union.

It is obvious that since national technical means of surveillance do not penetrate roofs sufficiently well, additional warheads and launchers of types tested earlier could be
produced clandestinely, but in view of the very large numbers
of existing warheads, small additions would not jeopardise
the strategic balance. Since, under a comprehensive ban, any
detected nuclear weapons-related activity would constitute a
violation, and since operational nuclear forces require a
chain of such activities, a comprehensive freeze - which
means zero activity - is more verifiable than quotas on
restrictions.

Jane Sharp[6] describes why a nuclear warhead ban is verifiable. In the USA all weapon-grade plutonium and tritium are
produced in four reactors, three of which are in the Savannah
River plant in South Carolina, and the fourth in the recently
reactivated reactor at Hanford in Washington State.   All
nuclear components are sent along known routes to a final
assembly plant, the Pantex plant at Amarillo, Texas.

The plutonium and tritium which are used as triggers in
thermonuclear warheads are assembled at the Rocky Flats plant
at Golden, Colorado, and the uranium and lithium deuteride in
the Y-12 plant at Oak Ridge, Tennessee. Jane Sharp maintains
that the nuclear weapons production cycle is 'at least as
concentrated in the Soviet Union'.

Three of the four plutonium and tritium production reactors
in the USA could be closed down if no new warheads were to be
produced. One reactor may have to be kept going in order to
produce tritium; because of its short half-life (12 years)
tritium reservoirs in nuclear warheads need to be replaced
periodically. This reactor, and the military nuclear
facilities producing enriched uranium for reactor fuel, would
have to be provided with safeguards against diversion for
weapons purposes.

Limits on the production of weapon-grade material could be

monitored if the USA and the USSR placed their civilian nuclear plants under IAEA inspection, since both (as well as Britain and France) have already promised to do so in some instances.

Hans Blix, Director General of IAEA, is optimistic that the IAEA safeguards could be increased to monitor a nuclear weapon freeze. In 1983 IAEAs safeguards budget was only $ 34 million. Even if it were doubled it would still be amongst the lowest costs of a comprehensive freeze. Karl Pieragostini[7] discusses tamper-proof, remotely monitorable sensors and other devices for the verification of non-proliferation.

Would a Verifiable, Comprehensive Freeze be Acceptable to the Soviets?

Much uncertainty regarding the Soviet attitude to the freeze was caused, until recently, by the almost complete avoidance of official endorsement of the bilateral freeze proposal. But this attitude appears to have changed. The top meeting of heads of WTO states held 28 June 1983 endorsed the freeze. Ambassador Victor Issraelyan, speaking at the Committee of Disarmament on 5 July 1983, endorsed the freeze 'as the first step which could initially involve only the USA and the USSR'. It ought to include declarations of cessation of the development of nuclear weapon systems and of a moratorium on nuclear tests; reductions would follow as the second stage and verification problems could be solved.

On 7 July 1983, in a statement following a meeting of a delegation of the USSR Supreme Soviet with a delegation of the House of Representatives of the US Congress, Tass stated:

Quite constructive support has been given by this meeting to the idea of freezing the nuclear arsenals, the speaker further stressed. This is quite understandable because it is the clearly expressed demand of our peoples. It is our profound conviction that the freeze is also in accord with the interests and security of both sides. True, there are those who would like the modernisation of nuclear weapons, that is, the nuclear arms race, to continue under the freeze as well. But this would make talks more difficult because the arms race would be outpacing the progress of the talks. It is important for the idea of the freeze to be practically embodied in the actions and agreement of our governments. As for the Soviet Union, this desire was clearly expressed by the session of the USSR Supreme Soviet.

Conclusion

As should be evident from all that, a comprehensive nuclear freeze would be the simplest and most effective arms control measure today. The main opposition to it comes from the Reagan administration which maintains that it would perpetuate a nuclear imbalance and would not be fully verifiable.

I believe that the perception of nuclear imbalance is wrong. When all strategic factors are taken into account, the USA is slightly superior. But a slight superiority in warfighting capability does not amount to much in a nuclear balance, nor do existing asymmetries. On the contrary, the nuclear balance is so stable that the Soviet Union could afford to project conventional military forces in Africa, Asia and elsewhere without significant immediate risks. This was part of the challenge which has caused the Reagan administration to strive for military superiority.

In my opinion the Soviet Union has not shown the kind of restraint in its use of conventional military power that a superpower, in a dynamic competition with another superpower, ought to have shown in order to avoid an increase in the arms race. The superpower conflict must be solved by other methods than a new spiral in the nuclear arms race.

The other counter-argument to freeze - that it is not fully verifiable - is one that has not been studied enough. Particularly, the two new features of freeze, a total ban on production of new nuclear warheads and fissionable materials, and a ban on weapons modernisation, need to be examined in greater depth. The path of nuclear weapons production is fairly well known in the USA but much less in the Soviet Union. The latter has not presented any concrete views on how the verification of freeze would be organised, except the general notion that it is possible.

Today, the biggest barrier to any arms control treaty is the lack of willingness by the superpowers to agree on rules of restraint in the use of military force for advancing their ideological and other interests in the Third World. If the two superpowers do not boldly tackle this problem probably nothing can save us from a new hectic arms spiral and all that results from it.

References

1. R. Forsberg, 'A bilateral nuclear-weapon freeze', Scientific American, (November 1982) pp. 32-41.
2. E.M. Kennedy and M.O. Hatfield, Freeze! How you can help prevent nuclear war, (New York: Bantam Books, 1982).

3. H.A. Bethe and F.A. Long, 'The freeze referendum - what next?', Bulletin Atomic Scientists, (February 1983) pp. 2-3.
4. R. Perle, New York Times, (7 September 1982).
5. C. Paine, 'Freeze verification: time for a fresh approach', Bulletin Atomic Scientists, (January 1983) pp. 6-9.
6. J. Sharp, 'Verifying a Warhead Freeze', Arms Control Today, (June 1983) pp. 4-7.
7. K. Pieragostini, 'Cooperative Verification', Arms Control Today, (June 1983) pp. 1-4.

Daniel Frei

International Crises Getting Out of Control: The Risk and its Origins

The spectre of a 'nuclear Sarajevo' is haunting the world[1]. It cannot be denied that local or regional international crises risk escalating in both intensity and geographic scope; sooner or later they may lead to an armed conflict with frightening consequences which, as in 1914, all or most of the actors concerned neither expect nor intend. Generally speaking, inadvertent or unintentional escalation may result from poor rationality[2], that is, suboptimal performance of either the national decision-making apparatus or the web of communications and procedural links existing between the opponents, as well as third parties. In other words, escalation is either something that a government unintentionally does or something that inadvertently happens[3]. If (in contrast to intentional 'strategic' escalation which is outside the scope of this paper) suboptimal performance constitutes the origin of an uncontrolled escalation process, one may say that the resulting evolution is highly unnecessary and undesirable. Both sides, as well as third parties, therefore have an interest in preventing such a course of events by evolving adequate crisis control measures. With a view to finding appropriate cures, it is indispensable to start with a systematic risk assessment. The risk of uncontrolled escalation as a consequence of suboptimal performance originates in a number of cognitive, behavioural, organisational, political, strategic and other factors conducive to the propensity of suboptimal performance. These factors have been amply elucidated in two decades of modern crisis research[4]. Summing up these findings in a nutshell, the following factors must be said to cause and/or aggravate the risk:

1. Individuals faced with a crisis situation suffer from stress generated by the severity of threat, time pressure and surprise. As stress tends to affect the cognitive ability,

decision-makers under stress may suffer from misperception and other kinds of cognitive maladaptation[5], such as:

selective filtering of incoming information;

random skipping of pieces of information;

reliance on past experience irrespective of the nature of the new situation;

narrowing of the choice of options considered;

reduced search for additional information;

tunnel-vision and loss of perspective;

simplification of the information by rigid structuring, based on beliefs, stereotypes, biases and preconceptions;

loss of complexity;

inadequate feedback control;

tendency to respond to ambiguity by irrelevant rationalisation and other psychological mechanisms indicative for intolerance of ambiguity;

rejection of inconsistent information;

aversion to information challenging existing policy beliefs and 'bolstering' of previously preferred solutions;

projections of hostility and scapegoating.

In a crisis situation, stress may trigger cognitive pathologies in the minds of the responsible decision-makers. As a consequence, they are often no longer in a position to interpret reality properly and arrive at an adequate judgement. As was pointed out by W.I. Thomas many years ago, if men perceive situations as real, then perceptions tend to become real.

2. Apart from cognitive distortions the urgency and stress as experienced in a crisis situation also tends to lead to a degradation of the behavioural performance of the decision-makers concerned. In particular, three tendencies can be observed:

- resort to simple procedures of problem-solving characterised by 'bounded rationality'; instead of considering, calculating and comparing alternatives they settle for the first acceptable option, that is, they 'satisfise' rather than optimise[6];

- tendency to resort to 'groupthink': in a crisis, a strong 'team' mentality tends to emerge; doubts and second thoughts are often submerged in the mutual reinforcement that knits the team together emotionally[7];

- shift to risk: in stress situations, groups are more likely, when deciding collectively, to adopt risky solutions and to have illusions of invulnerability[8].

3. Organisations (cabinets, crisis staffs, politbureaus) also suffer from stress and often respond by inadequate adaptation[9]:

- problems of coordination and control: as in any large

organisation, tasks are inevitably disaggregated and, therefore, the overall decision-making process may be difficult to control in an acute crisis situation characterised by a high degree of urgency;

- generation of additional time-pressure due to a contraction process taking place in the decision-making organisation: fewer persons have to handle more problems since the top decision-makers wish to control as much as possible; hence they suffer from overload problems that are hardly conducive to a careful and circumspect approach to problem-solving.

4. Pre-programmed routines and rigid standard operating procedures may not be able to cope with the nature of a crisis[10]:

- incomplete and insufficient routines, in turn, reinforce the time-pressure;
- standard operating procedures may create a logic of their own and, by their inherent rigidity, prevent solutions that otherwise have been beneficial; the rigidity of the Schlieffen plan in 1914 decisively contributed to the fatal escalation of the Sarajevo crisis;
- standard operating procedures determining low-level actions and continuing without knowledge of the top decision-makers may create undesirable precedents or even initiate a new yet unintended course of action;
- this risk is reinforced by the fact that, in the highly competitive situation of a crisis confrontation, any action of this kind immediately triggers a reaction by the other side. As members of President Kennedy's crisis team put it in retrospect: 'The gravest risk ... was not that either head of government desired to initiate a major escalation but that events would produce actions, reactions or miscalculations carrying the conflict beyond control'[11].

5. All the risks identified so far are increasingly aggravated by the nature of the modern strategic system:

- with the emergence of nuclear weapons, the threat of using force has attained a completely new order of magnitude, having virtually a terrorizing effect by creating expectations of a danger far beyond anything previously experienced; in an acute international crisis, this prospect inevitably generates stress and thus may lead to maladaptive behaviour[12];
- a similar effect is generated by the rapidly growing urgency of crisis decisions; the shrinking warning time available aggravates the risk that political leaders of the countries concerned, in the hectic situation of a crisis emergency, will no longer be capable of deciding

and acting entirely according to the requirements of the
complex and subtle logic of modern nuclear strategy;
- the modern arms race represents a continuous threat to
  the survivability and invulnerability of the deterrent
  forces; in other words, the more strategic stability is
  jeopardised, the more each side feels tempted to prevent
  a disaster by striking first, thus overriding the requirements of careful decision-making.

6. The symbolic use of force as a 'continuation of politics
by other means' is increasingly a standard pattern in contemporary crisis behaviour.   It aggravates the risk of inadvertent escalation[13]:
- although the risks inherent in any use of force are growing, the trend toward use of military means for symbolic
  purposes ('sabre rattling', 'showing the flag') is rapidly becoming common usage; in the nuclear age, by contrast
  to the pre-nuclear age, the number of armed confrontations short of war has increased[14]; correspondingly,
  the number of opportunities for inadvertent escalation is
  also increasing;
- the risks are particularly grave if nuclear weapons are
  involved; the use of demonstrative options such as
  various levels of alert status for missiles, dispersal of
  bombers and submarines is most dangerous[15];
- the acquisition of long-range intervention capacities by
  the major powers (Soviet Navy; US Rapid Deployment Force)
  for the purpose of 'global power projection' reinforces
  this tendency;
- crisis bargaining applying techniques of coercive diplomacy may go awry due to faulty calculations of manoeuvres, threats and counter-threats; the semantic structure of signalling each other's intentions and capabilities is not safe against misunderstandings[16]
  possibly followed by overreactions;
- coercive diplomacy also entails the risk of events getting out of control due to the 'logic of events', military necessity, low-level actions undertaken by subordinate commanders and confusion due to the malfunctioning
  of C^3 systems; there is not only a 'fog of war' problem
  - one may legitimately speak about 'fog of crisis'
  situations as well.
7. Additional crisis confrontations are pre-programmed by the
rapidly growing number of poorly defined commitments made by
the major powers in third world regions:
- ambiguous commitments for poorly defined 'assistance', in
  contrast to traditional alliance commitments, may tempt
  the opponent to try limited probes in order to find out

the limits of the adversary's commitment;
- similarly, the weaker partner in such a poorly defined relationship may feel tempted to overexploit the 'guarantee' obtained from the major power, which thereby becomes a prisoner of the smaller ally's policies;
- arms transfers from industrialised countries to third world countries create invisible bonds which may drag the supplier countries into a direct involvement and an unintentional armed confrontation in a crisis situation, due to the necessity of securing access routes for arms shipments and of not 'losing face' as a reliable supplier in critical situations; hence local conflicts may easily spread into other regions[17].

Existing Measures for Crisis Prevention and Control

The various risks described above are partly mitigated by unilateral, bilateral and multilateral measures and institutions aimed at both crisis prevention and crisis control. Together they constitute what might be called an international 'regime' for coping with crises. The following paragraphs present a kind of a checklist of these measures without examining their limits and potentials.

1. The governments undertake serious unilateral efforts to improve their performance in acute crisis situations:
- the responsible leaders still have the image of Hiroshima in mind and they are aware of the magnitude of the risks with which they are dealing; the emergence of nuclear weapons has led to increased caution and circumspection in crisis bargaining; in general, restraint in using force has been a predominant pattern in the nuclear age;
- the governments are also largely aware of the pitfalls germane to a decision-making apparatus in a situation of threat and surprise; the 'lessons of the past' are duly respected; as a consequence, governments have undertaken steps to upgrade performance of crisis decision-making centres, including training (crisis games), systematic contingency planning and improved C^3 facilities.

2. A number of bilateral and multilateral agreements provide approaches to prevent misunderstandings and misperceptions. To some extent they also contribute to defusing acute international crises, setting minimum standards of behaviour[18]:
- the 1963 Hot Line Agreement secures instant communication between major decision centres (Moscow, Washington, London, Paris);
- the 1971 Nuclear Accidents Agreement provides for immediate notification in the event of an accidental, unauthor-

ised incident involving a possible detonation of a nuclear weapon, immediate notification of the event by missile warning systems of unidentified objects, and advance notification of planned missile launches extending beyond the national boundaries;

- the 1972 Naval Incidents Agreement prohibits certain actions by subordinate commanders that might lead to critical situations;
- the 1973 Agreement on the Prevention of Nuclear War stipulates urgent consultations if a situation appears to involve the risk of war; there are, however, no operational implications to this agreement;
- the confidence building measures (CBMs) agreed upon in the 1975 Final Act of the CSCE provide for prior notification of major military manoeuvres and thus exclude one source of suspicion regarding strategic surprise actions;
- the significance of the 1972 Basic Principles Agreement is subject to controversy; while some authors think that it merely gave the erroneous impression that the USA and the USSR were in agreement on the 'rules of the game', other authors tend to assume that it reflects the existence of an otherwise informal and tacit, yet elaborated, 'code of conduct' or set of 'conventions of crisis'[19].

3. The utilisation of universal and regional international organisations (that is, the UN and bodies such as the OAU and the OAS) deserves special attention in view of both crisis prevention and crisis management; although they are still far from fully implementing the idea of peaceful resolution of conflicts and collective security, their involvement represents indispensable support for the efforts to prevent inadvertent escalation; in the past few years their utilisation has become increasingly flexible, thus leaving room for innovative functions[20].

Although no exhaustive assessment of the merits and demerits of existing measures can be provided here, a summary evaluation of their efficiency may be given by juxtaposing them with the risks (see Table 1). The conclusion cannot be avoided that the existing crisis management regime is able to cope with only a small fraction of the risks, yet most measures at least contribute to mitigating some of the risks. The analysis also clearly demonstrates that the crisis control regime mainly relies on unilateral measures while the domain of contractual and institutional arrangements remains largely underdeveloped.

Table 1. The Efficiency of the Existing Measures for Crisis Prevention and Control

the measures	the risks*						
	A	B	C	D	E	F	G
Unilateral restraint	(+)	(+)	(+)	(+)	(+)	(+)	?
Upgrading of decision-making apparatus	(+)	(+)	(+)	(+)	(+)	?	0
Hot Line Agreement	+	(+)	?	?	?	(+)	0
Accidents Agreement	(+)	(+)	(+)	+	+	+	0
Naval Incidents Agreement	+	(+)	+	+	(+)	+	?
Prevention of Nuclear War Agreement	?	0	0	0	?	?	?
CBMs	+	0	?	?	(+)	(+)	0
Basic Principles Agreement	?	0	0	0	?	?	?
'Conventions of crisis'	?	?	?	?	?	?	?
UN system	(+)	0	0	(+)	?	(+)	(+)
Regional organisations (OAU and OAS)	(+)	0	0	(+)	?	(+)	(+)

*Explanation of the risks: A = misperception; B = behavioural maladaptation; C = organisational maladaptation; D = inappropriate standard operating procedures; E = aggravation by nuclear strategy; F = symbolic use of force; G = poorly defined commitments.
Explanation of symbols: 0 = irrelevant; + = measure fully copes with the risks existing in the respective field; (+) = measure partly mitigates the risk; ? = mitigating effect may be possible but is not ascertained.

Possible Approaches for Improving Crisis Control Measures

Based on the foregoing analysis, a number of practical measures can be suggested to improve both the crisis prevention and crisis control capacity of governments and international organisations. In doing so, three prerequisites must be kept in mind if these proposals are to have any practical meaning:

- Given the multi-faceted nature of the risk, it is important to choose a combined and comprehensive approach simultaneously envisaging a multitude of measures; any single-item approach cannot be but insufficient as there is no panacea.
- The decisive criterion for evaluating the practicability of a measure, apart from its contribution to averting or mitigating the risk of unintentional escalation, is the interest of the parties concerned. Crises are not triggered in order to be solved - they emerge from a competitive relationship in which each party wishes to maximise its goals and is deeply concerned about its security. If proposals for improving crisis control measures are to be realistic, they must serve these interests, or at least must not impede the efforts undertaken for the sake of these interests. However, as most international conflicts are non-zero-sum games, there is always a cooperative dimension leaving at least some room for implementing policies aimed at controlling and solving the crisis.
- The potential for cooperative measures varies from crisis to crisis, depending on its intensity and the issues at stake. Hence, if a particular measure proves to be inefficient in one crisis, this does not necessarily mean that the negative conclusion must be generalised. For instance, in some crises, one or both parties may deliberately destroy communication and refuse to 'listen', while in other situations, they may feel the urgent need to communicate.

The following summary listing of possible measures has been drafted with the aim of drawing attention to a scope of action as broad as possible, ranging from unilateral measures to desirable improvements in the structure and function of international organisations[21].

Unilateral approaches: internal measures

1. In crisis situations, the decision-making group must be given the opportunity to deliberate confidentially, exempt from domestic pressures.

2. Firm control of all relevant elements of the governmental machinery must be assured. Respective preparations (definitions of competence, C^3 efficiency) must be made well ahead in peace-time.
3. In order to assure proper information processing and in order to prevent an undue reduction of cognitive complexity, it may be useful to consider introduction of the following systems or to explore and evaluate alternative courses of action: the formal options system, establishing a 'devil's advocate' role, and multiple advocacy.
4. More comprehensive contingency planning helps to avoid being surprised by 'improbable' events and offers a way out of rigid standard operating procedures.
5. This also includes training of responsible leaders and their staff in order to make them fit for responding instantaneously and without panic to crisis situations.
6. All deliberations and actions should be based on an accurate assessment of one's own interests and those of the opponent.
7. More attention should be paid to the links existing between local crisis spots in Third World regions and the delicate strategic relationship of the two major powers elsewhere. Dismantling mechanisms that automatically drag third countries into local conflicts is an urgent task.

Unilateral approaches: measures aimed at shaping relations with the adversary

8. Crises can be prevented if the potential adversaries clarify their intentions in a timely fashion.
9. It is of crucial importance to transform poorly defined commitments into more precisely delineated relationships.
10. Communication channels must be kept open under all circumstances.
11. Communications must be kept specific.
12. The intensity of a crisis can be reduced by fractionating the conflict.
13. It is useful to keep in mind that some types of actions may provoke the opponent to irrational escalation. Such actions to be avoided are: threatening the opponent's value system and leaving the other side with no other way out but war or humiliation.
14. More attention should be paid to the use of unilateral (tacit or explicit) confidence-building measures, such as limitation or reduction of troops in border regions or restrictions on the number of strategic bomber missions.

15. In coercive diplomacy, germane to most crisis bargaining situations, the parties concerned should at least refrain from making symbolic moves involving nuclear weapons (nuclear alerts, nuclear threats). It should also be made certain that the troops, ships and aircraft despatched to a crisis area do not carry nuclear weapons.

16. Contingency planning for crisis situations should focus on more options in the conventional field.

Bilateral and multilateral approaches

17. The Hot Line channels currently established between Moscow and Washington, Paris and London should be extended to other capitals located in potential crisis regions. The extension of similar communication links to military headquarters, as suggested by President Reagan, deserves implementation.

18. The 1972 Naval Incidents Agreement should be multilaterised and extended to submarine activity. It may serve as a model for similar agreements in other fields. More specific and further-reaching agreements of this kind may be negotiated for regional and subregional contexts or with regard to specific countries.

19. It is desirable that the nuclear powers attempt to forge a common approach to the problem of C^3 vulnerability. They should at least exchange views on this subject.

20. In arms control negotiations on both the strategic and regional level, special efforts should be undertaken to prevent the development and deployment of new systems that reduce warning time and thus create situations of extreme urgency, which prompt launch-on-warning and/or pre-emption policies. The removal, on a mutual basis, of such systems which have already been deployed deserves priority in the current arms control negotiations.

21. Confidence-building measures have a particular importance for crisis prevention and deserve extension in both geographic scope and the number of issues concerned. The 'post-Helsinki' CBMs discussed in the CSCE meeting in Madrid constitute an encouraging approach; however, additional steps may be envisaged towards mutually agreed access to information regarding the other side (exchange of observer teams, mutual aerial inspection, exchange of certain categories of information), prior notification of military activities other than military exercises (major troop movements, new weapons deployment or withdrawal), measures to restrict certain types of military activities (ceiling and sub-ceilings of troops and equipment, limitation of the stationing period for troops abroad, limit-

ation of the frequency of certain military activities such as military exercises).

22. Monitoring by satellite could 'play a positive role in preventing or settling international crises'[22]. The project of an international satellite monitoring agency (ISMA), therefore, deserves careful examination and further elaboration regarding its political feasibility.

23. The conventional arms transfer talks among supplier countries should be resumed at the earliest convenience with a view to limiting or reducing unforeseeable implications of supplier-receiver relationships. If no comprehensive agreement is available, a regional or country-by-country approach may offer opportunities for agreement.

24. Several authors have expressed the desirability of the major powers to reach agreement on a kind of 'code of conduct' applicable to international crisis confrontations. However, they tend to underestimate the acceptability of such an approach in a world characterised by competition and different social and political systems[23].The Soviet Union has made it clear that it could not agree to any 'division of the world into spheres of influence or spheres of special interest' and that it wishes to 'continue to support the struggle of the peoples for their social and national liberation.' Still, the idea of a code of conduct should not be abandoned; less far-reaching steps in this direction may have a fair chance of being more feasible.

25. While it may be difficult to reach agreement about a code of conduct pertaining to third parties, it may still be possible to reach agreement (either tacitly or, in some circumstances, also explicitly) on clearly defined spheres of abstention and, eventually, on a buffer zone or zones where qualified disengagement measures can be implemented stepwise.

26. It also seems desirable that the two major powers have at least a basic understanding of the types of commitments and actions that ought to be avoided on a mutual basis, that is, a 'negative' code of conduct.

27. Another approach to the idea of a code of conduct is for talks among experts from various countries, to be arranged within the framework of international professional organisations active in the field of social science. These talks should be held with a view to elaborating a set of rules ('conventions of crisis') on which agreement seems possible, perhaps formulated in a context-specific way, that is, focused on specific regions which seem crisis-prone.

28. An alternative starting point to be envisaged is the ex

post facto analysis of past international crises. International expert groups might study them in order to identify possible recurrent patterns emerging in the practice of past crisis management. To the extent that such recurrent patterns become fixed as norms of international behaviour, they approach the status of international law.

29. In this context, the various proposals put forward by the Soviet Union and other socialist countries regarding agreements or a world treaty for renouncing the use of force also deserve careful re-examination. Many Western observers tend to reject this idea as offering no solution of the intrinsic security dilemma which cannot be overcome by a mere 'paperwork' pledge. It cannot be denied that a simple pledge referring to intentions without corresponding measures aimed also at capabilities may be somewhat incomplete, yet, instead of simply rejecting or ridiculing the idea altogether, a more constructive approach might concentrate on precisely the corollary measures in the field of capabilities; in other words, it is desirable to discuss ways and means to guarantee the pledge by substantive steps in the field of arms control and disarmament.

Approaches within the framework of international organisations

30. It is fair to say that the United Nations system is currently under-utilised; especially the Security Council has a more substantive potential for a helpful role in crisis control, as suggested by Mr. Perez de Cuellar in his 1982 Annual Report: 'If the Council were to keep an active watch on dangerous situations and, if necessary, initiate discussions with the parties before they reach the point of crisis, it might often be possible to defuse them at an early stage before they degenerate into violence'[24].

31. The permanent members of the Security Council, having special rights and special responsibilities, may consider regular consultations at the highest possible level.

The following quotations from the Report of Mr. Perez de Cuellar are relevant[24]:

32. In order to avoid the Security Council becoming involved too late in critical situations, it may well be that the Secretary-General should play a more forthright role in bringing potentially dangerous situations to the atten-

tion of the Council.

33. The Secretary-General may also 'develop a wider and more systematic capacity for fact-finding in potential conflict areas'.

34. Moreover, the Council itself could devise more swift and responsive procedures for sending off good offices missions, military or civilian observers or a United Nations presence to areas of potential conflict.

35. UN peace-keeping operations could be 'strengthened by an increase in their military capacity or authority' or by underpinning their authority 'by guarantees, including explicit guarantees for collective or individual supportive actions'.

This catalogue of possible measures is not exhaustive[25]. It is also not presented without reservation in several cases. Its only purpose is to serve as a basis for further deliberations and to stimulate discussion.

References

1. M. Kahler, 'Rumors of War: The 1914 Analogy', in Foreign Affairs, 58 (1981) Number 2 pp. 374-396; The Independent (Palme) Commission on Disarmament and Security Issues, Common Security, (London: Pan Books, 1982) p. 62f.
2. For a definition of rationality in crisis behaviour, see Janice Stein, 'Can Decision-Makers Be Rational and Should They Be?', in M. Brecher (ed.), Studies in Crisis Behaviour, (New Brunswick: Transaction Books, 1978) pp. 316-339, especially p. 319.
3. R. Smoke, War. Controlling Escalation, (Cambridge, Mass: Harvard University Press, 1977) p. 21f.
4. D. Frei (ed.), Managing International Crises, (Beverly Hills: Sage Publications, 1982); D. Frei (ed.), International Crises and Crisis Management, (Farnborough: Saxon House, 1978); M. Brecher and J. Wilkenfeld, 'Crises in World Politics', in World Politics, 34 Number 3, pp. 380-417; G.W. Hopple and P.J. Rossa, 'International Crisis Analysis: Recent Developments and Future Directions', in P.T. Hopman et al (eds), Cumulation in International Relations Research, (Denver: University of Denver Press, 1981) pp. 65-88; D. Frei and C. Catrina, Risks of Unintentional Nuclear War, (Geneva: United Nations Publications, 1982) ch.V.
5. Cf. R. Cohen, Threat Perception in International Crisis,

(Madison: University of Wisconsin Press, 1979); O.R. Holsti, 'Theories of Crisis Decision-Making', in P.G. Lauren (ed.), Diplomacy, (New York: Free Press, 1979) pp. 99-136; A.L. George, Presidential Decision-Making in Foreign Policy: The Effective Use of Information and Advice, (Boulder: Westview Press, 1980); L.M.W. Brecher, Decision in Crisis, (Berkeley: University of California Press, 1980) p. 343; K.W. Deutsch, 'Crisis Decision-Making: The Information Approach', in D. Frei (ed.), Managing International Crises, (Beverly Hills: Sage, 1982) pp. 15-28; V.B. Lukov and V.M. Sergeev, 'Patterns of Crisis Thinking', in ibid. pp. 47-60; R. Jervis, Perception and Misperception in International Politics, (Princeton: Princeton University Press, 1976); I.L. Janis and L. Mann, Decision Making. A Psychological Analysis, (New York: Free Press, 1977); R.N. Lebow, Between Peace and War. The Nature of International Crisis, (Baltimore: Johns Hopkins University Press, 1981) ch.5 ('Cognitive Closure and Crisis Politics').

6. Stein op.cit. p. 321; George op.cit. p. 40
7. P.M. Morgan, Deterrence. A Conceptual Analysis, (Beverly Hills: Sage, 1977) p. 180f.
8. J. Kashi, 'The Role of Deterrence in Disarmament', in D. Carlton and C. Schaerf (eds), The Dynamics of the Arms Race, (London: Croom Helm, 1975) pp. 92-103; Morgan op.cit. p. 181.
9. J. Steinbruner, 'Beyond Rational Deterrence", in World Politics, 28 (1976) Number 2, pp. 223-245; Lebow op.cit. p. 282
10. G.T. Allison, Essence of Decision. Explaining the Cuban Missile Crisis, (Boston: Little, Brown, 1971); C. Smart and I. Vertinsky, Design for Crisis Decision Units: Pathologies and Prescription, (Berlin: International Institute of Management, 1977); G. Allison and M.M. Halperin, 'Bureaucratic Politics', in R. Tanter and R.H. Ullman (eds), Theory and Policy in International Relations, (Princeton: Princeton University Press, 1972) pp. 40-79.
11. D. Rusk, R. McNamara, G.W. Ball, R.L. Gilpatric, T. Sorensen and McGeorge Bundy, 'The Lessons of the Cuban Missile Crisis', in Time, 27 September 1982, p. 36f.
12. Cf. for a more detailed elaboration of this point Frei and Catrina op.cit. pp. 133-137; Lebow op.cit. p. 238ff.; D.S. Lutz, 'Kriegsgefahr und Kriegsverhutung in den 80er Jahren', in W. von Baudissin and D.S. Lutz (eds), Konflikte, Krisen, Kriegsverhutung, (Baden-Baden: Nomos, 1981) pp. 29-56.
13. P. Williams, Crisis Management. Confrontation and Diplomacy in the Nuclear Age, (London: Martin Robertson,

1976); A.N. Gilbert and P.G. Lauren, 'Crisis Management: An Assessment and Critique', in Journal of Conflict Resolution, 24 (1980) Number 4, pp. 641-664.

14. W.D. Eberwein, Militarische Konfrontationen und Eskalation zum Krieg, 1900-2000, (Berlin International Institute for Comparative Social Research, 1981); B.M. Blechman and S.S. Kaplan, Force Without War, US Armed Force as a Political Instrument, (Washington D.C.: Brookings, 1982); S.S. Kaplan, Diplomacy of Power. Soviet Armed Forces as a Political Instrument, (Washington D.C.: Brookings, 1981).

15. M. Leitenberg, 'Threats of the Use of Nuclear Weapons since World War II', in A. Eide and M. Thee (eds), Problems of Contemporary Militarism, (London: Croom Helm, 1980) pp. 388-395; G.H. Snyder and P. Diesing, Conflict Among Nations. Bargaining, Decision Making and System Structure in International Crises, (Princeton: Princeton University Press, 1972); J. Steinbruner, 'An Assessment of Nuclear Crises', in F. Griffiths and J.C. Polanyi (eds), The Danger of Nuclear War, (Toronto: Toronto University Press, 1979) pp. 34-42.

16. J.J. Kruzel, 'Military Alerts and Diplomatic Signals', in E.P. Stern (ed.), The limits of Military Intervention, (Beverly Hills: Sage, 1977), pp. 83-99; J.M. McConnell, 'The Rules of the Game', in B. Dismukes and J.M. McConnell (eds), Soviet Naval Diplomacy, (New York: Pergamon Press, 1979) pp. 240-280; R. Cohen, International Politics. The Rules of the Game, (London: Longman, 1981); D. Frei, 'Internationale Krisen als Wandlungsprozesse von Zeichensystemen', in Publizistik. Vierteljahreshefte fur Kommunikationsforschung, 27 (1982), Number 3, pp. 300-310.

17. R.K. Betts, 'Arms Trade Control', in R. Burt (ed.), Arms Control and Defense Postures in the 1980s, (Boulder: Westview Press, 1982) pp. 109-141; Frei and Catrina op.cit. pp. 148-153; B.M. Bechman et al, 'Negotiated Limitation on Arms Transfers. First Steps Towards Crisis Prevention?', in A.L. George (ed.), Managing US-Soviet Rivalry, (Boulder: Westview Press, 1983) pp. 255-284.

18. Cf. A.L. George, Towards a Crisis Prevention Regime in US-SU Relations, prepared for the Pugwash Workshop on Crisis Management and Prevention, Geneva, 1978); idem, Toward a Soviet - American Crisis Prevention Regime, (Los Angeles: Center for International and Strategic Affairs, 1980); J. Goldblat, Agreements for Arms Control, (London: Taylor & Francis, 1982); A.L. George, 'The Basic Principles Agreement of 1972', in A.L. George (ed.), Managing US-Soviet Rivalry, (Boulder: Westview Press, 1983)

pp. 107-117.

19. C.M. Bell, 'Decision-Making by Governments in Crisis Situations', in D. Frei (ed.),International Crises and Crisis Management, (Farnborough: Saxon House, 1978) pp. 50-58; idem, The Convention of Crisis, (Oxford: Oxford University Press, 1972).

20. Cf. G.I. Morosov, 'International organization and settlementment of international conflict', in D. Frei (ed.), International Crisis and Crisis Management, op.cit. pp. 89-100; H.R. Alker and F.L. Sherman, 'Collective Security-Seeking Practices Since 1945', in D. Frei (ed.), Managing International Crises, (Beverly Hills: Sage, 1982), pp. 113-146.

21. The proposals in the text are drawn from a large body of crisis literature (see the titles listed in the previous footnotes). In addition, the following publications have been used: R.K. Betts, Surprise Attack. Lessons for Defense Planning, (Washington D.C.: Brookings, 1982); A.J. Yefromov, Nuclear Disarmament, (Moscow: Progress Publishers, 1979); N.N. Inozemtiev (ed.), Peace and Disarmament 1980, (Moscow: Progress Publishers, 1980); U. Nerlich, 'Stabilisierend Massnahmen in Europa', in U. Nerlich and F. Bomsdorf (eds), Die Einhegung sowjetischer Macht, (Baden-Baden: Nomos, 1982) pp. 263-304; D.S. Mefford, The Soviet Use of Force, Ph.D. Thesis, M.I.T. 1982; Commission on the Organization of the Government for the Conduct of Foreign Policy, Appendices, 2, (Washington D.C.: G.P.O., 1975); K. Ruhala, 'Confidence-Building Measures', in W. von Baudissin and D.S. Lutz (eds), Kooperative Rustungssteuerung, (Baden-Baden: Nomos, 1981) pp. 139-158; W. Ury and R. Smoke, 'Beyond the Hotline: Heading off Crises', in International Reviews, November 1982, pp. 46-47; G.A. Trofimenko, 'The Third World and the US-Soviet Competition: A Soviet View', in Foreign Affairs, 59 (1981), Number 5, pp. 1021-1040.

22. UN study on the Implications of Establishing an International Satellite Monitoring Agency: A/AC206/14, 10 June 1981.

23. Cf. A.L. George, 'Crisis Prevention Re-examined', in A.L. George (ed.), Managing US-Soviet Rivalry, (Boulder: Westview Press, 1983) pp. 365-398.

24. UN Report of Secretary-General, 1982.

25. See also Common Security op.cit. p. 178.

12 AVOIDING NUCLEAR WAR; THERE IS STILL HOPE FOR HOPE

Victor Weisskopf

A tremendous danger hangs over the world: nuclear war between the superpowers of the East and West. Such a war would be the greatest catastrophe mankind has ever suffered. It would kill millions of people. It would destroy human civilisation as we know it. The damage would be incomparably worse than in any previous wars. The foreseeable consequences, such as radioactive pollution and dust clouds would be disastrous; it may make life practically impossible for the unfortunate survivors. The unforeseeable consequences may even be much worse than the expected ones. In spite of this the number of nuclear weapons increases every year. At present more than 50 000 warheads are deployed and thousands are added every year, with increased efficiency and improved means of delivery. It is a quantitative and qualitative race out of every reasonable proportion.

It is probable that because of this nuclear threat we have had no war between the great powers for 38 years, an unusually long period. But there is a mounting danger that this precarious equilibrium will collapse under the pressure of a crisis, by accidental releases of bombs, or by acts of desperation if one side feels an overwhelming threat.

A few useful but half-hearted steps have been made to stabilise this precarious situation, such as the atmospheric test-ban and the ABM treaty. Even these small steps are now threatened to be modified and weakened instead of being strengthened and enlarged.

The two superpowers are poised against each other by the forces of history, by conflicting ideologies and by mutual fear. There is a genuine fear on both sides that each superpower is out to obstruct and destroy the opponent, to make him powerless in order to change his social and political system.

The West fears that the Soviet Union is bent on spreading communism all over the world and to destroy what is called the capitalist system. The East fears a threat of encirclement, with hostile military bases all around its frontiers, and it observes a crusading spirit in the West, with the aim of banishing the evils of communism from the earth.

These fears are genuine, but they do not make much rational sense. Neither of the superpowers is threatened by the other since in the nuclear age any serious attempt to attack the other side must end in mutual annihilation. Nuclear blackmail is unworkable since nuclear victory is impossible. The only threat faced by the superpowers is the threat of internal difficulties, such as unemployment and economic stagnation in the West and mounting internal tensions in the East.

But the mutual fears are the primary cause of the escalating arms race: 'They did this, therefore we must do that which they also will do, therefore...'. It brought us into the present crazy situation, unique in history, where each side has more than a hundred times what is needed to destroy all of the opponent, knowing full well – and this is the difference from all previous arms races – that any actual use of those weapons means the annihilation of both sides.

Future generations – if there will be any – will regard this as a virulent case of collective mental disease. As long as the two superpowers are poised against each other in mortal fear that the other will use every opportunity to obstruct and destroy it, there will be no stopping of this madness.

Certain fundamental principles must be recognised before we can think of reversing the present deadly threat.

There is no defence against nuclear weapons, once they have reached the levels we have today. Since 100 bombs are enough to destroy the opponent, we would need a defence system that is more than 99 per cent efficient against 10 000 strategic bombs deployed. Such an efficiency cannot be expected from any military system.

In the present world loaded with nuclear explosives any use of nuclear bombs would be a crime against humanity. Nuclear explosives cannot be considered as weapons of war. Their only purpose is to deter the use by the other side, and for that purpose far fewer are good enough. It is senseless to avoid a nuclear war by preparing to wage it and prevail. The old slogan, 'Si vis pacem para bellum'('If you want peace prepare for war'), may have been true with old-fashioned arms. It is no longer true for nuclear weapons. One cannot wage war with nuclear arms. This is why the deployment of so-called nuclear battle-field or tactical weapons is extremely dangerous. If they ever were applied, the other side would apply them too and a nuclear war will be under way. It is often argued that such nuclear arms deter a conventional attack from the other side. But such deterrence

is not plausible - it implies the inadmissible risk of trans-
forming a conventional conflict into a nuclear holocaust.
Nuclear arms can only deter a nuclear attack. A conventional
attack can only be deterred with a well organised conventional defence, or by a mutual reduction of conventional
forces. Conventional defence is often regarded as too expensive for the West compared to a nuclear defence. How can
anything be too expensive that reduced the chances of a
nuclear conflagration?

An escalating nuclear arms race is no protection against a
nuclear war. The only possible protection is a reduction of
mutual distrust and fear, the driving elements of the arms
race, and the prevention of conflict situations.

This task is much more difficult than the solution of
scientific or technical military problems, which requires
only creative intelligence and technical ingenuity. The prevention of the nuclear holocaust is much harder. It requires, in addition, political and military insight, an
understanding of the psychology of the adversary, a readiness
to compromise and, most importantly, it requires a great deal
of wisdom. It must be based upon an absolute dedication on
ethical and moral grounds to the aim that a nuclear war
should not, cannot, and must not occur; a dedication that is
not always present in the leadership of the superpowers.

Two big superpowers confront each other in this conflict.
Each side has many reasons to oppose the other regime and to
condemn its activities. But the times are gone when objectionable regimes could be removed by force. World War II was
the last occasion. The existence of nuclear weapons has
changed the meaning of war. War between nuclear powers is no
longer acceptable. The only hope for change is a gradual
movement towards more sensible policies. But this is possible only if the superpowers cease to threaten one another.

Confrontation and threat by an ever increasing nuclear
arsenal diminish the security of both partners - they increase the fears on each side and the danger of desperate
acts. This is why confrontations and threats must be replaced by a greater interdependence between the adversaries,
by more cooperation in various fields, such as arms control,
Third World support, increased commerce, where one side becomes more and more dependent on the other, by common
scientific projects, such as a world accelerator, or a lunar
laboratory. It can be done; we had successful scientific
collaborations with Soviet science in the Antarctic, in the
study of fusion reactors and in other fields. It must be
done in spite of many justified criticisms of the political
system of the other side. Those criticisms should be
expressed publicly in many forms, and it is hoped that the

other side may change some of its measures in the interest of
mutual understanding. But non-cooperation because of dis-
satisfaction with the methods of the opponent will not get us
very far; it will make things worse, not better. Confrontation must be replaced by competition - not military, where
both sides can and will do the same - but in economic and
social actions and in human affairs. The aim must not be the
destruction of the economy and the political system of the
other side, but to show them and the rest of the world how
one can do better.

Is there any hope that either side will choose the way of
replacing confrontation by cooperation? We do not know. It
would be in the interest of both sides, and powers have
always served their own interests. One thing, however, is
certain: nothing will change if the relentless confront-
ational stand of today is pursued. It will get worse, as is
plainly visible today. We can only stop the arms race and
turn it around by finding ways of dealing which are to the
mutual advantage of both sides and which do not threaten the
existence of the other side. If the fear of being destroyed
by the opponent subsides, there is a possibility that the
policies will change. Fear has always been an important
cause of aggressive acts.

The reduction of this fear should be an important aim for
both sides. Neither side is able to annihilate the other.
Therefore, actions must be avoided that are perceived as a
threat.

When we face the risk of nuclear war annihilation it is not
important whether some small country is under a totalitarian
regime which is called leftist or rightist. Such details may
have been important before the existence of nuclear weapons.
Today they become secondary. The most obvious examples are
Central America and Afghanistan, but the Third World abounds
in similar cases. What is much more important would be an
improvement of economic conditions, a fight against the
abject poverty of most of the population in these countries,
and their age-old struggle for greater participation in
decision making. Such improvements would reduce the danger of
political violence which may lead to major conflicts. They
constitute an interesting opportunity for collaboration of
East and West. The present policy of the superpowers is on a
collision course. If it remains so, the chances of a nuclear
war are great. This is why it is imperative that the attitudes on both sides must undergo a change away from counting
weapons and bases, towards a more stable world by non-
military measures. Such changes are already beginning.
Questions are asked that were not asked before. There is a
strong and growing grass roots movement in the USA and in

Europe, including many professional groups and religious organisations. It expresses the revulsion of the people against the escalating nuclear arms race. A change in the people's attitudes will produce a change in the government's policies. Some such changes are already noticeable.

True enough, in the East the process will take other forms. The processes of social and political change are very different and cannot take the form of public pressure against the government. Nevertheless, a shift from confrontation to cooperation on one side might well induce similar shifts on the other side.

This process will not be a fast one. It takes time before old prejudices disappear and deep mistrust melts away. It will take equally long before the number of nuclear weapons can be reduced to a small fraction of the present one. I do not believe that nuclear weapons can be completely eliminated in the next decades. There will always be a fear that some country may construct them secretly. Maybe future generations will be able to understand the danger better and will be able to build a world without such weapons.

Some smaller changes for the better in the attitudes towards the problem of nuclear war have taken place in the past and give us hope that more of it may happen in the future. The initiative at the Pugwash meetings led to the atmospheric test ban and the ABM treaty; the two Academies of Sciences have held common discussions on the problems of the nuclear war danger; some common ideas on that subject were worked out under the sponsorship of the Pontifical Academy of Sciences, leading to a declaration for a halt in the production of new nuclear weapons and against their first use. It was signed by the presidents or their representatives of the most important Academies of Science in the West and East. But much more must be done along these lines and on a much broader basis. Our Soviet colleagues, some of whom are very influential, must also take a far more active part in curbing the excesses of the Soviet military-industrial complex.

Here is a summary of the main points that must be observed for the prevention of nuclear war.

There is no issue at stake which ever could justify resort to nuclear weapons.

Nuclear explosives are **not** weapons of war. Their only purpose can be deterrence of use by an opponent.

The nuclear arms race will continue as long as the superpowers are in mortal fear that the other will use every opportunity to obstruct and destroy it.

Today neither side can destroy the other without being destroyed.

Nuclear arms limitations and reducti ns are necessary but not sufficient.

Reduce mutual fears by replacing confrontation and threat by cooperation, by interdependence, by non-military competition, and by measures that benefit both sides.

Tolerate systems with opposing ideologies. Avoid conflict situations. Create stability by avoiding measures that are perceived as a threat, and by cooperation to reduce poverty, famine and exploitation in the Third World.

I strongly believe that Europe must play a more important role in this. A special responsibility falls on Europe. The two superpowers are locked in a struggle of military and nuclear competition. Their efforts towards arms control and cooperation are hampered by political considerations, by face-saving tendencies, by attempts to outsmart the other side and to put the blame on the opponent.
Europe is much less bound by the policies of the past decades. It is not stuck in the ruts of previous policies or propaganda. So far it has played the role of a bystander, leaving the initiatives to the superpowers. The unfortunate dual-track decision, of making the deployment of nuclear weapons in Europe dependent on the willingness of the superpowers, is a typical example. The future existence of Europe should not depend on the whims of the superpowers, whether they decide to bargain or to fight, to give in or not on some secondary items connected with numbers of certain missile types - numbers that are not relevant except when considered within the total range of the nuclear posture. Are a few hundred intermediate range warheads really of such importance when the number of strategic warheads is in the ten thousands?
Why does Europe leave the proposals, the counting, the decisions to the USA and the Soviet Union? European governments or groups of influential European personalities, should bring forward proposals for treaties and measures for the reduction of tensions, which are based on **their** judgments of relative strengths and relevance. They have most of the material, and the factual inputs to their disposition. The European governments could have their own observation satellites, their own evaluation centres, which are independent of those of the superpowers and, therefore, free from political bias.

So many non-negotiated treaties are on the shelves and not discussed today: the Comprehensive Test Ban, the Anti-Satellite Treaty, SALT II, and many more. Should the European community not take the initiative and ask for realistic discussions of such treaties?

Moreover, and most importantly, Europe must lead the superpowers towards cooperation and positive measures to reduce the mutual fears. Europe has already taken some of that initiative. There are many commercial contacts with the East which are useful and favourable for both sides.

Much more, however, should be done and can be done under European leadership. Europe is in the best position to create the new attitude of mutual interdependence and mutually advantageous cooperation. Europe has been the leader of western civilisation for 2000 years. This is not the moment to give it up. The world needs the experience, the tolerance and the wisdom, which has accrued here after 2000 years of bloody conflicts. Europe has achieved one remarkable success: wars between Italy, France, England and Germany are unthinkable now. They were the order of the day only 40 years ago. Therefore, Europe must take the initiative to show how this can also be done on a world scale.

If we do not succeed, our century will be remembered by the unfortunate survivors as the time of preparation for the great catastrophe, and science would be seen as the main culprit. Our century ought to be remembered as an age in which mankind acquired its deepest insights into the universe and learned to control its martial impulses.

Let us hope, strive and act, so that it will.

Part Three

Security in Europe

13   NEGOTIATIONS ON NUCLEAR FORCES IN EUROPE

Lawrence Freedman

It is easy to believe that the current problems besetting nuclear arms control in Europe are simply the result of an inflexible USA or Soviet stance. However, a backward look at the history of these problems provides no evidence that negotiators operating in a more favourable political environment found them much more tractable. These 'gray area' weapons have dogged strategic arms control from the start and often have been removed as an obstacle only by being deferred to a later stage in the negotiations.

It is also clear that if at last they can be encompassed in the agreement, a deal at Geneva will be less radical than the rhetoric surrounding the negotiations might suggest. This, in turn, casts doubt on the role that arms control negotiations can play in rationalising force structures.

SALT I

When the SALT talks began in November 1969, there were grounds for believing that nuclear weapons in Europe played a small and declining role in the strategic calculations of the United States and the Soviet Union. Nevertheless, these weapons raised a series of awkward questions which made it likely from the start that they would complicate the negotiations.

The first question they raised was that of the scope of the talks: was the concern with weapons of a particular range, able to travel intercontinental distances, or with weapons capable of reaching the territory of a superpower? Taking the first view allowed for a cut-off point by range, with due allowance for submarine-launched systems. This was favoured by the United States but was unacceptable to the Soviet Union, which felt directly under threat from British, French and Chinese systems, and from US weapons based in Europe as well as from US intercontinental systems.

This raised the question of responsibility to allies. The

Soviet view of the scope of the talks challenged the United States to negotiate on behalf of other countries and to accept restrictions on weapons that played a major role in the basic security guarantees it had made to its allies. Yet, the Soviet Union was not offering restrictions on its forces which directly threatened these allies. An added difficulty was the knowledge that the numbers and types of systems based in Europe were of a sort that would frustrate negotiations.

At the start of SALT neither side accepted the difficulties of setting limits to the negotiations. Both proposed partial limits on some of the European systems of the other side. The initial US SALT proposal, developed prior to the start of the negotiations, advocated a freeze on medium-range ballistic missiles (which only the Russians still maintained) and a ban on mobile versions thereof.

The Soviets argued that US fighter-bombers in Europe – the so-called forward-based systems – had the range to reach the Soviet Union and so were strategic and should be withdrawn before the talks could proceed. On similar grounds they argued for the removal of US forces in the Far East and on aircraft carriers. The exclusion of their own theatre forces was justified on the grounds that these could not reach the United States and were needed for defence against third countries. This latter point, of course, made it difficult for the Soviets to argue for inclusion of third-country forces. Yet it did so, in a muted way. The lack of conviction behind the effort was illustrated by the concentration on only submarine-based forces and the neglect of British and French aircraft.

The US and Soviet proposals on theatre forces led to an impasse which was responsible for a lack of progress at the talks. The Americans eventually proposed, in August 1970, that forward-based systems and medium-range missiles both be excluded, to permit progress on the basic issue of central strategic systems. This was supported by the allies. Whatever the West European view a decade later, at the time far greater priority was attached to keeping the US forward-based systems out of the negotiations than getting the Soviet missiles in. The Soviets dropped only their demand for the withdrawal of forward-based systems, but still insisted that these systems be properly taken into account in the main agreement.

This was not explicitly granted in the SALT I agreement of May 1972, but a number of tacit concessions may have been made by the United States in return for Soviet deferral of the forward-based systems issue. The agreement was far more limited than originally proposed and allowed the Soviets numerical superiority in offensive missiles. The Soviet

Union also seemed to think that it had been given some allowance for British, French and Chinese systems. In a unilateral statement of May 1972, which was not accepted by the United States, the Soviet team argued that any additional British or French missile-carrying submarines, in addition to the nine then deployed or planned, would justify a comparable Soviet increase in submarine numbers.

As the forward-based systems had not been formally included in SALT I, they were still available as a Soviet bargaining chip for SALT II. Once again the Soviets raised the issue. The November 1974 Vladivostok aide-memoire between Presidents Ford and Brezhnev excluded these systems but once again there were suspicions that some form of quid pro quo had been obtained by the Soviet heavy bombers and the abandonment of attempts to reduce the Soviet heavy-missile arsenal.

Throughout this period, the issue of nuclear weapons in Europe was not dealt with head-on. It was seen as peripheral to the main concerns of SALT and the weapons themselves as something of a relic of a bygone age. For the Soviets, leaving the forward-based systems issue unsettled kept it available as a bargaining chip, while formal agreement might legitimise the US presence in Europe and draw attention to the imbalance in theatre forces. The Americans for their part wanted to keep forward-based systems out of the talks because of potential difficulties with allies. While justifying their exclusion by reference to the Soviet position on its own theatre forces, there was little disposition to push the linkage so as to achieve a clear trade between Soviet missiles and US aircraft. Thus, over the first few years of SALT, the issue declined rather than grew in importance.

SALT II

The trend moved dramatically in the opposite direction during SALT II. The main reason for this was the advent of a new category of weapons – known as 'gray area' systems – that could not be properly termed either strategic or theatre. The principal weapons in this category were the Backfire bomber and the cruise missile. The Backfire problem was rather like that of forward-based systems in reverse, in that the aircraft was primarily intended to fulfil a theatre mission but was technically capable of striking the opposing homeland.

Throughout 1975 the United States pressed for Backfire to be included in SALT, while the Soviets remained adamantly opposed. Primitive cruise missiles were still around from the early stages of the nuclear race, and prompted some ironic exchanges in SALT before the modern potential of the weapon was recognised. In 1969 the United States had proposed a freeze on submarine-launched cruise missiles, which only the Soviets then retained. The chief Soviet negotiator, intent on ridiculing US concern, compared cruise missiles to 'prehistoric animals of the Triassic period'.

The US programme in the 1970s focused initially on submarine-launched cruise missiles, comparable to those of the Soviet Union, but the emphasis soon shifted to air-launched programmes. It became clear that the new weapons could be extraordinarily versatile, performing strategic or theatre roles, delivering nuclear or conventional munitions from a variety of platforms and with phenomenal accuracy. A worse complication from the arms control point of view was that the range and payload of any given type seemed impossible to verify. The initial SALT involvement with cruise centred on the twin issues of range restrictions and counting rules. The Soviets used an imprecise statement in the Vladivostok accords to press for a ban on all cruise missiles over 600 kilometres in range. The United States, while prepared to forgo systems which had intercontinental range in their own right, was wary of any greater constraints.

The issues of Backfire and cruise were the principal obstacles to progress in SALT II for nearly three years after the Vladivostok summit. It was natural, then, that a trade-off should be attempted to break the deadlock. On two occasions, once in February 1976 and again a year later, the United States proposed that the twin problems be deferred to SALT III to enable an interim agreement to be reached. The Soviet Union, however, was not prepared to leave cruise missiles unconstrained, and it became obvious that some more complex solution to the gray area problem was required.

In the end, in SALT II, Backfire was not made subject to major constraints. The Soviet Union had steadfastly resisted US demands that it should count as a heavy bomber, or that its deployment should be limited to 'peripheral' areas such as Europe. All the United States obtained was a written promise not to increase the Backfire production rate from 30 per year (a level which it has not at any rate met in recent years), nor to convert the aircraft to an intercontinental role. One way in which the United States reconciled itself to this setback was to assert its right to counter the Backfire by a similar US system, the FB-111.

The United States accepted limits on the air-launched cruise missile, in terms of effective numerical ceilings. The ground- and sea-launched versions were viewed by the Soviets as much more threatening, but a protocol to the Treaty which prohibited their deployment for three years did no more than state a physical fact. This protocol served as a device to put off difficult issues for future negotiations, while putting down a marker for the content of these negotiations, reinforced by a declaration of principles on SALT III.

Moscow expected, or at least hoped, that the protocol would set a precedent for the future, and US and European critics were anxious that this might be so. Washington described the protocol as virtually meaningless, but President Carter was forced to give a positive assurance that the weapons could be deployed in Europe once the three-year period expired.

Far from setting a precedent, the protocol helped precipitate the modernisation decision. More paradoxically still, European worries over the cruise missile helped to prejudice the very arms control process which was fast becoming a political necessity for the success of the theatre nuclear force programme.

The real root of increased NATO sensitivity was the shift from stagnation in the theatre stockpiles to an accelerating arms race. The Europeans did not want SALT to prejudice any weapons system which might conceivably be needed to counter the new Soviet build-up. Europeans were worried that, because of its preoccupation with its own vulnerability, the United States would leave the **theatre** capabilities of Backfire and SS-20 unconstrained by SALT, while bargaining away any Western response.

Meanwhile, by codifying a sort of symmetry at the strategic level, SALT was enhancing the importance of asymmetries lower down the line. Last, but by no means least, it was believed by many defence planners that, irrespective of what the Soviets were up to with the SS-20, NATO had to improve its own theatre forces because of the age of existing capabilities, in particular the F-111 and the Vulcan bomber.

SALT II to INF

There was a growing consensus in the late 1970s that theatre nuclear weapons should be directly involved in future arms control negotiations. The development which forged this consensus was that the two blocs at last were prepared to pay for restrictions on opposing theatre nuclear forces by accepting constraints on their own arsenals:

- The Americans were concerned that the technological ambiguity of gray area systems, together with the resurrection of the forward-based systems issue, would prevent any further progress in SALT unless the theatre nuclear forces problem was tackled head-on.

- The Europeans wanted to remove or to counter the growing threat posed by Backfire and SS-20s and had learned from the furore met over the neutron bomb that any programme for new nuclear deployments had to be accompanied by substantive proposals for arms control.

- The Soviets were extremely worried about the military and political implications of having cruise and Pershing missiles stationed in Western Europe.

In December 1979 NATO ministers approved a programme to base 464 Tomahawk cruise missiles and 108 Pershing II ballistic missiles in Europe during the 1980s. The opportunity to justify the modernisation programme by reference to the SS-20 was too good to miss, and the future of the two programmes was seen to be linked. This encouraged the view that it was necessary to produce an arms control proposal in **parallel** to the plans for force modernisation. The agreed proposal involved the following conditions:

a) any future limitations on US systems designed principally for theatre missions should be accompanied by appropriate limitations on Soviet theatre systems;
b) limitations on US and Soviet long-range theatre nuclear systems should be negotiated bilaterally in the SALT III framework in a step-by-step approach;
c) the immediate objective of these negotiations should be the establishment of agreed limitations on US and Soviet land-based long-range theatre nuclear missile systems;
d) any agreed limitations on these systems must be consistent with the principle of equality between the sides; therefore, the limitations should take the form of de jure equality both in ceilings and in rights;
e) any agreed limitation must be adequately verifiable.

Adopting SALT as the most appropriate forum acknowledged that cruise missiles were already bound up with SALT, and that completely separate talks on central and theatre systems could symbolise a break in the link between the major US nuclear arsenal and the defence of Europe. The unwillingness of the British and French to expose their small nuclear forces confirmed the bilateralism. Only US missiles from the NATO side were to be discussed. Restricting future negotiations to 'land-based missiles' reflected the popular perception of the issue at hand. It would also keep matters simple by excluding aircraft. There was, however, a disposition against regional ceilings, on the grounds that only a global ceiling could take in most of the relevant SS-20s.

The actual substance of the proposal reveals the preoccupation with parity. The use of the term de jure equality, indicated that NATO would be more interested in establishing a right to equal ceilings than in actually creating an equality in practice.

The problem lay in combining two conflicting objectives. The culture of arms control and popular perceptions of the issues stressed the importance of missile parity. Yet, the military objective had not been to match the SS-20, missile for missile, but merely to provide a credible response, reflecting established requirements. More important in doctrinal terms, the notion of a separate regional balance implied by parity reflected exactly the sort of uncoupling from the central strategic balance that West Europeans had been trying to prevent.

After the NATO decision it was unclear whether the Soviets would agree to talk at all. The initial reaction was that the basis for talks had been destroyed, but by July 1980, and the visit of West Germany's Chancellor Schmidt to Moscow, a new basis had been found. The new Soviet position was stated in Pravda on 7 July 1980:

> Without withdrawing the proposals put forward earlier, (the Soviet Union) could also agree to a discussion of issues relating to medium-range weapons even before ratification of SALT II. At the same time, the discussions must involve not only medium-range missiles, but also US forward-based nuclear weapons. Both these problems must be discussed simultaneously and in organic connection...Possible accords could be implemented only after the SALT II Treaty comes into force.

INF

From October to November 1980, preliminary discussions between US and Soviet teams on theatre nuclear arms control took place in Geneva. In May 1981 Secretary of State Alexander Haig agreed, in Rome, that negotiations should resume before the end of the year; the time would be settled when he met Soviet Foreign Minister Andrei Gromyko at the UN General Assembly in September.

Before the start of the negotiations proper in November 1981, it was possible to identify the problems that would create the greatest difficulties:

- NATO wanted to concentrate solely on missiles, whereas the Soviet Union wished to include aircraft. The United States argued that its F-4s and carrier-based A-6s and A-7s were dual-capable and generally unsuitable for strikes into Soviet territory.

- The Soviet Union wished to confine discussions to forces actually based in Europe. The United States could not accept that; at a minimum, the SS-20s able to cover both Western Europe and China in sites just east of the Urals would have to be included.

- NATO envisaged limitations on relevant systems currently facing China. The Soviets held that these SS-20s and bombers have nothing to do with the European theatre, but from the NATO perspective these systems could be turned against it, either as a result of a Sino-Soviet rapprochement, or just through reinforcement measures in an emergency. It has been suggested that SS-20s could be transported to new sites by air.

The Soviet Union had always seen itself as **demandeur** on the issue of nuclear weapons in Europe, because of the importance it attached to weapons that could attack Soviet territory as against those which could merely attack the territory of its allies. If Soviet weapons of comparable range to the US forward-based systems were included, then a comparison of US and Soviet inventories put the Soviet Union far ahead in numbers. Thus, if the argument were to be phrased in terms of **equality**, the Soviets would have to make all the concessions.

It was too much for the Kremlin to move from a situation where the United States had to make all the concessions to one where the onus was on the Soviet Union. The Soviet leadership, therefore, argued that the basic position was equal and that the two sides should make equal reductions and eschew one-sided increases; parity existed and had to be preserved.

NATO had, in the past, resisted notions of separate European balances, but the culture of arms control and the logic of its own arguments was forcing it towards such a balance. The initial negotiating offer reflected the history of European systems being seen as complicating factors in the central strategic balance, to be dealt with either as part of a broader deal or as a once-and-for-all trade between two equally awkward - if not strategically comparable - systems. This depended on being able to view cruise/Pershing and the SS-4, -5 and -20 in isolation from other systems in Europe.

Such a position might have been possible while negotiations on central systems provided the dynamic to arms control; but it was hopeless once these theatre negotiations had to stand on their own. Given the long-standing Soviet position on forward-based systems, the inclusion of aircraft was inevitable. NATO too was being forced to argue for equality in Europe, despite all its doctrinal misgivings about such a course. To justify extra missiles coming in on the NATO side, it could not be accepted that parity existed; for NATO, parity was now desirable but had to be created.

Negotiations began in November 1981. It has become a truism that the United States and the Soviet Union have been gearing their statements as much to Western public opinion as to the other side. The Soviet Union has had grounds for hoping that the cruise/Pershing programme would be scuttled through domestic opposition - so obviating the need for concessions on its part. The United States, for its part, assumed that it was only when it seemed likely that the NATO programme would go ahead that Soviet concessions would be forthcoming. Its positions have thus been designed to secure support from domestic opinion, even if they were unacceptable to the Soviet Union.

Despite initial promises from the negotiating teams of discreet, businesslike diplomacy, the continual playing to the gallery by the national leaders has undercut traditional diplomacy. Bold statements demanding quick rebuttals are rarely conducive to the solution of complex issues. In fact, the process of public debate has served to reinforce the original positions which can now probably only be reconciled, if at all, through intensive private diplomacy.

The opening US position was the so-called 'zero option', by which NATO would forgo the cruise and Pershing programme if the Soviets abandoned all of its SS-4s, -5s and -20s, including those in the Far East. The episode demonstrated the European governments' preoccupation with getting the Americans to provide a negotiating spectacle, especially one that appropriated the slogans of the disarmament movement, without devoting much thought to the content of the negotiations. This approach was always vulnerable to a Soviet veto, which could deny any position the image of **negotiability**. This fate befell the zero option and is now likely to be suffered by the new compromise - the **interim solution**. In the latter, both sides have equal numbers of missile warheads, at a level as close as possible to zero but probably around 300. In doctrinal terms this is more acceptable but no more negotiable, and carried with it the strong suggestion that somewhere, somehow, cruise and Pershing missiles will have to be installed. In September 1983 President Reagan moved some way towards easing a few secondary points of contention: by offering compromise solutions on Soviet systems based east of the Urals (a US right to match Soviet numbers with a promise not to exercise it); by acknowledging that one day aircraft will have to be included; and hinting – but not promising – a possible compromise on the European balance (maybe something less than parity such as disproportionate cuts of Pershing).

The basic construction of the Soviet position is quite bogus. It claims an existing equality of aircraft and missiles in Europe – at just under 1000 apiece. However, it can only construct this equality by disregarding its own counting rules at difficult moments. Thus, it imposes a geographical restriction to keep out of negotiations its own aircraft and systems facing China (which **could** be moved to face Western Europe in a crisis), yet it wishes to include US FB-111 aircraft, plus A-6 and A-7 aircraft or carriers, both based outside of its own guidelines area.

The Soviets set a minimum range of 1000 kilometres, which would exclude US F-4s but include the Soviet SU-19 Fencer; yet it tries to bring in the former and keep out the latter by playing games with calculations of combat range. (They do this essentially by suggesting that the US F-4s need not worry about Soviet air defences and could fly at a continual high altitude, while the Soviet SU-19s **would** have to worry about their own defences and fly continually from base at a low altitude!). And finally, Moscow wants to include British and French submarines, even though by its own previous arguments as well as those of the countries concerned these should be discussed, if at all, as strategic forces.

The Soviet position as laid down in a draft treaty of May 1982 would have the two sides going down to 300 aircraft and missiles within five years of the treaty coming into force. In terms of their calculation, the Soviets could keep a reasonably healthy SS-20 and Backfire force while all US aircraft would be expelled from Europe, and there would even have to be a reduction in the number of US based FB-111s.

In December 1982 Yuri Andropov modified the formula to allow for a specific deal, relating the number of SS-20s to the 162 British and French missiles. The offer underlined the Soviet preoccupation with getting the Americans out of Europe rather than cutting the European forces. For the first time Moscow offered a specific limit on numbers of SS-20s, but it did not involve a move away from the previous position, which included aircraft. Aircraft would still have to be reduced.

In April 1983 Andropov offered to count warheads rather than launchers. This would have been a concession if combined with a greater concession on accepting new US missiles in Europe, but as an extension of the established Soviet proposal it seemed to reach exactly the same conclusion as before. The same was true of an August offer which later seemed to be qualified, to **eliminate** SS-20s later from

Europe rather than move them east of the Urals. Anything else would have been preposterous. What is notable is that there has been no movement from the refusal to sanction any new US missiles. The preoccupation with British and French missiles has also become something of a fixation. The speed of Andropov's rejection of President Reagan's September 1983 compromise does not suggest a willingness to legitimise the new US missiles even though the Kremlin must by then have known that their arrival was inevitable.

Conclusion

This saga provides an illustration of how not to go about arms control. The problem might have been more tractable in the early 1970s when the forces seemed reasonably settled. Whatever opportunity there might have been was lost through the natural disposition to put off awkward issues of low salience. By the time it had become impossible to defer the issue any longer, the political, strategic and arms control context had become much less propitious. As with many other areas of political activity, attitudes are often struck more with regard to immediate pressures and short-term effect than with regard to long-term considerations. The history of arms control is littered with lost opportunities, as weapons still at the early stage of development, or issues of great potential relevance but of slight contemporary interest, passed by.

It may be that until arms control can escape the dead hand of parity there is always the possibility of a repeat performance. Parity is a natural concept for diplomats. In practice it involved attempting to match complex force structures that may be essentially similar in broad functions and overall capability but are not at all comparable in detail. The effort to squeeze these distinct forces into contrived categories is not only extraordinarily difficult but it is also controversial and can create far more bad feeling than any success can dissipate. Already many in the field want to entangle battlefield nuclear weapons in the arms control net. Obviously, these weapons are not wholly benign and deserving of protection from interference; but arms control, as now conceived and practiced, with its neat but arbitrary accounting methods is the least promising method for addressing the problems that they create.

It is not possible to turn the clock back and restart the arms control enterprise on the basis of more modest and clearer ambitions. With the INF negotiations now bearing an enormous political burden - for the state of alliance cohesion as well as of East-West relations - there is a need for a fix of some sort.

It is unlikely that the formal position of either side can serve as a basis for a future agreement. At some point the structure of an eventual deal is not hard to work out; it would probably follow the famous Nitze-Kvitsinsky 'walk in the woods' compromise of July 1982. The basic arrangement in that deal was that the Soviets gained the cancellation of Pershing and a freeze instead of reduction in its Far Eastern deployments, while the United States was allowed some 300 cruise missiles in Europe with a reduction of SS-20s to 75, with 225 warheads. Conceding the introduction of any new NATO missiles will be difficult for Moscow, as will tolerating a further delay in dealing with aircraft. For Washington, the main difficulty may be in accepting the abandonment of Pershing. It is a better missile, though not as dramatic in its implications as suggested in Soviet propaganda.

If an agreement were to be reached, it would not be equivalent to a treaty. Given the vexed issues of definition, noncircumvention and verification, which will all take months to sort out, all one could hope for in 1983 was an agreed framework, a la Vladivostok, with a promise to expedite consideration of the details.

As I have argued, the attempt to construct a separate framework for a European nuclear balance was, if anything, an aberration. It was a result of the exhaustion of the negotiations on central strategic systems, political enthusiasm for an INF negotiating effort, doctrinal absentmindedness by the West Europeans, and a crude misrepresentation of the existing balance by the Soviet Union.

Even if the attempt is sustained, there are many years of fruitless wrangling ahead, continuing to poison European politics, in order to achieve an elusive and artificial construction of minimal strategic significance. The concentration on Europe suggests the importance and distinctiveness of the relevant systems. The great disparities born of the Soviet Union's more consistent interest in intermediate and medium-range systems cannot be readily overcome by compromise even if the will was there to compromise. Moving into aircraft offers no relief. The disparities remain and even get worse as the range is lowered. The problems are aggravated by difficulties of definition and restriction with dual-capable systems. Battlefield systems will inevitably be drawn in, rendering counting and verification even more difficult, adding to the chaos. For the longer term, therefore, the need is to draw a clear line to avoid further complications from further systems.

The Americans should acknowledge that their F-111s, FB-111s and sea-launched cruise missiles will have to fit in, in return for inclusion of the Soviet Backfire, Badger and Blinder aircraft. Having identified these extra systems - along with the ground-launched cruise missile and SS-4s, SS-5s and SS-20s - it should be made clear that all other systems - including US Phantoms and Soviet Fencers - are unsuitable for traditional methods of arms control. The designated systems should then be put back into the strategic arms pot where they have always belonged.

Although it is possible to design schemes for this re-merger the position has been greatly complicated by the sorry state of strategic arms control and the various complicated formulae being advanced by the United States at the START negotiations (now being revamped following the Scowcroft Report on the basing of the MX ICBM). It is possible that warheads will emerge as a sole unit of account which is fine for missiles but causes immense problems for aircraft. Although the asymmetries in START are by no means as marked as in the INF negotiations, each specific issue tends to carry with it great domestic baggage in the United States. There can thus be no confidence that INF or START can be merged with, as it were, balanced books on either of the sides, let alone both sides. Whether a merger between two confused and incomplete negotiations would intensify or ease the agony will depend on the political circumstances of the time. It is not a matter for dogmatism. What is clear is that if nuclear arms control is ever again to prosper, some overall framework must be found.

14   THE REAL PROBLEMS ABOUT NUCLEAR FORCES IN EUROPE

Anders Boserup

For reasons we have discussed many times, it was always clear
that the INF talks were very unlikely to yield useful results. In fact, they seem well on the way to becoming an un-
mitigated disaster, leaving us only with increased sensitivity about perceived imbalances, with East-West tensions
and recriminations, with deep divisions in the Western
alliance, with full deployments on both sides and with the
prospect for further counter and counter-counter deployments
on both sides.

As in other cases the negotiations have tended to drift
towards certain pseudo-issues: attempts to define some 'fair'
deal or some 'balance' for the weapons considered. For the
category of intermediate-range missiles the search for such a
'fair' 'balance' is particularly meaningless, yet it seems to
be precisely this that both sides are now aiming for.

As a counter to the tendency for real problems to be pushed
aside, for ambitions to shrink and for pseudo-problems to expand as negotiation deadlines approach, it is useful to try
to list afresh the basic problems in the field of INF weapons
as they appear at the present juncture, and to consider what
it is that a worthwhile agreement ought to achieve. As I see
it there are four main problems.

1. Pershing II presents a problem in two ways. First, it
undermines the basis of the strategic balance of terror by
threatening (part of) Soviet warning, command and communications installations with instant annihilation. It is an
ideal 'decapitation weapon' whose introduction (whatever the
numbers) violates the **principle** of equal security.
Presumably **any** agreement legitimising some Pershing II
deployment would be worse than no agreement for the Soviet
Union.

Second, this missile which is a prime instrument of first-
strike attack and a prime target of pre-emptive attack is
vulnerable in base, much less so when dispersed. This further
aggravates the pressure for fast action in times of crisis

and it will make Western crisis management very precarious –
acts of prudence being undistinguishable from war
preparations. Altogether this is a highly destabilising
weapon, at the strategic level and at the level of crisis
management. For this latter reason it is not at all certain
that Pershing II deployment, as was the intention, will give
greater moral strength to the FRG government in times of
crisis. Giving the Soviet Union some leverage on public fears
in the FRG, deployment could have the exact opposite effect,
making the FRG government more, not less susceptible to
pressure. The threat from the SS-20 may be more credible and
may thus be felt more strongly in the FRG when Pershing II
has been installed. These issues seem to have been largely
ignored thus far.

2. With the cruise missile there are also two types of
problems. First, the introduction of long-range cruise missiles, as everybody seems to agree, will make future quantitative limitations impossible to verify. This has long been
regarded as the main reason that made a total ban on long-
range cruise missiles so urgent. It must be recognised,
however, that with current US plans to deploy thousands of
ALCMs and SLCMs, the deployment of some hundreds of GLCMs
makes little difference either way. The cruise missile
problem can no longer be solved within the INF context. Nor
can the Soviet Union be expected to make any great
concessions to avoid GLCM deployment, unless it be part of a
wider package comprising ALCM and SLCM as well.

There is another important problem with the long-range
cruise missile which seems to have gone largely unnoticed in
all the excitement about the nuclear version, namely the
effect that non-nuclear (conventionally armed) long-range
cruise missiles would have on military stability in Europe. A
surprise attack with a few hundred long-range cruise missiles
armed with conventional warheads would probably suffice to
paralyse or throw into disarray the defences on the other
side. Whereas a disarming first-strike against nuclear forces
is fiction and will remain fiction – dangerous fiction, but
fiction all the same – a paralysing first-strike against conventional defences is a distinct possibility. With nuclear
warheads it is a reality. If the same can be achieved with
conventional warheads – and a cruise missile would be an
ideal weapon for this purpose – this would undermine the
nuclear umbrella, put a premium on pre-emption, and make
security in Europe very precarious. If the Soviet Union were
believed to have such a capability for deep non-nuclear
strikes against Western defence installations – that is, if
it initiates a sizeable cruise missile programme – it is not
hard to imagine the reactions of panic this would give rise

to in the West and the arms build-up it may trigger. The fact
that the West might have a similar capability is little com-
fort, as it would not 'balance' a presumed Soviet advantage
but merely aggravate overall instability.
    3. The SS-20 presents an altogether different kind of prob-
lem. It is not destabilising in the same way as cruise and
Pershing. It cannot threaten the retaliatory forces of the
USA and it cannot 'creep under' the nuclear threshold like
the cruise missile. It is not substantially different in
capability from other missiles in the Soviet arsenal. The
problem it poses is essentially political: it has been
perceived as provocative in the West and has caused enormous
commotion, but no-one has shown convincingly that it
constitutes a novel threat. Judging by what is known about
its accuracy and warhead yield it is certainly not a
surgical-strike weapon by any stretch of imagination. By
the same token, however, it must be regarded as perfectly
superfluous from the point of view of Soviet security. If
Western reactions to the SS-20 have been excessive, so has
the Soviet reluctance to scrap it.
    It should have been obvious long ago that the proper re-
action to the SS-20 deployment is not counter-deployment to
achieve some wholly meaningless 'eurostrategic balance' but
insistence that SS-20 be counted under SALT. Whether the
Soviet Union wants to target US allies rather than the USA
itself with some of its quota under SALT is best left to
itself to decide. Anyway, we have no means of knowing it,
except when missiles are specially built for a restricted
role, as in the case of the SS-20. True, the SS-20 can be
justified in part by the existence of French and British
forces. For that very reason it belongs in SALT. There, some
allowance might reasonably be made for the French and British
forces which these countries themselves admit to being
strategic. If the Soviet Union is concerned about **where**
the USA deploys **its** quota (that is, whether Pershing II
is deployed on its periphery), that too is an issue which
properly belongs in the SALT context.
    4. The last major problem has to do with the self-made
difficulties with which NATO is now confronted. From the
double-track decision itself, through the zero option, to the
latest round of declarations of unfaltering resolve by NATO
ministers, Western policy has been less than intelligent and
less than far-sighted. The NATO governments have trapped
themselves in a situation where it is very difficult to find
any way out that would not create profound divisions among
the NATO countries and within them. The disarray and instability that could result from a deep crisis of confidence in
and within NATO will improve the security of no-one, East or

West, neither in the short nor in the longer term. The military aspects of the INF issue were never all that important. The primary motivations were political all along, but they seem to have backfired badly. Many Western governments must by now be realising that it is time to get priorities straight, and that the problem overshadowing all others is to get through the present crisis without excessive damage to alliance cohesion and without catastrophic erosion of popular support for the alliance in general and for its nuclear policies in particular. It would seem that this can only be done by somehow redefining the issues, lifting them out of the narrow constraints of the INF talks.

What is needed in the near future is, first of all, an agreement on **how to proceed,** how to get negotiations onto a more promising track, that is, a combination of an actual agreement on certain steps and interim measures together with a protocol of intentions that holds out realistic prospects of progress on genuinely important issues. This seems to be the only way of reconciling the locked positions of most Western governments with the aspirations of the public.

It is suggested, therefore, that we might usefully discuss how a package lifting most of the issues out of the INF context and into a SALT/Freeze/START context might look.

Keeping in mind the problems identified above, a package consisting of the following elements is suggested for consideration:

a) a substantial cut-back (mothballing) of SS-20, together with an agreement that these and similar intermediate-range systems will be accountable under new SALT ceilings to be negotiated;

b) Pershing II, which would also become SALT-accountable, to be mothballed in the USA, pending discussion in SALT on whether or not to restrict deployment areas for SALT-accountable nuclear vectors;

c) a low ceiling on western GLCM deployment, together with an agreement of principle to include a complete ban of long-range cruise missiles as part of a SALT package;

d) a unilateral, voluntary USA moratorium on cruise missile deployment while SALT negotiations go on or for some specified period of time.

Sverre Lodgaard

Disengagement in Central Europe: Objectives

A nuclear weapon-free zone (NWFZ) in Europe would in effect be a buffer zone. The declared aims of all proposals for such zones has been to contribute to moderating the East-West confrontation, halting the arms race, and alleviating the political and humanitarian problems caused by the division of Europe in general and of Germany in particular. A zone arrangement is a means of achieving political and military ends, not an end in itself. In relation to most of these ends, it would be artificial to draw a sharp distinction between nuclear disengagement and withdrawal of other military forces. In Central Europe three objectives stand out as particularly important: to raise the nuclear threshold, to reduce the danger of surprise attack, and to facilitate political change (in particular, a more satisfactory, lasting solution to the German problem)[1].

Raising the Nuclear Threshold

There is widespread agreement that, in the military contingency planning for Europe, too much emphasis is put on the use of nuclear weapons. Measures to raise the nuclear threshold are therefore in great demand.

The disengagement zone represents a **hardware** approach to raising the nuclear threshold. If nuclear and eventually also major conventional weapons were removed from specified areas, military doctrines would obviously have to place less emphasis on the early use of nuclear weapons. The **software**-approach - to de-emphasise the early use of nuclear weapons by rewriting doctrines and war manuals - can also lead to subsequent withdrawal of nuclear arms. This is the logical, and perhaps also the likely consequence of no-first-use commitments[2]. The two approaches are different but may have similar effects; they certainly promote the same objective.

130

If the peace movements remain strong, the main question in the security debate of the 1980s may not be whether nuclear weapons should be used first or only in retaliation, but whether nuclear weapons should be deployed at all in countries which are not themselves nuclear-weapon states. Nuclear disengagement is a more tangible proposition than no-first-use, and attracts more public support. Withdrawal of all nuclear weapons a certain number of kilometres east and west of the dividing line in central Europe is a possible first step towards a comprehensive withdrawal of nuclear arms from Europe. On an optimistic note, it may turn the trends of military planning and political thought.

Even a modest beginning - for instance, along the lines suggested by the Independent Commission for Disarmament and Security Issues[3] - may raise the nuclear threshold significantly. It may reduce the danger of inadvertent escalation to nuclear war and, in particular, reduce the 'use them or lose them' dilemma. From a military point of view, it also has the attraction of putting the authorisation schedules for the use of nuclear arms on a more realistic basis. Politically it may provide some greatly needed mutual confidence.

Reducing the Danger of Surprise Attack

Any proposal for nuclear disengagement has to be combined with some agreement on conventional forces and/or unilateral changes of conventional defences. The link with the conventional sector is a complex question which can be solved in a variety of ways. In an atmosphere of East-West rapprochement, a nuclear disengagement zone might have been tied to a Mutual Force Reductions (MFR) agreement; the MFR is itself a zonal concept. However, given the present period of high tension, an accord in Vienna must probably wait for substantial improvement of East-West relations and increased mutual confidence. The parties must be willing to codify parity in the Central European sub-region; at present they do not seem prepared to do that. Therefore, it is doubtful that the Vienna negotiations can be expected to break the ice. Consequently, to link the establishment of a nuclear disengagement zone to an MFR accord may mean deferring it indefinitely.

Another possibility is to remove both nuclear and major conventional weapons from the zone. To some extent the conventional forces within the zone would have to be changed anyhow; for instance, effective verification may require withdrawal of dual-capable systems. Such withdrawal may be necessary to ensure the credibility of the arrangement and to achieve the desired confidence-building effect. However, some of these systems, dual-capable artillery units in particular, are numerous, and constitute a major part of the conventional fire power. So how can they be removed from the zone without at the same time making conventional defence much more difficult if not impossible? The answer may be to extend the restrictions into the conventional field by removing those conventional systems suitable for offensive uses. Tanks, medium and heavy artillery, multiple rocket launchers, bridging equipment, and so on, could be removed from the zone, leaving only weapons which are unsuitable for offensive strikes. Possible limits could be set at 100 mm calibre and, say, a 20 tonne weight limit for armoured fighting vehicles[4]. With present nuclear technology this would exclude dual-capable artillery from the zone. In addition, restrictions on weapon systems rather than personnel would be easier to verify and militarily more meaningful.

A disengagement zone along these lines would not only raise the nuclear threshold, but also lessen the possibilities and incentives for surprise attack. An attacker would have to mass its forces and move them through some 200 km of more or less congested roads, which may be interdicted by the defender, at least for the last 100 km, before coming in direct contact with the major forces of the opponent (unless the opponent decides to enter the zone in counter-action). The logistical complications would make a surprise attack more difficult, and other defensive measures within the zone could further increase the obstacles. For instance, some variation of the concept of **Raumverteidigung** (area defence) might be applied; large numbers of militia-type 'techno-commandos' could be spread all over the zone, in small groups and with light anti-tank and anti-aircraft precision-guided munitions (PGM). These forces would avoid a decisive battle, but would inflict attrition on the enemy so that he would have to fight the defender's heavy units in a reduced state.

A disengagement zone of this kind would fit the European variation of the Air-Land concept in two essential regards. First, it would allow interdiction strikes against the enemy's front and follow-up echelons, over distances of 100 km or more, at a stage when the enemy would be in marching rather than in dispersed battle order and would have to pass various check points. Second, rather than being tied up in a static, linear defence, the withheld major combat units may be kept intact and ready for manoeuvring strikes against the enemy, who would have to reveal his main avenues of approach.

Facilitating Political Change

An historical review shows that **political** change in East-West relations necessitates a parallel change in the

military East-West confrontation in the region. And because of the overriding importance of nuclear weapons, both as military means and as instruments of policy, it follows that political change away from the status quo requires a disengagement of the great nuclear powers, first and foremost in Central Europe. There is a distinction between agreements providing for great power disengagement and agreements of a purely military status quo character. The latter would enhance great power control of their respective positions in Europe, and would tend to strengthen the political status quo rather than change it. Of course, this applies to the conventional as well as to the nuclear field[1].

Denuclearisation of the two German states would be a precondition for any solution to the German problem – whether on the basis of neutrality or in the form of a confederation between the two states. However, in elaborating the concept of **Ostpolitik** Bonn explicitly ruled out neutrality. The salient principle of non-singularity is, moreover, applied both ways: on the one hand, the nuclear burden should be shared among the allies and not fall exclusively on the Federal Republic; on the other hand, singling out the two Germanies for exclusive denuclearisation is also objectionable. A zone of 300 km depth, as suggested by the Soviet Union and the GDR, would just about cover the two German states (and Czechoslovakia). Precisely for that reason, the suggestion is unacceptable to the FRG, because it would establish a special status for it within NATO and, to some extent, untie it from the rest of the Atlantic Alliance. A zone of some 150 km depth, covering approximately half of the country, would avoid this problem. After all, the doctrine of forward defence does not make it mandatory to deploy nuclear weapons in the immediate vicinity of the intra-German border, or within any fixed distance from it. Neither would such a zone presuppose any restraints on FRG participation in NATO nuclear planning.

The first step towards nuclear disengagement in Central Europe should, therefore, be functionally designed. A look at the tactical weapons presently deployed indicates that there is a 'natural' range threshold somewhere around 150 km; many systems fall below that limit, while others far exceed it. Following that parameter, the depth of a disengagement zone providing for the withdrawal of nuclear arms would have to be 150 km or more. If withdrawn that far, the bulk of the tactical nuclear weapons – nuclear artillery and short-range ground-to-ground missiles – could not reach targets on the other side. If major conventional arms suited for offensive operations were removed as well, there would be few, if any, targets left in the zone which would be sufficiently lucra-

tive for nuclear attacks. Therefore, the depth of a disengagement zone of that type might be 75 km or more.

The Functions of NWFZs in Northern and Southern Europe

No nuclear weapons are currently stationed in the five
Nordic and six Balkan countries (Albania, Bulgaria, Greece,
Romania, Turkey and Yugoslavia; Cyprus is also included in
the zone proposals) that are contemplated for inclusion in
NWFZs, except for Turkey. In these areas, the functions of
NWFZs would, therefore, differ from those of a zone arrangement in Central Europe. In the north and in the south of
Europe NWFZs would primarily be confidence-building
measures. They would have some military significance but
greater political importance. In time of crisis they would
function as early-warning systems - in the political rather
than in the military sense. The procedural provisions regarding withdrawal or suspension of treaty obligations should be
drafted so as to enhance this early-warning role.

It is not difficult to conceive of NWFZ arrangements which
would strengthen the security of the Nordic countries and
those of the Balkan Peninsula. Neither is it difficult to
generate political support for NWFZs in the prospective
members states. The problem is to find designs which are
acceptable to the major powers as well. A special difficulty
arises from the fact that an NWFZ in one sub-region would
force NATO to adopt different nuclear doctrines for different
parts of Europe. A differentiated doctrine - keeping some
countries 'in' while letting others 'out' - is particularly
hard to adopt in periods of high East-West tension, when
reliance on large numbers of nuclear weapons is a military
'must' for some, and politically opportune for others. Then,
the domino effects of an NWFZ in a sub-region of Europe may
seem particularly threatening.

Since the Nordic area has become more sensitive to the
strategic nuclear build-up and to major power rivalry in
other parts of the world, it follows that the Nordic NWFZ
proposals must aim at confidence and stability also in relation to the **global** ramifications of military activities
in the sub-region. One of the main thrusts of the arms race
is displayed in the vicinity of the Nordic countries -
notably on the Kola Peninsula and in the Barents and
Norwegian Seas - so efforts to avoid tension and enhance confidence should no longer be confined to the Nordic-Central
European framework.

For the USA and the USSR, the intermingling of strategic
and local forces in the north implies a danger of inadvertent
escalation[5]. Collateral measures to a Nordic NWFZ, limiting

the presence of battlefield nuclear weapons, may reduce that danger somewhat and, therefore, be in their interest[6]. Strengthening the barrier against inadvertent or accidental escalation by removing tactical nuclear weapons from the chaos of warfare is a function that a Nordic zone arrangement would have in common with a battlefield NWFZ in Central Europe. With the latter this is the main point. With the former it would be a modest achievement that could be enhanced by regional confidence-building measures comprising also the inner seas of Europe and waters adjacent to Europe[7].

Characteristics of NWFZs

There are three main characteristics of an NWFZ: non-possession, non-deployment and non-use of nuclear weapons. The non-possession requirement is met by Nordic, Central European and South European countries alike; except for Albania they have all ratified the NPT. The non-deployment obligation, however, presents various kinds of difficulties for the countries involved.

Non-deployment

Participation in an NWFZ requires an **unqualified** position against the deployment of nuclear weapons, applying in times of both war and peace, and embodied in an international legal instrument. While Norway's and Denmark's policy of non-deployment in peace time has never been challenged by other NATO members, non-deployment in times of crisis and war would impose more substantial restraints on NATO nuclear planning for northern Europe. In important respects, Norway, Denmark (and Iceland) would be decoupled from NATO's nuclear strategy, and their participation in NATO's military planning and organisation might have to be reconsidered in other respects as well.

In the Balkan area, only Turkey still accepts nuclear weapons on its soil in peace time. However, Turkish participation in an NWFZ does not necessarily presuppose elimination of all nuclear weapons from that country. It is conceivable that Turkey would be included only in so far as its European territory is concerned (the European territory being defined, for instance, as it was in the Helsinki Document on confidence-building measures[8]).

In Central Europe, any NWFZ would require substantial re-deployments. In peace time, the United States has relatively few nuclear weapons closer than 100-150 km from the inter-German border; on the eastern side there may be some.

Information about Soviet nuclear weapon deployments in eastern Europe is scant and controversial. The main difference that an NWFZ would make applies to times of crisis, aiming at a higher nuclear threshold in times of war. With the establishment of an NWFZ, there would be no nuclear weapons within the specified number of kilometres east and west of the border, whereas current plans prescribe that large numbers of nuclear weapons should be coupled with forward deployed delivery vehicles in tense international situations. If major conventional weapons were to be withdrawn from the zone as well, force deployments would also look very different in peace time.

If it can be convincingly argued that a combined nuclear and conventional disengagement will improve the conditions for effective conventional defence, this idea may attract substantial political support on both sides. The political and military establishments may then be willing to relinquish the present postures of forward defence which are rather strictly adhered to by the West, and which have deep historical roots in Soviet military thinking.

Negative security assurances

Today, non-use assurances are integral parts of the proposals for an NWFZ in both northern and southern Europe. If extended they would make it more difficult for nuclear-weapon states to **threaten** to use nuclear weapons in time of crisis. To some extent, the political functions of nuclear weapons would be constrained. In Central Europe there is no similarly strong case for non-use assurances in relation to a zone extending a specified number of kilometres on either side of the East-West border. The main military rationale for such a zone - to raise the nuclear threshold - does not presuppose any non-use commitment. Neither would such a withdrawal of nuclear weapons preclude continued adherence to a first-use doctrine.

In connection with the UN Special Session of 1978, the nuclear-weapon states made unilateral non-use declarations. The Committee of Disarmament subsequently tried to turn these (conditional) pledges into a uniform, legally binding commitment for all nuclear-weapon states, but without success so far. The lack of progress has led to a certain lack of interest in the entire matter. It is not very attractive to pursue a proposal which is both difficult to attain and at the same time relatively insignificant. In relation to NWFZs, assurances containing far-reaching qualifications may turn out to be of little value for the zonal states.

The renewed interest in no-first-use commitments offers a

different and in many ways more satisfactory solution to the
quest for negative security assurances[9]. If all nuclear-
weapon states committed themselves not to be the **first** to
use nuclear weapons, non-use assurances would largely become
superfluous. Moreover, no-first-use commitments are likely to
have military implications of a stabilising nature, which
non-use obligations would not.

Even in a general setting of no-first-use commitments there
might, however, be a need for additional security assurances
to non-nuclear-weapon states. For instance, a no-first-use
pledge may cease to apply in relation to all states participating in an attack where nuclear weapons are actually used
by one or two states only; in this case there would still be
room for additional and more absolute assurances to participants in an NWFZ. These assurances should cease to apply only
in relation to zonal states which allow the stationing and/or
use of nuclear weapons on their territories, that is, give up
their nuclear weapon-free status[10].

Nuclear Disengagement Region-Wide

A disengagement zone in Central Europe may be considered in
close conjunction with the proposals for NWFZs in northern
and southern Europe.

The proposals to give European countries non-nuclear
status, or enhance that status, vary according to the
character of the area. For instance, the idea of limitations
on nuclear weapons which are deployed in the neighbourhood of
the prospective zone and which are well suited for use
against targets within it carries more weight in the Nordic
than in the Balkan context. Some such limitations may easily
be contemplated east, north and west of a Nordic zone, as
more or less integral parts of a zone arrangement. However,
to ask for limitations in Schleswig-Holstein and in the
northern parts of the GDR and Poland seems far-fetched;
nuclear weapons deployed in those areas are part of the
Central European balance, so to require their withdrawal on
behalf of a Nordic NWFZ would neither be reasonable nor gain
much respect. The solution probably lies in the establishment
of a disengagement zone in Central Europe which is geographically contiguous to a Nordic zone.

The need for such a link is particularly obvious in the
case of Denmark. Together with FRG, Denmark is responsible
not only for the defence of Denmark and the straits but also
for Schleswig-Holstein, under joint command for that purpose.
Should Denmark take part in a Nordic NWFZ and extend its 'no'
to nuclear weapons in peace time to include also crisis
situations and time of war, the common doctrinal platform on

which FRG and Danish forces operate today would be eroded.
However, a look at the map shows that a Central European zone
extending 150 km into either side (as proposed by the Independent Commission on Security and Disarmament Issues[3])
would cover virtually all of Schleswig-Holstein. This would
not eliminate the problem, but a disengagement zone in
Central Europe would go a long way towards solving it. More
ambitiously, a geographically contiguous NWFZ running all the
way from the northern edge of Europe to its southern parts
may be envisaged, with special provisions for each of the
three sub-regions. An NWFZ on the Balkan Peninsula would be
geographically contiguous with a Central European zone via
neutral, non-nuclear Austria.

Apart from FRG territory, the only territories in Central
Europe available for deployment of NATO nuclear forces are
the Dutch and the Belgian. However, the Netherlands aims at
reducing its involvement in NATO's nuclear posture, and
Belgium would like to move in the same direction. To have
nuclear weapons in one of these countries to satisfy the FRG
stress on non-singularity, but not in the other, is hardly a
practical proposition. With some modifications for southern
Europe (mainly Italy and Turkey) there is, therefore, no
great difference between a battlefield NWFZ and withdrawal of
all nuclear weapons for **all** European states which do not
themselves possess such arms. The latter would allow for the
continued existence of nuclear weapons on Soviet, French and
British territory, including US weapons in Great Britain,
and has the advantage of being simple and unambiguous[11].
In the process of making Europe nuclear weapon-free, there
may be no convincing alternative between a contiguous
disengagement zone running north-south with a battlefield
NWFZ in the middle, and the removal of nuclear weapons from
all European non-nuclear-weapon states.

References

1. M. Saeter, 'Nuclear disengagement efforts 1955-80: politics of status quo or political change?', in S. Lodgaard
   and M. Thee (eds), Nuclear Disengagement in Europe,
   (London: Taylor & Francis 1983) pp.53-69.
2. A. Myrdal, The Game of Disarmament, How the United States
   and Russia run the Arms Race, (New York: Pantheon Books,
   1976).
3. Common Security. A Programme for Disarmament, The Report
   of the Independent Commission on Disarmament and Security
   Issues under the Chairmanship of Olof Palme, (London: Pan
   Books, 1982) pp.146-150.
4. S. Lodgaard and P. Berg, 'Disengagement and nuclear

weapon-free zones: raising the nuclear threshold', in Nuclear disengagment in Europe, op.cit. pp.101-114.
5. B. Rosen, 'Inadvertent nuclear war? Escalation and NATO's northern flank', International Security, 7, No.2, (Fall 1982).
6. J.J. Holst, 'A nuclear weapon-free zone in the Nordic area: conditions and options - a Norwegian view', Bulletin of Peace Proposals, No.3, (1983).
7. J. Prawitz, 'A Nordic nuclear weapon-free zone: model and procedure', in Nuclear Disengagement in Europe, op.cit. pp.191-198.
8. SIPRI, World Armaments and Disarmament, SIPRI Yearbook 1976, (London: Taylor & Francis 1976) pp.324-425.
9. J. Goldblat, 'The Nuclear Non-Proliferation Treaty and No First Use of Nuclear Weapons', Bulletin of Peace Proposals, 13, No.4, (1982).
10. A. Rosas, 'Non-use of nuclear weapons and NWFZs', in Nuclear Disengagement in Europe, op.cit. pp.221-230.
11. Annexe Two (by Egon Bahr) to the Palme Report, op.cit, pp.182-183.

Nansen Behar and Ivan Nedev

The theoretical model for creating nuclear weapon-free zones in different parts of the world has its historical precedent in the demilitarised zones of the past in which a partial or total ban on the deployment, production or use of particular weapons or troops was established. These demilitarised zones were temporary and had limited scope, in most cases encompassing only parts of the warring countries, whereas nuclear weapon-free zones include in principle whole countries, groups of countries, parts of the globe and even space.

A nuclear weapon-free zone is a relatively new term in international relations. According to J. Evensen[1] the concept rests on four main pillars:

a) The country, or countries, must undertake a **legal obligation** under international law not to produce or deploy nuclear weapons on their territories, nor to permit other countries such deployment. This obligation must be equally valid in times of war as in times of peace.

b) The nuclear weapon states, on their part, must undertake to respect strictly the status of the zone and to refrain from the use, or from the threat to use nuclear weapons against states of such a zone.

c) An international control apparatus or system must be set up in order to ascertain that the parties to a nuclear weapon-free zone, as well as the nuclear weapon states, comply with their commitments.

d) Nuclear weapon-free zones must be so established and administered that they will strengthen the atmosphere of detente in the world.

Recently, the issue of establishing nuclear weapon-free zones in Europe, where nuclear confrontation is most intensive has acquired a special importance in relation to the problem of nuclear disarmament. The conditions now existing on the 'old continent' make it both imperative and conducive to go over from theoretical models of nuclear weapon-free zones to concrete practical steps. These conditions include:

a) the existence of a sufficient number of countries whose governments have expressed readiness to participate in such zones;
b) the intention expressed by the European countries at the Helsinki Conference to strengthen their collective security by avoiding the arms race and taking measures to limit nuclear proliferation;
c) the existence of geographical regions where no nuclear weapons are stationed or in which the majority of countries have no nuclear weapons on their soil.

Typical examples in this respect are the proposals for nuclear weapon-free zones in northern Europe and in the Balkans, as well as the recent proposal by the Swedish Prime Minister Olof Palme of a tactical-nuclear-weapon-free zone in Central Europe. In this paper, the emphasis is on the idea of a Balkan nuclear weapon-free zone.

Origins of the Idea

The idea of turning the Balkan peninsula into a nuclear-free zone is not new but the proposal to establish such a zone has gained fresh importance in the light of the deterioration of international relations and the deployment by NATO of medium-range theatre nuclear weapons (cruise and Pershing II missiles) in Europe. This is of direct concern to the Balkan states since they - especially the two Warsaw Pact members, Romania and Bulgaria - will be within the range of the new nuclear missiles.

It was in this context that Bulgaria supported the establishment of a Balkan nuclear weapon-free zone (BNWFZ). Elaborating on this proposal, T. Zhivkov, State Council President of Bulgaria, emphasised on 20 October 1981:

We warmly support the idea of turning the Balkans into a nuclear-free zone. We propose that a meeting of the leaders of the Balkan states be held as early as next year to discuss this problem. The turning of the Balkans into a nuclear-free zone would correspond to the interests of our peoples. It would be a substantial contribution to the improvement of the international climate, to the gradual transformation of Europe into a continent free of nuclear arms; it would be one more victory for peace[2].

The idea of a BNWFZ thus turned into a practical proposition, which remained high on the list of priorities not only of Bulgarian diplomacy but also of different public organisations and bodies, such as the Bulgarian Academy of Sciences, the Agrarian Party, the Fatherland Front, and the Bulgarian youth organisations. These groups have organised symposia and meetings on the BNWFZ idea with participation from different Balkan countries. It has become an object of discussion among the governments of the Balkan states and gained support from Romania, the Greek Government led by Andreas Papandreou and Yugoslavia.

The practical discussions have moved further ahead with the meeting in Athens early in 1984 of a group of experts from the Balkan countries to prepare the conditions for a summit meeting at which the BNWFZ proposal will be further debated and eventually decided upon. The positive response of all Balkan countries, with the only exception of Albania, has raised hopes for further practical progress towards freeing the peninsula of nuclear weapons.

It should be mentioned that a proposal essentially similar to the idea of a BNWFZ was made as early as September 1957 by Romanian Prime Minister K. Stoyka. It aimed at making the Balkans a region without foreign military bases. Although nuclear weapons were not directly mentioned, there was an affinity to the idea of a BNWFZ because the removal of US bases from the Balkans would be tantamount to freeing the region of nuclear weapons. At that time – as now – there were no Soviet military bases in the Balkans.

The Conceptual Framework

The idea of creating a Balkan nuclear weapon-free zone has important political, strategic and economic aspects.

From a political point of view, the establishment of such a zone would not only contribute to regional security but may create an impulse for new processes aiming at all-European security. Every regional multinational NWFZ has the potential for a chain-reaction effect in international relations. A regional NWFZ tends to increase the degree of confidence both between its member states and with neighbouring countries. Since most of the small and medium-size states in Europe belong either to one or the other of the two main military blocs in the world – NATO and the Warsaw Pact – regional NWFZs could also contribute to greater confidence between the main military powers and in this way make a global impact.

The creation of a BNWFZ would be in full accord with the principles of the Final Document of the Helsinki Conference because some of the causes of regional tension would diminish; confidence-building as well as stability in inter-state relations would be prompted; the use and the threat of use of force against the territorial integrity and political independence of states would be eliminated; and the danger of military conflict by misunderstanding or miscalculation, and of a surprise attack with or without the use of nuclear weapons, would become less likely.

The establishment of a BNWFZ has singular international policy implications. Unlike the situation in other regions of Europe, the seven Balkan countries cover a relatively small area but have a variety of political and military affiliations outside the region. The establishment of a BNWFZ may foster cohesion and stimulate political harmony and economic cooperation.

It should be noted that the Balkans consist of countries with no nuclear weapons on their territories, as well as countries (members of NATO) which probably have such weapons on their soil.

From a **strategic** point of view the BNWFZ would become a kind of a buffer between the nuclear powers of the two military blocs - a sanctum in one of the most sensitive areas of the globe on the crossroads between Europe, Asia and Africa. It could become an important link in a disengagement belt linking a Northern nuclear weapon-free zone and a denuclearised Central Europe with a nuclear weapon-free Balkan region. The non-nuclear axis running from the north to the south of Europe would separate the main forces of the military groupings; it would make the European continent safer and arms control in Europe more credible.

Political and Economic Premises

Historians have dubbed the Balkans 'the powder keg' of Europe because of the many past conflicts and armed confrontations. Recently, however, the Balkans have been turning into a zone of peace. Mutual trust and good neighbourliness are being consolidated. The road towards this goal is full of diversions, sudden reverses or temporary increases of tension but the dominant tendency in the Balkans today is towards détente and cooperation. Distrust between the countries with different social systems is steadily being reduced, and a new community of interests - promoted primarily by the aspirations to live in peace - is coming into being. The Balkans can serve as a fairly good example of the promotion of good neighbourliness between countries with different social orders, in accord with the spirit of Helsinki. In particular, Bulgaria's policy during the last two decades has been one of the factors contributing to this development.

Economic cooperation on a bilateral basis plays a key role in the advancement of this process. Thus, Bulgaria has developed mutually advantageous economic relations with its neighbours.

A Tentative Outline of a BNWFZ

The difference between the present and earlier denuclearisation proposals lies not so much in their substance as in the urgency imposed today by the escalation of nuclear armament in Europe. There is a widespread apprehension of the increased threat of nuclear weapons, and a realisation of the implications of their use in Europe. The goal of averting nuclear war has gained paramount importance. We believe that although our region represents a micro model of the world political scene, there exist opportunities to safeguard peace on the peninsula and to strengthen further cooperation between the Balkan states. The establishment of a BNWFZ would be conducive to this end.

Although no detailed blueprint for the establishment of a BNWFZ has yet been elaborated, there were many ideas and concepts. The following is a brief, tentative outline of the main elements of a BNWFZ, as seen by us:

- All Balkan states should become members of the zone. Except Albania, they are all signatories of the Nuclear Non-Proliferation Treaty.
- The delimitation of the BNWFZ should follow political and not strictly geographical boundaries of the region.
- The nuclear weapon-free status of the zone should be guaranteed by nuclear powers, especially all European nuclear powers, the United States and China.
- Under an agreement to establish a BNWFZ the Balkan states should undertake: not to manufacture, acquire or test nuclear weapons and their delivery systems, or other nuclear devices, and not to try directly or indirectly to gain control over such weapons or devices; not to give any support to other countries in actions that might infringe upon the nuclear weapon-free status of the zone.
- The nuclear powers should commit themselves: a) not to provide member states of the BNWFZ in any direct or indirect way with nuclear weapons and their delivery systems, or any other nuclear devices; b) not to aid, support or encourage the member states of the BNWFZ to produce, acquire or test nuclear weapons and their delivery systems, or to gain control over them; c) not to deploy or store nuclear weapons and their delivery systems

on the territories of the BNWFZ; and d) not to use or threaten to use nuclear weapons against the territory of the member states of the BNWFZ.

All these measures should be accompanied by adequate control provisions which would guarantee that all countries fulfil their obligations under the agreement for a BNWFZ. The scope, form and method of control might be discussed in detail when an agreement is reached in principle for the establishment of such a zone.

In our opinion, the idea of a BNWFZ, as well as of national security in general, should be considered in close connection with political and economic issues. The following points might be taken into consideration:

- the rejection of the view that armaments, including nuclear armaments, guarantee peace and stability between nations particularly in the case of small nations;
- the development of indigenous economic, scientific and technological potentials as a basis for broader equality in international relations; more advanced economies naturally enhance international trade and involve more active participation in the international division of labour;
- the establishment of a BNWFZ should not create difficulties for the peaceful use of nuclear energy;
- participation in the BNWFZ should not be incompatible with membership in defence alliances.

The Verification Problem

Some critics of the BNWFZ have pointed out the difficulties of the verification of the treaty in view of the fact that the members belong to two military blocs - NATO and the Warsaw Pact.

The problem of verification has two aspects, a military-technical and a political one. We are of the opinion that for a zone of relatively small size, as the Balkans, the technical aspect of the verification would not be difficult to resolve. Some elements of suspicion, due to past experience, would have to be overcome but present day technology offers means for effective control of the movement of nuclear weapons and their means of delivery.

More important is the political aspect. Given the political will to establish a NWFZ, mutually acceptable means of control, which could make easier the verification of the treaty, can be devised. As far as the military blocs are concerned, their guarantee to abide by the nuclear weapon-

free regime of the zone should include acceptance of the
verification measures agreed upon by the participating
countries. In any case, the problem of the verification of
the treaty should not be turned into an obstacle for its
conclusion.

Favourable Conditions

There are several factors which create favourable conditions
for the setting up of a BNWFZ:

- No Balkan country possesses nuclear weapons of its own or
  the potential to produce such weapons.
- All Balkan countries, except Albania, are signatories of
  the Non-Proliferation Treaty and have accepted the safeguard obligations of the International Atomic Energy
  Agency.
- Four of the countries in the region: two member states of
  the Warsaw Pact (Bulgaria and Romania), one member of NATO
  (Greece) and one non-aligned country (Yugoslavia) have on
  different occasions expressed support for the BNWFZ idea.
- Public opinion in the Balkan countries has recently shown
  growing support for the BNWFZ idea.
- Last, but not least, despite the deterioration of the
  international climate, all major achievements of detente
  in the region have remained alive, as proved by the
  frequent high-level visits among the Balkan states.

However, from the point of view of the feasibility of the
BNWFZ idea, one must also take into account some potential
negative factors. The Balkans are, in a way, a micro model of
the world. Not only does the line dividing NATO and the
Warsaw Pact cross the peninsula, but almost all the different
shades of opinion in both sides are present in the region.
Even those Balkan states which accept the BNWFZ idea have
different concepts as to its framework. Furthermore, the
United States and NATO regard the BNWFZ idea as a step which
would change the military balance in favour of the Warsaw
Pact. Consequently, pressures are being applied on the NATO
allies in the region to reject the BNWFZ idea.
It would be naive to expect that the implementation of a
BNWFZ would be a quick and easy process. Its success will
depend largely on the general evolution in the international
climate. But given the self-interest involved - the overriding interest of all Balkan states to prevent nuclear war
in the region - the proposal bears weight.
We do not share the opinion that the situation in the
Balkans and the setting up of the BNWFZ depend only on the

general state of East-West relations, and that the BNWFZ idea
should await a general agreement on nuclear disarmament. On
the contrary, we believe that at the present state of world
affairs, small countries, such as in the Balkans, have the
responsibility and could effectively contribute to lessen
tension and diminish the threat of a nuclear catastrophe.
This is exactly what a Balkan nuclear weapon-free zone is
about.

References

1. J. Evensen, 'The establishment of nuclear weapon-free
   zones in Europe: proposals on a treaty text', in S.
   Lodgaard and M. Thee (eds), Nuclear Disengagement in
   Europe, (London: SIPRI, Taylor & Francis, 1983), p. 172.
2. T. Zhivkov, Speech delivered at the Ceremonial Meeting
   Dedicated to the 1300th Anniversary of the Founding of the
   Bulgarian State, Sofia, October 20 1981, (Sofia Press
   Agency, 1981).

17.   MUTUAL FORCE REDUCTION NEGOTIATIONS

Jane Sharp

Background to the Negotiations

The Vienna talks on Mutual and Balanced Force Reductions
(MFR) stem from a NATO invitation to the Warsaw Treaty Organisation to negotiate mutual and balanced reductions of forces
in Europe, issued from a North Atlantic Council meeting in
Reykjavik in June 1968. But the antecedents of MFR can be
traced to various disengagement proposals after World War II,
when the crucial problem for both East and West was how to
re-absorb Germany into the international system: divided or
reunified, disarmed or armed, aligned or non-aligned. NATO's
goals in 1968 were first, to halt unilateral force reductions
by those allies with forces in central Europe, and second, to
counter the Warsaw Pact proposal for a pan-European Security
Conference with a more pragmatic arms control measure.

The Soviet and East European response was cautious. Soviet
leaders made WTO participation in MFR conditional on NATO
participation in the ESC - later convened as the Conference
for Security and Cooperation in Europe (CSCE) - and on conclusion of a series of agreements between the Federal Republic of Germany and the Soviet Union, the Democratic Republic
of Germany, Poland and Czechoslovakia, the essential feature
of which was Bonn's acceptance of the political and territorial realities of post-1945 Europe, however painful these
were in terms of perpetuating the division of Germany.

Exploratory MFR talks began in Vienna in January 1973,
where establishing the status and number of the participants,
and the boundary of the reduction zone, took until June;
foreshadowing the difficulties of negotiating an agreement
which would both satisfy the two superpowers and reassure
their allies.

The reduction zone comprises the territory of the three
northern tier countries of the WTO: GDR, Poland and
Czechoslovakia, and for NATO: FRG and the three Benelux
countries.

States with forces deployed in this zone are the direct participants in the negotiations. For NATO: the USA, Canada, UK, FRG, Belgium, Luxembourg and the Netherlands; for WTO: the USSR, GDR, Poland and Czechoslovakia. WTO southern tier states - Hungary, Romania and Bulgaria - and NATO flank states - Norway, Denmark, Italy, Greece and Turkey - are all designated 'special' participants. All participants - direct and special - attend weekly plenary sessions, but the weekly informal sessions, where serious business is conducted, are attended only by direct participants - the USA and the USSR - each accompanied on a rotating basis by two of their allies. In the weekly intra-NATO sessions both categories of participant attend with equal voice, but four NATO members are neither direct nor special participants in Vienna. Portugal, which was in political turmoil when the talks began, has 'observer' rights, which the Portuguese Ambassador to Vienna exercises infrequently. Spain, which was not a member of the alliance when the talks began, has 'wondered aloud' about participation but has not pressed the issue. Iceland has no military forces, and France deplores the bloc-to-bloc format of the talks but keeps a close watch on NATO's MFR policy through NATO sessions in Brussels.

In setting an agenda the exploratory talks did not go beyond designating the Vienna forum: 'Negotiations on the Mutual Reductions of Forces and Armaments and Associated Measures in Central Europe'. Despite some obvious shared interests in an agreement which would not only reduce the high level of military confrontation in central Europe, but add an important military element to the political detente which developed in Europe in the early 1970s, and reduce the spiralling costs of defence for both sides, NATO and the WTO nevertheless approached the MFR negotiations with different priorities.

NATO's initial objective in proposing the talks was to stem the trickle of unilateral Western force withdrawals which plagued the alliance in the mid to late 1960s, or at least to obtain reciprocal Soviet force reductions to maintain the balance at lower levels. NATO's military leaders also hoped the Vienna talks might establish procedures which would reduce the risk of surprise attack by opening up the WTO to regular inspection. The Soviets' primary interest was in imposing constraints on the Bundeswehr and on NATO's technologically superior armaments, both nuclear and conventional.

The Negotiations to Date: Agreements Reached

Based on a view that the Soviet Union enjoyed significant military advantages in manpower, tanks and proximity to

Eastern Europe, NATO's opening position in Vienna called for
unequal cuts in NATO and WTO forces to a common manpower
ceiling in the MFR guidelines area. American and Soviet
forces would be reduced in a first phase agreement to be
followed in a second stage by reductions by the other direct
participants. By contrast, the Soviet Union, while acknowledging differences in the NATO and WTO force postures,
asserted that the two sides were essentially balanced in the
MFR zone and proposed equal percentage reductions to maintain
the same balance at lower levels. The Soviets wanted indigenous forces reduced early, national manpower sub-ceilings, and
limitations on arms and military equipment as well as troops.
    Through the 1970s MFR negotiations wrestled with
disagreements in three main areas: the nature of the NATO-WTO
balance and the need for an agreed data base, the phasing and
scope of reductions sought, and the measures necessary to
verify an agreement. By June 1983, however, a substantial
measure of convergence had been achieved and both sides now
agree on the following elements of an MFR treaty:
- the goal is to reach common alliance manpower ceilings,
  within the reduction zone, of 900 000 for ground plus air
  forces, and 700 000 for ground troops alone;
- reductions should be phased;
- in the first phase only stationed Soviet and American
  forces would be reduced;
- at the same time all direct participants in the negotiations would be committed to reduce at a later stage;
- stationed forces must be withdrawn within national
  boundaries to locations which do not threaten the security
  of states with 'special participant' status.
Measures to monitor compliance with a treaty will include:
- periodic exchanges of data after force reductions;
- notification of the beginning and end of reduction steps;
- pre-notification of large military movements into and out
  of the reduction zone;
- permanent observation posts at the exit and entry points
  of the reduction zone;
- non-interference with national technical means (NTMs) of
  verification, for example, satellite photography;
- supplementing of NTMs by on-site inspections;
- establishment of a consultative commission to resolve any
  ambiguities about treaty complicance.
    Both sides have made compromises. The Soviets accepted,
after initial resistance, the concept of common alliance
ceilings instead of equal percentage reductions, and relaxed
their original effort to impose individual national
sub-ceilings on manpower. The Soviets also moved from their
original position on verification which was to assert that

national technical means were adequate to monitor an MFR agreement. Now, the Soviets accept the establishment of permanent observation posts on the borders of the reduction zone and have even accepted the principle of on-site inspections by military personnel of the opposing alliance. For its part, NATO seems to have accepted in practice, after initial resistance, the Soviet view that Hungarian territory – on which two Soviet divisions are stationed – should be excluded from the reduction zone, at least in a first agreement. In addition, NATO now accepts, after some reluctance, that all direct participants should commit themselves to reductions coincident with the first stage reductions of stationed Soviet and American forces, and that the forces of direct participants should be frozen between reduction stages. NATO has also dropped its initial insistence that Soviet reductions be made in the form of an entire tank army.

Issues Still to be Resolved

Manpower Ceilings: Both sides seek a common alliance ceiling of 900 000 for ground and air forces combined, with a sub-ceiling on ground forces of 700 000. WTO would also impose a sub-ceiling of 200 000 on air forces, but NATO would permit more than 200 000 air force personnel if ground forces dropped below 700 000.

WTO would not allow any state to contribute more than 50 per cent of the manpower in its alliance ceiling of 900 000 in the reduction zone; a provision designed to limit the Bundeswehr from making up the shortfall of any other NATO ally, but which is of substantial interest to many NATO states, since it would also prevent the Soviet Union from increasing its proportion of the WTO ceiling. Resistance to this proposal in the FRG has prevented its acceptance by NATO as a whole.

The Phasing of Reductions: NATO proposes reductions in four phases over seven years, imposing a freeze on all participants' forces in the area after the second stage. WTO would reduce in two stages, with all direct participants freezing their forces coincident with the first phase reductions of Soviet and American troops.

Limits on Armaments: NATO has vacillated on the question of armaments over the ten years of the talks. Initially NATO proposed that the Soviets withdraw their arms and equipment but American forces leave theirs in place to compensate for the geographical advantage enjoyed by the Soviet Union (proximity to Central Europe). Later, in December 1975, NATO proposed trading NATO nuclear weapons for Soviet tanks, and

in the latest draft treaty proposal of July 1982 NATO omits
armaments altogether.

The Soviet position has been consistently that arms and
military equipment should be withdrawn when the troops with
which they are associated are reduced. The WTO draft treaty
of February 1982 proposed a special protocol to deal with
armaments.

The Data Discrepancy (see Table 1): NATO continues to
insist that both sides agree to a data base on pre-reduction
forces before a treaty can be signed. NATO asserts that WTO
has over 150 000 more ground troops in the reduction zone
than the Soviet Ministry of Defence admits. Some of this
difference can be accounted for by definitional differences -
perhaps as many as 100 000, mainly East European, forces -
but this still leaves 50 000 Soviet troops, the equivalent of
over four divisions, unaccounted for. Nevertheless, the WTO
argues that agreement on data should focus on verifying
residual force levels after all phases of reductions are
complete.

Necessary Degree of Inspection: Beyond the permanent
observation sites at exit and entry points, WTO still views
on-site inspections within the reduction zone as more of a
privilege than a right. Whereas NATO wants an agreed annual
quota of up to 18 inspections, WTO thus far has only accepted
on-site inspection by invitation if one side challenges the
other.

Notification of Reductions and Related Activity: WTO
wants notification of all troop movements of more than
20 000, and would prohibit manoeuvres involving more than
40 000 to 50 000 troops; a move designed to curb NATO's large
annual exercise each autumn. NATO wants pre-notification of
troop movements in and out of the reduction zone on an annual
basis in order to get better intelligence on the rotation of
Soviet troops into and out of Eastern Europe. NATO also seeks
prior notification of all out-of-garrison activity by one or
more division formations, not only in the Eastern MFR
reduction zone but also in the western military districts of
the Soviet Union; offering in return to provide proportional
coverage beyond the Western MFR zone. Though the Soviets have
accepted similar proposals in principle at the CSCE review
conference in Madrid, they have not yet done so in the MFR
context in Vienna.

Exceptions: NATO is seeking permission to allow the
United States to use the Western MFR zone as a stopping place
for the Rapid Deployment Force and to permit large infusions
of troops for the annual NATO exercises each autumn. WTO
resists this and insists that ceilings imposed following
reductions should not be exceeded for any purpose.

Table 1. The Data Discrepancy in Vienna
(Two Sets of Figures Introduced at Vienna, June 1980)
(in thousands)

	Western view		Eastern view	
	ground	air	ground	air
NATO				
United States	200[a]	35[b]	210[f]	37[f]
Great Britain	55[c]	11[c]	58	10
Canada	3[c]	2[b]	4	2
Belgium	63[c]	20[c]	66	21
FRG	335[c]	106[c]	336	108
Netherlands	75[c]	19[c]	66	18
Luxembourg	1[c]	–	–	–
NATO HQs	4g	–	8	–
France	51[c]	–	45	–
Totals	787[d]	193[d]	793[e]	196
Total ground and air:	980[d]		989	
Warsaw Pact				
Soviet Union	470[a]	60[b]	403g	40g
Czechoslovakia	140[c]	46[b]	140	41
GDR	108[c]	36[b]	95	30
Poland	210[c]	62[b]	160	70
Totals	928[a]	204	798[e]	181[e]
Total ground and air:	1132		979	

Notes
a. ACDA Annual Report 1980.
b. J.G. Kelliher, The Negotiations on Mutual and Balanced
   Reductions, (New York: Pergamon Press 1980).
c. IISS, Military Balance 1980-1981, (figures for July 1980).
d. These figures obtained by adding, but ACDA Annual
   Report says 790 000 total for ground forces.
e. G. Yergenyev and I. Melnikov, in Moscow Novoye Vrema,
   20 August 1982, cited by FBIS-SU, 26 August 1982.
f. Figures supplied by non-governmental expert, for all
   individual Eastern view of NATO ground and air figures.
g. Figures supplied by US source, for all individual Eastern
   view of Warsaw Pact ground and air figures. Known to be
   accurate within 5 per cent.

Source: The Arms Control Reporter, Institute for Defense
   and Disarmament Studies, (Brookline, Mass. 1982).

Prospects for an Agreement

Arguably,   given a growing shortage of Russian males of draftable age, the continuing tension with China, and the occupation of Afghanistan, the Soviet military might be more interested in a MFR agreement now - to stabilise the Soviet presence in Eastern Europe at lower levels - than when the talks began in the early 1970s. On the NATO side, the FRG government also faces negative demographic trends and there is a growing sentiment across the political spectrum in the United States for reducing American troops in Europe. For a variety of reasons Presidents Reagan and Andropov could both benefit from an arms control success. If high level attention in both East and West were focused on the Vienna negotiations, the following issues could be resolved relatively quickly. Technical solutions exist; all depends on political will.

The Data Discrepancy (See Table 1): To date, NATO has insisted that an agreed data base for pre-reduction force levels must be established for Western governments to have any confidence in a MFR agreement. WTO, by contrast, has argued that it is necessary only to agree on the level of post-reduction forces to verify an agreement. Essentially the Soviets are saying: 'trust us to reduce the appropriate number of troops to reach a common ceiling even if you do not accept the current Soviet data'. The Soviets have also suggested reductions by 'mutual example' outside the framework of a formal treaty in an effort to ease the data problem. Soviet reluctance to be more forthcoming on dis-aggregation of the WTO data has been frustrating to the other delegates in Vienna, but there are several plausible explanations. To do so might, for example, reveal serious undermanning of divisions, and expose weakness rather than the superiority which NATO claims the Soviets enjoy. In any event, the recent Soviet position accepting permanent observation posts at exit and entry points to the MFR zone, and the principle of on-site inspections in Eastern Europe, should make it easier to reach a compromise on data.

Analysts at the Defense Intelligence Agency (DIA) and the Congressional Research Service (CRS) in Washington are developing statistical tools with which to estimate total forces deployed in each side's reduction zone, by random inspections of military units for which a range of acceptable size will already have been agreed by each side[1]. If this could be developed into an effective monitoring procedure, NATO should be able to back off from its insistence on pre-reduction data. While this would meet the Soviet criterion that the focus should be on post-reduction levels, it will require detailed unit-by-unit information on the composition of each alliance manpower ceiling of 900 000. Such disclosures could face resistance not only from the Soviet military establishment but also from the FRG which is hypersensitive to anything that smacks of a national sub-ceiling.

Inspection Quotas: In the early 1960s, Soviet, American and British negotiators were unable to resolve their differences over the appropriate number of annual inspections to monitor a comprehensive test ban. This led to a much weaker limited treaty, permitting underground testing. This experience should inform and guide the participants in MFR. It would be tragic indeed if MFR ran aground on the inspection issue after the Soviets had reversed their earlier resistance to on-site inspection. If the Soviets can now go the extra mile and agree to an annual quota of on-site inspections, instead of their current position of inspection by invitation only, then NATO should be willing to modify the number of inspections it considers adequate to monitor a MFR agreement, and perhaps also relax the requirement to monitor out-of-garrison activity unconnected with the reduction schedule.

Limits on Armaments: As noted, NATO has vacillated on the issue of arms reductions and limitations at MFR. The reasons advanced for omitting them from the latest NATO draft treaty include: negotiations are so close to completion on a manpower agreement that it would be foolish to delay and complicate matters by including armaments; NATO needs to preposition equipment for American forces returning to Western Europe in a crisis, so arms and equipment associated with American forces should not be withdrawn; the Soviets have more (even if technologically inferior) arms in the reduction zone.

While NATO does not include armaments in its proposals currently on the table in Vienna, several former members of the United States delegation in Vienna have recommended MFR as the logical forum in which to negotiate a follow-on agreement on short-range battlefield nuclear weapons, most of which are deployed in the reduction zone. With the Soviets threatening to introduce new battlefield nuclear weapons into Eastern Europe in response to the deployment of NATO's new long-range cruise and Pershing, setting limits on short-range nuclear weapons might have broad appeal.

All the WTO states have endorsed Olof Palme's proposal[2] for a nuclear-free strip in central Europe, recommending that it be widened to 600 km, and suggesting Vienna as the logical forum at which to negotiate the details of an agreement. A simpler, and certainly less time-consuming procedure, would be to remove NATO nuclear systems from Western Europe for which there are no Soviet equivalents in Eastern Europe -

nuclear armed artillery pieces for example – then codify a form of 'zero-solution' before any similar Soviet systems were introduced, that is, NATO could offer to do with short range systems what it has urged the Soviet Union to do with medium range missiles. It would represent a levelling-down-to-parity, for a change. The alternative looks like being a new spiral in the modernisation of short range nuclear systems on both sides, despite the fact that many NATO military leaders are on record as saying the weapons in question have no military utility.

The Issue of Sub-Ceiling: NATO reluctance to date to accept the 50 per cent solution is ironic, since this compromise measure was first raised in Western circles – and discussed at length at the Pugwash conference in Varna in 1978. It is an eminently practical suggestion since it codifies the status quo; the Soviet Union currently contributes approximately 50 per cent of WTO forces in the zone, and the Bundeswehr comprises approximately 50 per cent of NATO forces in the Western zone. Furthermore, it meets tacit but long-standing concerns on both sides, by setting de facto limits on Soviet forces in Eastern Europe and on the Bundeswehr in NATO. It seems unlikely that an MFR agreement would be held up over this issue, since the Soviets could always deal with it in a unilateral statement if necessary.

References

1.   S. Sloan, 'East-West Troop Reductions in Europe: Is Agreement Possible?', US Congressional Research Service, (Washington DC, 1983)
2.   Common Security. A Programme for Disarmament, The Report of the Independent Commission on Disarmament and Security Issues under the Chairmanship of Olof Palme (London: Pan Books, 1982.)

EUROPEAN SECURITY

Robert Neild

A variety of measures to improve European security are in the air. There are the negotiations between the United States and the Soviet Union over intermediate range nuclear forces. There are the private proposals floated in the United States for a no-first-use declaration by NATO. There are various proposals for nuclear-free zones in Europe, some of which have been around for a long time.

For conventional forces, we have the Mutual Balanced Force Reduction talks in Vienna which have dragged on for years; some confidence-building measures have been introduced and more proposed; and now we have a spate of proposals in the NATO countries for a strengthening of conventional forces in order to reduce reliance on nuclear weapons.

How is one to make sense of all these measures and decide what to advocate?

Clearly the motivation for them derives from fear of nuclear war. The object of the measures relating to nuclear weapons - such as nuclear-free zones or a freeze - is directly to push back nuclear weapons and ease that fear. The object of the proposals to strengthen conventional forces is indirectly to achieve that result.

But the question that matters is, will the measures proposed increase or reduce our security?

Admittedly security is an ambiguous expression. Increased security could be defined as a diminished risk of nuclear war. But it might be possible to reduce the risk of nuclear war by measures which increased the risk of conventional war. In that case we would have to assign weights to the two risks and minimise their weighted sum. In practice, what we seek are policies which reduce the risks of both conventional and nuclear war. It is with these that we are concerned here.

Let us start with the NATO perception of the problem of security. NATO's conventional forces are perceived to be inferior to those of the Warsaw Pact. The inferiority is off-set by the policy of the flexible response, whereby NATO would be ready to be the first to use nuclear weapons. But that policy is seen to be a legacy of the days when NATO enjoyed nuclear superiority. It is seen to have become increasingly unsafe and untenable since the Warsaw Pact achieved nuclear parity - some would say superiority.

The reaction is to be found in the unofficial proposal that a policy of no-first-use be adopted; and, secondly, in the proposal, coming from both official and private mouths, that the conventional forces of NATO be strengthened so that reliance on nuclear weapons is reduced.

The adoption of a declared policy of no-first-use has, however, been criticised on the grounds that on its own (that is, without an improvement in conventional forces) it will not add to security, and may detract from it by appearing to suggest that NATO is reluctant to fight in self-defence. It could similarly be argued that a nuclear-free zone on the central front might not add to NATO's security in so far as there is a conventional imbalance which would be exposed more nakedly.

The proposal for a strengthening of conventional forces, on the other hand, has been received with widespread approval and little criticism in NATO countries.

Yet, there is obviously a risk that the result could be an accelerated conventional arms race alongside whatever is happening in the nuclear arms race.

Whether improved conventional forces would lead to an arms race and would reduce or increase security is commonly thought of in terms of the relative levels of arms and relative levels of expenditure (which determine the rate of change in the level of arms). That is the basis of our models of an arms race, from Richardson onwards. But instead attention should be turned to the characteristic of forces.

Anders Boserup[1] has emphasised, and others have echoed, the importance of differentiating between forces with offensive potential (for example panzer divisions), which make your enemy feel threatened and cause him to arm in reaction to your arms and, on the other hand, forces with defensive potential (for example dispersed anti-tank forces) which are less provocative to your enemy. The former are likely to aggravate an arms race, the latter to calm one.

A further important distinction is that between forces which are concentrated and, therefore, vulnerable to weapons (nuclear or conventional) that cause destruction over an area, and forces that are dispersed.

The prime examples of concentrated forces vulnerable to area weapons seem to be:

a) concentrated armoured and mixed armies on the battlefield, aircraft on airfields, and naval bases;

b) concentrated movements of troops (and supplies) at the
   time of mobilisation;
c) concentrated movements of troops (and supplies) to
   reinforce or relieve troops at the front once war has
   begun.

If one nation, A, possesses forces which offer rich targets
of this kind, its opponent, B, is likely to feel the need of
nuclear weapons (or conventional substitutes) to destroy A's
forces before A attacks him. And if two nations possess
forces of this kind, there will be a temptation for each to
use his concentrated forces (for example aircraft on airfields) to destroy the enemy's forces (aircraft on airfields)
before the enemy acts in that way.

Let us consider in this light the policies now being proposed for NATO. The most complete exposition is to be found
in 'Strengthening Conventional Deterrence in Europe:
Proposals for the 1980s', the report of the European Security
Study, a private but authoritative group of American, British
and German experts and recently retired senior officers from
NATO, supported by the American Academy of Arts and Sciences
and others[2]. It subscribes to the policy of forward defence
and proposes that this can be achieved, and the nuclear
threshold raised, by making use of new technologies. It looks
to the prospect of 'smart' conventional weapons (that is,
precision-guided area munitions) which are as effective as
small nuclear weapons. These weapons could be used against
Warsaw Pact air bases, against second echelon forces coming
up along supply routes, and against forward formations. The
relevant paragraphs in the main report read as follows[3]:

17. New advanced technologies for target acquisition and
conventional weapons can provide a far more effective
conventional means than is now available for carrying out
NATO's critical defensive missions. These include area
impact and guided conventional submunitions; accurate
delivery means for guided submunitions by surface-launch or
air-launch non-nuclear missiles and by other stand-off
weapons; and techniques for near real-time surveillance and
target acquisition. These new technologies would be
particularly useful for the attrition of Warsaw Pact air
power interdicting and disrupting Warsaw Pact follow-on
forces; and helping to counter the initial Warsaw Pact
attack by the selective engagement of forward Warsaw Pact
formations. In addition they can greatly enhance the
effectiveness of NATO aircraft against Warsaw Pact armored
ground forces by equipping the aircraft with modern
dispensers and sub-munitions.
18. These advanced conventional technologies have been

designed; many have been tested and others are being
tested; and a few are already in production in the Federal
Republic of Germany, France, and the United Kingdom, as
well as in the United States. We calculate that the new
technologies to provide a capability to suppress Warsaw
Pact air bases and interdict Warsaw Pact choke points could
be acquired and deployed by 1986. Those that would provide
a capability for the disruption of Warsaw Pact follow-on
forces could be made effectively available by 1988.

Two further points in the report are worth noting;

a) The report states that implementation of the policies it
proposes to strengthen NATO's conventional forces 'would
not remove the necessity for NATO to retain a nuclear capability. The threat of nuclear weapons would still be important in compelling Warsaw Pact forces to operate in a
"nuclear scared" mode and in deterring Soviet theatre
nuclear strikes.'[4].

b) In a workshop report supporting the main report it is
emphasised that 'A fundamental conclusion of this Workshop
report is that NATO can best bolster its conventional
deterrent by concentrating on defeating Soviet strategy,
rather than on simply attriting Soviet forces.'[5].

In a supporting paper by a German expert, Dr. Stratmann, it
is argued that 'If the capabilities of Western forces were
limited to the delaying and attriting function, NATO's objective of restoring the integrity of allied territory (not to
mention the possible interests in acquiring "tokens" of Pact
territory) would become unattainable.'[6].
It is noteworthy that no consideration is given in the
main report, nor anywhere in the published supporting reports
and papers, to the possible reactions of the Soviet Union and
Warsaw Pact to the policies proposed for NATO. The possibility that there is an arms race and that the actions of one
side will induce reactions in the other is not considered.
The question, what will happen when the Warsaw Pact develops
the same 'smart' weapons, is not asked.
Let us try to think how this policy must look from the
Soviet side.
The prospect that NATO will acquire the ability to knock
out, with conventional weapons, Warsaw Pact airfields, second
echelon tanks and troops coming up through Poland and GDR to
reinforce the first echelon, and concentrations of forces on
or near the battlefield, is bound to produce an alarming
feeling of potential nakedness. Worst-case analysis will

suggest that by the use of these weapons NATO might achieve a position where, having neutralised a large part of the forces opposing it, it could advance into Warsaw Pact territory, forcing the Soviet Union to consider first use of nuclear weapons. It is vital to note, however, that this worst-case scenario depends on one characteristic of the policies proposed for NATO: that it should not go for defensive forces which have limited mobility and depend primarily on attrition, but should retain armour so as to be able to drive out the enemy. If a policy of defensive forces and attrition were adopted in combination with the smart long-range weapons, NATO's forces **viewed as a whole** would not have an offensive potential. The ability to destroy second echelon forces, airfields and concentrated forces would ease the task of attrition. The whole might constitute an effective defensive stance, that is, in dissuading the Warsaw Pact from attacking. Instead, we have a combination of forces which compared with present forces will look more offensive.

This illustrates the importance of the characteristics of forces and the need to restructure them in a defensive manner. It is an illustration written by someone from a NATO country in criticism of policies now proposed for NATO and their effects on the Warsaw Pact. In this sense it is an exercise in self-criticism. It would be extremely interesting and valuable to see a critique, along similar lines, of Warsaw Pact policy by someone from the Warsaw Pact.

In the meantime, it may be useful to say something about Soviet and Warsaw Pact strategy as it is presented in the West by Western experts who follow the Soviet military literature. The concern here is not with interpretations of Soviet **intentions**, that is, whether it plans or is likely to attack us; for intentions are a subject on which speculation is bound to be rather wild and consequently rather uninteresting. Instead, the concern is with what can be called military **doctrine or strategy**, that is, how the Warsaw Pact would fight, **supposing** a war began for some reason or other.

The view of Soviet strategy we are offered in NATO countries is apparently based on Soviet writings in books, military journals and similar publications where military problems are openly debated. Whether the Western experts have interpreted these writings correctly is another matter. In fact, one can find various interpretations by different authors. But the 'mainstream' version goes something like this:

a) the best means of defence, at least in Europe, is to take the offensive and swiftly destroy NATO's ability to fight;

b) for this purpose, armoured forces supported by artillery and aircraft would, in the event of war, attack on many fronts seeking to achieve 'break-throughs' on several axes deep into NATO territory, so as to disrupt its defences and command structure;

c) the large number of tanks and armoured vehicles, the strong river-crossing capability of Warsaw Pact forces, and other features of those forces, all fit in with this picture; they show that the Warsaw Pact has a strong offensive capability.

At another level, there is speculation about why this strategy is maintained. The explanations offered are fairly numerous:

a) it is a strategy of re-fighting the last war, a posture the military of all countries commonly adopt, as a result of inherent conservatism and the lack of any compelling experience (that is, another war) to make them change their ways;

b) the Soviet Union, after its terrible experiences in World War II, has an understandable instinct to keep war off its territory and push it into that of the enemy;

c) in the early post-war years, the Soviet Union countered the risk of nuclear domination by the United States by posing the threat of conventional domination in Europe, that is, an asymmetrical deterrent; the conventional strategy has lived on, although nuclear parity has been achieved.

One could go on. But what matters is the effect of the reported Warsaw Pact strategy on the minds of people in NATO countries. It is similar to the effect which the proposed NATO strategy is likely to have on the minds of people in Warsaw Pact countries. Indeed, the Report of the European Security Study, referred to above, describes the offensive nature of Warsaw Pact strategy as a justification for the proposals it makes for strengthening NATO.

A final question: how can we generate a debate in which both sides examine critically the effect of a conventional strategy and force structure of their own side and the reactions it is likely to induce on the part of the other side, and then exchange ideas about how to do better?

References

1. A. Boserup, 'Deterrence and Defence', Proceedings of 31st Pugwash Conference (1981) pp. 111-113.
2. 'Strengthening Conventional Deterrence in Europe: Proposals for the 1980s', Report of the European Security Study (London: Macmillan 1983).
3. ibid pp. 34-35.
4. ibid p. 29.
5. ibid p.41.
6. ibid p. 178.

Marian Dobrosielski

The attention of governments and public opinion, both in the East and the West, is now mainly concentrated on the **military** aspects of European security. This is understandable because the most immediate, gravest threats to our security are posed by the continuously accelerating quantitative and qualitative arms race, in nuclear and conventional weapons. Therefore, to diminish these threats and dangers is the principal task of responsible governments, as well as of all of us. But we tend to forget that this is only one aspect, a negative one, of the security problem.

We must strive to achieve, through genuine disarmament measures, not only common military security, but also common security in the socio-political, economic, scientific, cultural, informational and many other fields. Pugwash has very often emphasised the complex, many-sided and close interrelationships of these different security elements, for instance the complementarity of political and military detente. Without neglecting the military aspect, we should devote more of our attention to these problems.

The Madrid CSCE Meeting

In the shadow of the unsuccessful and hopeless negotiations on nuclear weapons in Geneva, and on conventional forces in Vienna, there is one ray of hope, the positive ending of the Madrid Meeting of the Conference on Security and Cooperation in Europe (CSCE). For the first time after many years we have not only a reconfirmation by all CSCE participants of the principles and provisions of the Final Act from Helsinki[1], but also a step which should lead towards their better and fuller implementation. The Concluding Document of the Madrid Meeting[2], if fully implemented by all participants, could mean a renewal of the policy of detente and cooperation. This document contains provisions which, to many of us, would have seemed impossible to have been agreed upon at a period of such strong international tension.

I should like to recall that the task of the periodical Madrid-type meetings, as defined in the Final Act from Helsinki, is to have a thorough exchange of views of the participating states both on the implementation of the principles and provisions of the Final Act, and on the enhancing of their mutual relations, improvement of security, and development of cooperation and the process of detente[3]. Different countries put somewhat different interpretations on this provision. Most of the Western countries, especially the USA, stress the thorough exchange of views on the implementation of the Final Act as the main task of such meetings, whereas the Eastern countries – while not denying the importance of such exchange – believe that the working out of measures concerning further development of cooperation and detente should be their principal task.

When the Final Act was drafted the participants did not define the duration of such meetings, but it was assumed that they should last no longer than several weeks. However, the first of these meetings, in Belgrade 1977, actually lasted several months, and the Madrid meeting lasted almost three years. (The preparatory meeting started on 9 September 1980 and the main meeting on 11 November 1980). There were several adjournments, the longest one from March to November 1982. The long duration of the meeting led some delegates to quip that CSCE stands for 'Can Start, Can't End'. It is worth recalling that Stage II of the CSCE, during which the Final Act was worked out, lasted less than 2 years, a year less than the Madrid meeting.

Opening statements were made inter alia by Ministers and Deputy Ministers of Foreign Affairs of a number of participating states. Negotiations were held mostly at the ambassadorial level. Some 200 delegates participated in them. Contributions were also made by: Algeria, Egypt, Israel, Morocco and Tunisia.

A very important characteristic of the Madrid meeting was that the military aspects of European security, which were practically ignored in Belgrade, came to the forefront of interest. Already on 6 December 1980, Poland put forward a thoroughly worked out proposal for convening a conference on military detente and disarmament. The next day, France tabled a proposal concerning a conference on disarmament in Europe. The peculiarity of the French proposal is that, except in the title, it did not deal with disarmament questions at all, but only with so-called military confidence-building measures. Later, Romania, Sweden and Yugoslavia put forward proposals concerning a conference on military aspects of European Security. The Polish proposal was endorsed from the beginning by all WTO countries. The French proposal was endorsed by the NATO countries, with the very lukewarm and late support of the USA.

Altogether, more than one hundred proposals concerning all 'baskets' of the Final Act were tabled by the participating states for inclusion into the Concluding Document. It would take too long to give a detailed analysis of the proceedings of the Madrid meeting, its ups and downs, and to assess the role played by specific countries or groups of countries. But it is necessary to stress the very positive role played during these meetings by the group of neutral and non-aligned countries, trying several times to prepare, on the basis of all proposals, drafts of the Concluding Document which could be acceptable to all.

It should also be mentioned that, as in the past, when everybody was convinced that all the major obstacles for agreement have been overcome, Malta created new obstacles, abusing the rule of consensus and declining to give its assent to the agreed text, unless the document provided for the convening of a conference on security, arms and armaments reduction in the Mediterranean, with the participation of the states of that region. This proposal was considered by practically all the other CSCE participants as being Utopian for the foreseeable future, and endangering the whole CSCE process.

The Concluding Document of the Madrid Meeting

The agreed Concluding Document, finally adopted by the Foreign Ministers of the participating states on 7 September 1983, is structured similarly to the Final Act. It is 40 pages long. Apart from the introduction, it consists of five chapters on: questions of security in Europe; cooperation in the field of economics, science and technology and the environment; questions of security and cooperation in the Mediterranean; cooperation in humanitarian and other fields; and follow-up of the Conference. There are also two annexes.

The reading of the Concluding Document makes for a pleasant surprise. It is difficult to perceive that a formulation permeated with such a spirit of cooperation and detente was possible to be agreed upon at a time of such deep mistrust and tension in East-West relations. If only one could believe that these measures will be implemented by all participants in good faith. If this were so, one would not need to worry too much about the future. Alas, past experience cautions us that for some countries, agreements are one thing, and the international political practice is something very different. I suspect, for instance, that the US government gave its

assent to the Concluding Document only in order not to alien-
ate its allies and to show the world public opinion that it
is not against any agreements. I do not think that the
international political conduct of the US government will
change overnight after the adoption of the Concluding
Document.

I utter these words of caution not to minimise the achievement of the Madrid meeting, but to stress my belief that for
a real breakthrough in international relations to be achieved
it is essential to have a genuine halt to the arms race and
an agreement on disarmament measures in both nuclear and
conventional forces. Only this would make it possible for
such documents, as the one we are discussing here, to play an
important role in strengthening international security and
cooperation.

The Concluding Document contains not only noble and pious
declarations but also several important decisions. The introduction gives a formal description of the activities of the
Madrid meeting. It contains a re-affirmation of the commitment to the continuation of the CSCE process, and of the
importance of security and genuine detente; a commitment to
the implementation of all provisions and respect for
all the principles of the Final Act.

The chapter dealing with questions relating to security in
Europe includes the following formulations:

- to exert new efforts to make detente an effective, continuing, increasingly viable, comprehensive process,
  universal in scope;
- to seek solutions to outstanding problems through peaceful means;
- to develop relations of mutual cooperation, friendship
  and confidence, refraining from any action which might
  impair such relations.

There is in this chapter a strong condemnation of terrorism, including terrorism in international relations, linked
with an obligation to prevent the territories of the participating states from being used for the preparation, organisation or commission of terrorist activities. There is also an
emphasis on the universal significance of human rights and
fundamental freedoms and the determination to develop laws,
and their effective exercise, in the field of civil,
political, economic, social, cultural and other human
rights.

One of the most important decisions of the Madrid meeting
was to convene a **Conference on Confidence and Security-
building Measures and Disarmament in Europe.** The first
stage of this Conference, scheduled for January 1984 in
Stockholm, will be devoted to the negotiation of a set of

confidence and security-building measures designed to reduce the risk of military confrontation in Europe. The adopted measures would cover the whole of Europe, as well as the adjoining sea and ocean area and air space; they should be militarily significant, politically binding, and provided with adequate forms of verification.

The next follow-up meeting of the CSCE, to be held in Vienna in November 1986, will assess the progress achieved during the first stage of the Conference, and eventually consider the mandate for the next stage. This means that **real** disarmament negotiations will, at best, not start before 1987. Do we really have so much time? How is it possible to discuss and agree on genuine confidence and security-building measures in the shadow of the fervent installations of new nuclear rockets and missiles in Europe? These questions are put not to diminish the importance of the proposed meetings but to stress the point that in the field of negotiations we are moving at a snail's pace, while at the same time the arms race is accelerating incredibly fast. Refraining from the installation of Pershing IIs and Tomahawks in Europe, and the scrapping of a large number of SS-20s, would produce more mutual confidence than the CSCE meetings can achieve.

The Concluding Document also contains other decisions about meetings and seminars of the participating states. Thus it was agreed to hold a meeting of experts to deal with the examination of peaceful settlements of disputes; this will take place in March 1984, in Athens. In October 1984 a seminar will be held in Venice on economic, scientific and cultural cooperation in the Mediterranean. A meeting of experts on questions concerning respect for human rights and fundamental freedoms will be held in May 1985, in Ottawa. A 'Cultural Forum' will take place in Budapest in October 1985. A meeting of experts on human contacts will be convened in Bern in April 1986.

Of the many excellent provisions dealing with economic, scientific, technological and environmental cooperation, only a few will be mentioned. There is a reiteration of the resolve to pursue and intensify cooperation irrespective of the economic and social systems of the participating states. There are obligations to develop trade and industrial cooperation between all the participating states to reduce and eliminate obstacles and barriers to trade expansion and industrial cooperation, and to promote stable and equitable economic relations. There is an acknowledgement of the necessity to establish a new international economic order and to conduct global negotiations relating to international economic cooperation.

The actual practice in East-West relations, especially the economic restrictions and sanctions imposed for political reasons by the United States on Poland and other socialist countries blatantly contradict these provisions. Will the USA change its attitude after the adoption of the Concluding Document? I personally doubt it.

Similar provisions, intended to facilitate cooperation in the field of energy, agriculture, environment, science, culture, education, information and human contacts, abound in the Concluding Document. Let us hope that, sooner or later, they will be put fully into practice. This could contribute to the creation of a system of positive common security through the elimination of discriminations, restrictions and sanctions in political, economic, scientific and other fields, and through increased cooperation instead of confrontation.

The Role of Scientists

The UN has proclaimed 1986 as the Year of Peace. Pugwash scientists could, and should, make an important contribution in this respect. Until now we have dealt mainly - and rightly so - with dangers arising from the misuse of scientific and technological progress. We tried to make governments and public opinion aware of the threats to international peace and the survival of mankind inherent in the nuclear arms race. Many other organisations and peace movements in the world have taken up this message. Thanks to this, the nuclear arms race is no longer an esoteric matter restricted only to military technologists and strategists. It has become a public, universal concern, a most urgent political issue. Most people are aware by now that the greatest danger threatening mankind is a global nuclear war, and that this threat is immeasurably larger than any real or illusory threat stemming from our different ideological, political, economic or social systems.

People are aware of this danger and they are frightened. But genuine peace cannot be built on fear. Fear is often the source of irrational and desperate actions. Pugwash should try, through a collective scientific effort, to bring new hope to people by showing how progress in science and technology could be used to solve positively different global crises and problems which are facing mankind; how science and technology can contribute to ensuring a genuine and lasting peace based not on terror but on cooperation.

We have tried to show, with some success, that in the nuclear era war can no longer be considered as 'the continuation of policy by other means'; that no positive political, economic, moral or any other goal can sanction the use of nuclear weapons or be achieved through the use of these weapons. For these reasons, among others, the use or threat of the use of force should be forever eliminated from international relations. The next step is to develop a positive, realistic and specific philosophy of peace. Peace should not be understood only as a negation, the absence or even elimination of war. We should give this notion a precise positive, humanistic, social, economic, philosophical meaning.

Today, the main task in international relations is to prevent, by all peaceful means, a nuclear holocaust, to put an end to the arms race and achieve disarmament. This is a necessary if, in itself, not a sufficient condition to maintain and strengthen peace. It is not enough for scientists to be against war and the arms race. We must fully understand and clearly explain the dangers threatening mankind stemming not only from the absurd arms race, but also from the crisis in the world economic and financial order, from the demographic, ecological, social, political and moral crises. It is necessary to create a common consciousness that these and other global crises and problems need a common, global approach for their solution, which can be found only by peaceful means, through dialogue and cooperation, and not through conflict and confrontation; through the creation of a global system of common political, economic, military, social security for all. By doing this, we will follow Bertrand Russell's appeal: 'Remember your humanity, and forget the rest'.

References

1. Final Act of the Conference on Security and Cooperation in Europe, Helsinki, 1 August 1975.
2. Concluding Document of the Conference on Security and Cooperation in Europe, Madrid, 7 September 1983.
3. M. Dobrosielski, 'Europe after Belgrade - Problems and Prospects' in W. Gutteridge (ed.) European Security, Nuclear Weapons and Public Confidence, (London: Macmillan 1982) pp. 3-10.

Part Four

Problems of Regional Security

Krishnaswami Subrahmanyam

Introduction

In the current international environment, a local conflict is difficult to define. It has been calculated that from the end of World War II up to the end of the Falklands conflict, there have been 148 conflicts, all but about ten of them having taken place in the developing world. Prof. Istvan Kende[1] has calculated that in the wars that took place up to the end of 1976, there were interventions by capitalist countries in 64 wars, by the socialist countries in six and by other Third World countries in 17. Similarly the Brookings Institution[2] has calculated that in the period 1946-1975 there had been 215 instances of the use of force without war by the United States and 195 instances by the Soviet Union.

According to SIPRI[3] in the period 1978-82 only 3.6 per cent of the Third World's arms supplies originated from the Third World, the rest coming from the developed world. Obviously, therefore, most of the conflicts in the Third World would not be sustained over a period of time were it not for the overt or covert support from the industrialised nations. In these circumstances, it is difficult to define a strictly local conflict in the Third World. There have been a few, but they are not likely to be high-profile conflicts. Most of the conflicts in the Third World have linkages with the superpower confrontation, or with some regional hegemonic power which in turn depends on a superpower for weapons and equipment.

The Role of Nuclear Weapons in Third World Conflicts

Nuclear weapons can feature in Third World conflicts in two ways. A recognised nuclear-weapon power can threaten to use the weapon in a Third World conflict situation. Alternatively, a clandestine nuclear-weapon power, such as Israel or South Africa, may do so. The US declaration in regard to the use of nuclear weapons highlights this possibility:

> The United States will not use nuclear weapons against any non-nuclear State party to the non-proliferation Treaty or to any comparable internationally binding commitment not to acquire nuclear explosive devices, except in the case of an attack on the United States, its territories or armed forces, or its allies, by such a State allied to a nuclear-weapon State or associated with a nuclear-weapon State in carrying out or sustaining the attack[4].

The phrase 'associated with a nuclear-weapon State' can be interpreted according to one's convenience and inclination. The attack by an adversary state need not be a nuclear attack to justify the USA resorting to nuclear weapons, and the declaration is vague as to whether an attack on the US armed forces also includes a counter-attack by a country when US forces launch an attack on it.

Up to the present, the USA has considered the possibility of using nuclear weapons in Vietnam, following the fall of Dien Bien Phu, in the Quemoy-Matsu crisis, which was a local clash between China and Taiwan[5], and it resorted to a nuclear alert during the Arab-Israeli war[1]. Use of nuclear weapons was also contemplated during the Korean and Vietnam wars[5]. In all these instances the use of nuclear weapons was envisaged against an adversary who had no nuclear weapons. The interventionism of the industrialised nations, particularly the nuclear-weapon powers and especially the superpowers, and their tendency to resort to nuclear threats are the primary reasons underlying Third World nuclear insecurity - an aspect which the apologists for interventionism seek to obfuscate, attributing prestige as the most important factor in proliferation.

The second category of nuclear threats in the Third World arises out of the clandestine arsenals of nuclear weapons in the hands of nations like Israel. Professor Stephen Cohen[6] describes Pakistan, which is making efforts to reach nuclear weapons capability, in the following terms:

> Pakistan belongs to that class of states whose very survival is uncertain, whose legitimacy is doubted and whose security-related resources are inadequate. Yet, these states will not go away, nor can they be ignored. Pakistan (like Taiwan, South Korea, Israel and South Africa) has the capacity to fight, to go nuclear, to influence the global strategic balance (if only by collapsing).

All the five states that Professor Cohen mentions have close links with the United States, and their military establishments are to a considerable extent influenced by US military doctrines. Apart from the above, the only other developing nations which are classified as coming within the category of near-nuclear-weapon powers are India, Argentina and Brazil.

For certain Western writers, it is fashionable to highlight the possible dangers arising from developing nations acquiring nuclear weapons, at the same time maintaining that nuclear weapons in the hands of the five recognised nuclear-weapon powers are quite safe. The fiction book 'The Fifth Horseman' exemplifies this, but historical evidence does not lend support to such a view. Indians and Pakistanis, as well as Arabs and Israelis, have fought a number of wars. Deplorable as these were, relatively speaking they were fought with great restraint, unlike the war in Vietnam where megatons of explosives were used - more than throughout history up to that date. The use of indiscriminate bombing as a way of fighting a war was part of Western conventional military doctrine, and city levelling through a thousand bomber raids logically led to Nagasaki and Hiroshima. Seymour Hersh in his 'Price of Power'[7] describes a drunken President talking of 'nuking' the Vietnamese. During the last days of the Nixon administration, James Schlesinger had to instruct the armed forces not to carry out orders relating to nuclear weapons coming from the President, without prior clearance with him. Scaremongers, for whom a Qaddafi with a bomb is the ultimate in terror, have to ponder the terrible risks of Nixon's presidency. According to Daniel Ellsberg[8], the authority to use nuclear weapons has been delegated since the days of President Eisenhower. There has been mention of 'prior release' orders in regard to tactical nuclear weapons if the threat of nuclear weapons in a tactical scenario is to be credible[9]. There is no reason to believe that the leadership of any developing country acquiring nuclear weapons is likely to be more rash in resorting to the weapons than the leadership of the industrialised countries.

Professor Kenneth Waltz writes[10]:

New nuclear states will confront the possibilities and feel the constraints that present nuclear states have experienced. New nuclear states will be more concerned for their safety and more mindful of dangers than some of the old ones have been. Until recently, only the great and some of the major powers have had nuclear weapons. While nuclear weapon powers have spread, conventional weapons have proliferated. Under these circumstances wars have been fought not at the centre but at the periphery of international politics. The likelihood of war decreases as deterrent and defensive capabilities increase. Nuclear weapons, responsibly used, make wars hard to start. Nations that have nuclear weapons have strong incentives to use them responsibly. These statements hold for small as for big nuclear powers. Because they do, the measured spread of nuclear weapons is more to be welcomed than feared.

The Likelihood of the Use of Nuclear Weapons

How likely is it that nuclear weapons would be used by any developing nation acquiring them in the near future? The risk that the recognised nuclear-weapon nations would use these weapons in intervention operations in the developing world remains significant. While China and the Soviet Union have offered a no-first-use pledge, the Western powers maintain their first use doctrine, which is not necessarily restricted to the European context or even to nuclear adversaries.

The use of nuclear weapons in certain contingencies in the Korean peninsula and in the Persian Gulf region has been discussed in the literature[11]. The Israelis, according to Amos Perlmutter[12], have perhaps 200 nuclear warheads. Given Israel's superiority in sophisticated conventional weapons and the total US commitment to Israel, the probability of Israel being compelled to resort to nuclear weapons against its Arab neighbours appears to be low. South Korea has at present no access to weapon-grade plutonium and may not be able, in the near future, to produce nuclear weapons of its own. Taiwan can, but since its adversary is China which has an enormous nuclear capability, it would appear that Taiwanese weapons, if developed, would be used only as a deterrent to resist forcible annexation by China.

Even if Brazil or Argentina acquired nuclear weapons it is difficult to envisage contingencies in which they would find it necessary or advantageous to use them. The British deployment of nuclear submarines and the torpedoing of the 'General Belgrano' may persuade the Argentinians of the desirability of nuclear-propelled submarines, but resort to the use of nuclear weapons by Argentinians does not appear to be within the realm of rational possibility.

Again, in the Indo-Pakistan context, if both countries were to develop nuclear weapons the probability is that a situation of stable mutual deterrence would evolve. India is a status quo power which does not favour any alteration of existing boundaries by use of force. Within Pakistan the view is gaining ground that the Kashmir problem should be left to be settled by a future generation. There is clear realisation

in Pakistan that if it were to go nuclear, India would over-
take it both in size and sophistication of arsenals. The history of the last four wars shows that neither side is inclin-
ed to resort to indiscriminate and excessive use of force
even under war conditions. Millions of divided families live
on both sides of the border and this would be one of the
major restraining factors.

There has been concern in Israel about the development of a
Pakistani nuclear arsenal which might be made available to an
Arab country. This appears to be an exaggerated fear for two
reasons. First, the Arabs are aware of the size and capability of the Israeli nuclear arsenal. Many Arab capitals
are within striking distance of Israel. Second, Pakistan
knows full well that if ever a nuclear weapon were used
against Israel the origin of the weapon would be attributed
to Pakistan which would have to face retaliation from the USA
whose nuclear forces are readily deployed in the Indian Ocean
area. Therefore, this possibility is also ruled out.

That leaves the possibility of South African use of
nuclear weapons against the frontline black African states.
This is the most credible among the scenarios of the possible
use of nuclear weapons in the developing world. Racism and
genocide go together. As the pressure on the South African
white minority increases through an armed struggle, the
racist regime may attempt to blackmail its neighbouring
states to prevent them from extending support to the freedom
fighters within South Africa. One cannot rule out the
possibility of a demonstrative use of a nuclear weapon to
deter the frontline states.

In the foreseeable future, that is the next ten to fifteen
years, the use of nuclear weapons in the developing world is
probable only in respect to intervention operations by
nuclear powers against developing countries, and by South
Africa against black African states. In the former case, the
neutron bomb, which is alleged to produce high casualties
with little collateral damage, may be a preferred weapon.

The Non-Proliferation Treaty

The 'Non-Proliferation' Treaty (NPT) legitimises the possession and use of nuclear weapons, and their unlimited proliferation, by the recognised nuclear-weapon powers. As already
mentioned, there has been clandestine proliferation by Israel
and South Africa. Nineteen nations of the world have re-
affirmed their right to resort to nuclear weapons, in
defiance of the demands by the international community to
declare the use and the threat of use of nuclear weapons as a
crime against humanity[13]. The users of nuclear weapons

are more likely to be among these nations. The vast literature on the so-called proliferation problem in the sixties
and seventies has served to divert attention from the gallop-
ing proliferation in nuclear arsenals and the emergence of
two clandestine nuclear arsenals. Most of the discussion
about the use of nuclear weapons in the developing world, by
countries which are yet to acquire the capability to produce
even a field gun (they would supposedly fabricate nuclear
weapons with reactor-grade plutonium with which no country in
the world has ever made an operational weapon), appears to be
the continuation of the exercise in obfuscation that started
in the early sixties.

In dealing with the issue of nuclear proliferation, there
is an unconscious racist bias. All the industrialised nations
of the world rely on nuclear war doctrines for their security
but deny that right to other nations. The two clandestine
nuclear-weapon powers who got away with it, are European
settler nations. Whereas frequent reference is made to the
large number of wars and major instances of inter- and intra-
state violence in the developing world, the interventionism
of the industrial powers in a majority of those instances of
violence hardly attracts attention in the literature. Of late
there has also been a trend to focus excessive attention to
the development of defence industries in the developing
world, at a time when the industrialised world moves into
sophisticated technologies which are likely to make
interventionist wars cheaper.

Nuclear weapons are unjustifiable in anyone's hands. But if
the countries which occupied vast areas of the world in the
colonial era and exploited the majority of humanity are going
to use these weapons in defiance of the overwhelming opinion
of the international community, then this attempt at domination and perpetuation of the weapons culture must be opposed
with various measures, including the development of deterrent
nuclear weapons by nations which are victims of such domination. Those who support the legitimacy of nuclear weapons in
the hands of a few nations cannot logically and credibly
preach that other nations should not have them. The argument
that the NPT constituted a step-by-step approach towards a
disarmed world is patently fallacious, as seen by the rapid
proliferation in the post-NPT period. Between 1968, when the
NPT was signed, and 1982 the number of nuclear warheads in
the US and USSR arsenals rose from 5350 to 19 000[14]. The
NPT is an extension of the doctrine of the 'white man's
burden'. The fact that it has been accepted by a large
number of nations does not make it any more legitimate than
imperialism which, in its day, was also accepted by a
majority of the people of the world.

It is necessary to draw attention to the pernicious nature of the NPT since it legitimises the use of nuclear weapons by a few powers. Unless it is resisted, more and more nations will be compelled to accept the legitimacy of the use of nuclear weapons. It will no doubt be pointed out that there is a rising trend of opinion in favour of no-first-use. But the fact remains that even as this trend developed, the use of nuclear weapons is discussed in areas where nations have acceded to NPT (Iran and South Korea), armed forces are being increasingly nuclearised, and nuclear war-fighting doctrines are being advanced. The anti-nuclear feeling in Western Europe and North America, which as yet is not strong enough to make an impact on the policies of the governments, is a welcome but not a sufficient safeguard for the developing world against the use of nuclear weapons. It was at the time when anti-imperialist feeling was widespread and imperialism retreating that the bloodiest colonial wars (Algeria, Vietnam, Southern Africa) occurred.

Conclusions

While murder is recognised as a crime, killing in self-defence is considered legitimate in law. In the case of possession and use of nuclear weapons, if this is lawful for a few nations which have had a record of imperialist behaviour, and which continue their hegemonism by possessing nuclear weapons, then it should be so for others as well, especially for self-defence against interventionism. Those who are against the spread of nuclear weapons should start denouncing the legitimacy of the existing nuclear arsenals. Those interested in reducing the danger of the use of nuclear weapons by interventionist powers and the two clandestine nuclear-weapon powers, should mobilise themselves collectively in the cause of delegitimising nuclear weapons. Such a campaign requires two essential steps. First, there must be pressure on the NATO nations and their allies to join the rest of the international community in declaring in the UN General Assembly that the use and the threat of use of nuclear weapons are crimes against humanity, and accede to the proposed convention to ban the use of nuclear weapons along the lines of the Geneva convention on chemical weapons. Second, if the NATO nations and their allies do not accept the above, the developing nations signatory to the NPT should serve notice that they would withdraw from it. The NPT can be deemed a legitimate step only if it is universally accepted that the use and threat of use of nuclear weapons are illegitimate and that the nuclear-weapon powers are committed to a time-limited schedule to reduce their arsenals. Other-

wise, the NPT will continue to be an instrument to legitimise
nuclear arsenals and unlimited proliferation. Most of the
signatories to the NPT are not in a position to acquire
nuclear weapons and their accession to the treaty has only
served to legitimise the nuclear arsenals and proliferation.
The withdrawal of these countries from the NPT will not
increase the risk of proliferation but will constitute an act
of political protest against the continuing proliferation of
nuclear weapons. Thus, the weakness of the non-nuclear-
weapon nations would be converted into a strength through the
act of withdrawal. The threat of such withdrawal would
reinforce the peace movements in those nations which continue
to assert the legitimacy of the use and threat of use of
nuclear weapons. The Secretary-General of the Organisation of
African Unity recently urged that African nations should
develop nuclear weapons as a deterrent against South
Africa[15]. This is not a feasible proposition. On the
other hand, a collective threat by the African states to
withdraw from the NPT would be a more feasible and credible
event in promoting the delegitimisation of nuclear weapons.

References

1. I. Kende,'Wars of Ten Years', Journal of Peace
    Research, 15, (1978) 3.
2. B.M. Blechman and S.S. Kaplan, Force Without War, The
    Brookings Institution, (1978).
3. SIPRI Yearbook 1983, (London: Taylor & Francis, 1983)
    p. 272.
4. Quoted in the UN Report Comprehensive Study of Nuclear
    Weapons, (New York: United Nations, 1981) p. 144.
5. K. Subrahmanyam, 'The Role of Nuclear Weapons in Inter-
    national Relations', Journal Institute for Defence
    Studies and Analyses, 3, (1970) 1.
6. S.P. Cohen, 'Identity, Survival, Security : Pakistan's
    Defence Policy', in E.A. Kolodziej and R. Harkavy (eds)
    Security Policies of Emerging States : A Comparative
    Approach, (Boston: 1982)
7. S. Hersh, 'The Price of Power', (Summit Books, 1983)
    p. 396.
8. Nuclear Armaments, An Interview with Dr. Daniel
    Ellsberg, The Conservation Press, (Berkley: 1980).
9. Lord Zuckermann, in F. Griffiths and J. C. Polanyi
    (eds), Dangers of Nuclear War, (University of Toronto
    Press, 1979) pp. 164-65.
10. K. Waltz, 'The Spread of Nuclear Weapons : More Maybe
    Better', Adelphi Paper 171, (London: The International
    Institute for Strategic Studies, 1981).

11. 'No First Use', A Report by the Union of Concerned Scientists, (Cambridge Mass., 1983).
12. A. Perlmutter, Bangkok Post, 14 May 1982.
13. UN General Assembly, Resolution 36/92 I, 9 December 1981.
14. 'Nuclear War : What is in it for you', Ground Zero, (New York: Pocket Books, 1982).
15. E. Kedjo, quoted in Hindu (Madras), 11 June 1983.

21 NUCLEAR PROLIFERATION AND NUCLEAR WEAPON-FREE ZONES IN THE MEDITERRANEAN AND MIDDLE EAST

Shalheveth Freier

Nuclear Proliferation

There is a danger of nuclear proliferation in the area. More especially, until it joined the Non-Proliferation Treaty Libya openly but vainly shopped for bombs. But I doubt that this switch in declaratory stance amounts to a change of intent. Israel is alleged to have a nuclear weapon potential the consummation of which depends on a political decision. Irrespective of the near universal criticism of the destruction of the TAMUZ I reactor near Baghdad by Israel, no satisfactory explanation has been given for Iraq's initial request to France for a plutonium-producing 500 megawatt natural uranium gas-graphite reactor, or for Iraq's readiness to accept one of the largest research reactors in the world, when denied the initial choice. I do not know whether the Iraqis would have been able to mount a nuclear weapon within five years of reactor start-up as claimed by Israel, but I find it difficult to believe that anything but a nuclear military potential was the principal purpose of the purchases and programme.

Pakistan cannot remain unmentioned in this context, even though it is outside the Mediterranean and the Middle East. Pakistan depends heavily for financial aid on the wealthy Arab States, and especially Saudi Arabia; it has reportedly the technical potential to go through with a military nuclear programme; and it has nuclear cooperation agreements with a number of Arab States.

Western European nations have not been overly fastidious in checking the credentials of Iraq and Pakistan before supplying them, or undertaking to supply them, with sensitive installations. The impression which emerges is one of a region pregnant with nuclear proliferation, with the mitigating difference that years rather than nine months are the period of confinement, in most instances.

This evolution is of course fuelled by the compelling

desire of many of the Middle Eastern and North African States
to eliminate Israel; by the volatile and internecine character of the relations between these states themselves
(Iran-Iraq; Libya-Chad+Sudan+Egypt; Syria-Iraq, and so on);
and by the unrestrained flow of advanced means of warfare
into the region. Indeed, Saudi Arabia and Libya are the first
and second largest arms buyers in the Third World.

The bitter hostility which suffuses relations on the southern littoral of the Mediterranean and in the Middle East make
this area an unlikely candidate for a regional arrangement,
such as a nuclear weapon-free zone, the chief ingredient of
which is lasting mutual reassurance of neighbouring countries
that they will not resort to war in order to settle present
or future disagreements.

On the northern side of the Mediterranean, Portugal, Spain,
France, Italy, Greece and Turkey consider themselves part of
the Atlantic Alliance and though their associations with NATO
vary in character it is manifest that they seek protection
within the NATO shelter. France is a nuclear power, and the
nuclear stance of the other countries does not, for the time
being, indicate the urge to proceed with an indigenous
nuclear weapon programme.

Nuclear Weapon-Free Zones

Between the universal renunciation of war as a means for
settling conflicts - at present unrealistic - and the random
proliferation of nuclear arms which would make wars more
devastating, two intermediate concepts have emerged, which
ostensibly commit their adherents not to make nuclear weapons
and thus reduce the destruction attendant on wars, if such
are unavoidable. These concepts are embodied in the Non-Proliferation Treaty (NPT) and the establishment of nuclear
weapon-free zones (NWFZ). Both have the same goal but are
dissimilar in nature, and this dissimilarity is reflected in
their differing record of apparent success. Almost 80 safeguards agreements are in force under NPT, but only Latin
America has succeeded in establishing a NWFZ by the Treaty of
Tlatelolco, despite proposals often supported by UN resolutions to establish such zones in Central Europe, the Balkans,
South Pacific, Nordic Countries, Africa, the Indian Ocean,
South Asia and the Middle East.

For the purpose of this discussion, I disregard the unin-
habited 'zones', the only ones except for the Treaty of
Tlatelolco, where the 25 years effort directed at establishing NWFZs has yielded formal treaties: Antarctic (1959),Outer
Space (1967), Sea-Bed (1972). Common to NPT and NWFZ is the
pledge by the non-nuclear weapon signatories not to have

nuclear weapons of their own. Since the pledge is coupled with an inspection of its credibility, it is certainly a substantive pledge. But there the similarity ends.

Adherence to NPT is a message to the international community that the adherent country abjures nuclear weapons for its own use. In so doing it adds a noticeable increment to the rather elusive notion of international security. But one cannot gloss over the diversity of aspirations which find shelter within this framework. It embraces, of course, states which have genuinely opted against the employment of nuclear weapons of their own or on their behalf. But NPT also includes some nuclear-weapon states, states which have nuclear weapons stationed on their soil, states which shelter under a nuclear umbrella without weapons on their territory, states which want to reap the benefits of easy access to nuclear materials and technology without actually forgoing the military option in the long run, and others which are still a long way from any serious interest in nuclear matters altogether. This diverse assortment coupled with the conditional nature of IAEA inspection illustrates that, for all its undoubted blessings, NPT promises more than it performs.

The NWFZ is a different proposition altogether. It expects countries of a limited region, some of which might be potential adversaries in a local war, not to develop nuclear weapons, let alone possess them. To the countries of such a region this commitment attests essentially to the readiness of all to compose their differences peacefully. For it is inconceivable that they would contemplate a future fraught with local wars, and the parallel quest for improved means of warfare, without considering the eventuality of nuclear weapons, if the nuclear arms race continues unabated. On this assumption it is equally manifest that they cannot content themselves with a conditional commitment, such as withdrawing on three months' notice as provided for in the NPT, or with mere IAEA inspection, where prior agreement by the inspected country is required about the identity of the inspector and the time and object of his visit. The candidate countries for such a regional arrangement will presumably insist on a more enduring commitment and on intrusive and unconditional inspection by the nationals of the region upon one another (as provided for in the case of the Antarctic Treaty).

Lastly, a regional arrangement cannot come about except by negotiation and an agreement among the states of the region themselves. Such is the history of the Tlatelolco Treaty and such is the procedure envisaged in all the other proposals for NWFZs, except where the Middle East is concerned. Here, Israel proposed formally in 1980 that the same procedure - of direct consultation between parties concerned - be set in motion for the examination of a NWFZ in the Middle East. But most of the Arab states would have no truck with Israel on anything, and an Egyptian proposal was overwhelmingly and repeatedly adopted at the UN proposing that all states of the region adhere first to NPT, place all their facilities under IAEA safeguards, and that once all this had come about a NWFZ could be negotiated. Whereas in all other instances the very consultation among the parties concerned was to be the primary confidence-building measure, in the Middle East it was relegated to the place of an inconsequential adjunct.

Put crudely in my own words, the proposal said: let us first make sure that the alleged Israeli nuclear potential is invalidated, then settle our accounts with that country, in our own good time, and forget about negotiating with Israel altogether.

It seems to me surprising that the Arab States did not test the earnest of the Israeli proposal by agreeing to sit down and begin to negotiate. The Israelis went further. They realised that, like other proposed NWFZs, the Middle Eastern zone was not well defined and that states of the region might not abhor in a uniform manner the idea of negotiating with them. Israel stated, therefore, formally that even a small number of states would do for initial consultation, that such consultations could be preceded by a meeting of experts from those states in order to sense intentions, discuss ideas, and hopefully recommend procedures for the official negotiating teams. There has been no response so far to any of this.

Let me illustrate two of these problems. Libya is not part of the Middle East but presumes to leadership in the fight against Israel and, in addition, threatens by subversion or overt action both Egypt and the Sudan which are in the Middle East. Moreover, as mentioned earlier, Libya is known to have openly shopped around for nuclear weapons until it joined the NPT. It is at present unlikely that a NWFZ in the Middle East would turn a blind eye on Libyan designs in the nuclear realm despite its endorsement of NPT.

Another problem is the feasibility of a credible NWFZ in the Middle East if non-recognition of Israel and preparations for recurring conventional wars are considered legitimate. In my view, such conjunction is absurd.

Proposals

The IAEA 'overview of nuclear-weapon-free zones'[1] attests to the difficulties this concept has encountered, and the rather special circumstances which made the Treaty of Tlatelolco a remarkable singular instance rather than a precedent, despite the admissibility of peaceful nuclear explosions (PNE) and the scope of the Brazilian and Argentinian nuclear programmes, which will make such PNEs possible.

There appear to be a number of conditions which have to be met in order that a NWFZ can be contemplated.

a) Initiative and negotiation between the parties of the region. Even the Palme Report insists on this precondition[2].
b) Renunciation of war of any kind to settle differences between the prospective partners in a NWFZ.
c) Unlimited duration of eventual engagement.
d) Unhampered on-site verification by nationals of the contracting partners upon one another.
e) No PNEs.

It is completely unlikely that these conditions will appear acceptable, or be credible if accepted, in the very unstable situation in the Middle East.

There appears to be only the one possibility, that some militarily important states in the region will recognise the dangers of nuclear proliferation to them all and decide that it is preferable to work towards a peaceful future, of which a NWFZ would be a part.

Sitting down and talking about the issues among the potential partners would by itself confer a blessing on the region, which it has been denied hitherto.

The alternative of a NWFZ for the Mediterranean and the Middle East would amount, in practical terms, to the Indian suggestion for a NWFZ throughout the world. Appealing but not feasible.

References

1. G. Delcoigne, 'An overview of nuclear-weapon-free zones', IAEA Bulletin, (June 1982), pp. 50-55.
2. Common Security: A Programme for Disarmament, Report of the Palme Commission, (London: Pan Books, 1982).

22 NAVAL DEPLOYMENTS AND STABILITY IN THE MEDITERRANEAN

Maurizio Cremasco

The Changing Strategic Situation of the Mediterranean

The quantitative and qualitative strengthening of air and naval forces of the riparian countries must be included among the factors which, in recent years, have contributed towards reducing the geostrategic dimensions of the Mediterranean.

It is an important phenomenon which must be evaluated, both with respect to the present situation of the Mediterranean area, rich as it is in latent tensions and endemic crises, and with respect to its future evolution under the stimulus of two concomitant developments: the institution of 'Exclusive Economic Zones' (EEZ) up to 200 miles from the coast and the extension of territorial waters from 6 to 12 miles; and the progress of extractive technologies, which will render the exploitation of the sea beds much more feasible and economically advantageous.

The problem in the Mediterranean seems particularly complex. Given the geography of the Mediterranean, the creation of the EEZs will bring, inevitably, a series of overlaps and hence possible causes of controversy in establishing the limits of each EEZ. On the other hand, the progress of extractive technology, and therefore the more extended possibilities of research and exploitation of submarine resources, will tend to make more difficult the agreements between countries with an overlap of their respective EEZs. It is probable that, in the future, not only the politico-economic controversies connected with the determination of sovereign rights (for example, the unresolved questions between Greece and Turkey regarding the limits of sovereignty on the continental shelf of the Aegean Sea, or between Malta and Libya in relation to the central Mediterranean), but also the contrasts regarding those rights of free and innocent passage which are identified with freedom of navigation, will increase.

The Growing Militarisation of the Mediterranean

It is in this framework, of the present instability and future new elements of controversy, that the growing militarisation of the Mediterranean must be projected.

An analysis of the increase in air and naval forces of the riparian countries from 1970 to 1982 leads to a series of observations.

- The strengthening of these forces (in particular those of North Africa and the Middle East) has been achieved both in terms of arms and equipment, and in terms of greater military capacity.

- Air forces have generally benefited more than naval forces. Today all the Mediterranean countries (with the exception of Albania, Morocco, Spain and Tunisia) possess air forces with a total of over 300 fighter aircraft.

- The qualitative strengthening of air forces has been impressive in many ways. Today, the air forces of the Mediterranean countries deploy medium bombers (Egypt Tu-16 'Badger' and Libya Tu-22 'Blinder') and a whole series of last generation fighters and fighter-bombers: F-15, F-16, 'Kfir' C-2, Tornado; Mig-23, Mig-27 and Mig-25; Su-20 and 'Mirage' F-1. Furthermore, the older but still operational F-4, F-104G and F-104S, 'Mirage' III and 'Mirage' V. The weapon systems consist of both air-to-air missiles and air-to-surface missiles of advanced technology.

Of course, the sophistication of the craft and their effective operational capability do not always correspond. In different countries the training of the ground crews and pilots is not such as to allow these weapon systems to be utilised to their full capacity. Besides, the scarce technical and logistic support does not permit the sustaining of prolonged military operations.

Nevertheless, the overall threat in the Mediterranean has grown in terms of greater cover, higher speed of intervention, and broader distribution of modern aircraft, endowed with enhanced firing accuracy and high destructive potential.

For the naval forces, the situation may be summarised as follows:

a) Greater dispersion of submarines.

b) Increase in the number or ex-novo acquisition of frigates. In the past ten years, the navies of Algeria, Syria, Tunisia and Morocco have been equipped with frigates.

c) Large increase in light missile units (corvettes, 'fast attack craft' (FAC) and hydrofoils). This is the most evident development of great military significance. The

FACs are able to carry out tasks of patrol and control
of sea areas surveillance of the EEZs; interdiction or
harassment of commercial maritime traffic; attacks on
naval formations. The anti-ship missiles with which
they are equipped, and their high speeds, make them a
dangerous threat also for large and fully armed
warships.

Nevertheless, the FACs seem particularly vulnerable to air
attack and destined to operate in zones not too far from the
coasts and in reasonably calm sea conditions. Thus, the FACs
seem suited for operating around the straits, in stretches of
sea rich in choke points and obligatory passages, in the
gulfs, and for patrolling the EEZs.

This picture, albeit roughly sketched, gives an idea of the
military capacities present in the Mediterranean basin. The
picture becomes even more complex if one considers the
American and Soviet air and naval forces, and if one takes
into account the trends toward further militarisation which
emerge from an examination of the arms acquisition programmes
of the Mediterranean countries, the policy and programmes of
American military aid, and the Soviet Union's readiness to
provide arms to the countries of the region.

In particular, the strengthening of the air and naval
forces, even of the small riparian countries, gives rise to a
series of problems. In the Mediterranean, the old concept of
high seas linked to the freedom of navigation, the fishing
rights, the rights of conducting research and exploitation of
the sea's minerals, seem ever more likely to come under discussion.

Limits on Freedom of Navigation

There might be situations in which, for declared motives of
security, navigational safety, or pollution control, limitations of transit might be enforced in certain sea zones.

The outbreak of conflict, or the particular internal situation of a country threatened by guerrilla movements, could
provide an incentive to create security zones within which
navigation would be subject to rigid control measures, with
the possibility that ships in transit might be stopped,
searched and possibly confiscated. Particularly, in cases of
conflicts between two riparian countries, ample stretches of
sea could be considered - implicitly or by explicit declaration - as war zones, that is, zones dangerous for navigation
by any type of ship, even those of non-belligerent countries.
For political reasons, naval blocks or limits of transit
could be imposed by neighbouring countries, in support of one
or the other of the countries in conflict, in order to dis-

courage or impede the shipment of military aid and/or rein-
forcements.

Furthermore, there might be situations in which a country
intends to impede the activity of information-gathering by
ships or planes along its coasts, even beyond the limits of
its territorial waters.

Could this mean that the Mediterranean will eventually become a sea which would be not only geographically, but also
militarily and politically compartmentalised? Could it bring
about a different formulation, not so much of the concept of
international waters, as of the operations which have always
been permitted, limiting their nature and/or extension?
Could it mean that the use of naval forces for political
ends, that is the diplomatic use of naval power, would no
longer be possible?

From a **technical** viewpoint, that is in terms of
military capacity, the riparian countries are theoretically
capable, albeit with varying degrees of efficacy, of creating
and managing situations of the type described above.

The proliferation of advanced technology weapons has aug-
mented the vulnerability of the surface naval forces and has
substantially reduced the 'low density threat' areas of the
Mediterranean, that is those zones in which it would be
possible to operate without too many risks and with few
losses.

The recent Anglo-Argentinian war for the Falkland Islands
has demonstrated the efficacy of the air forces in an anti-
naval role and the lethal nature of modern missile systems.
This is an element destined to weigh considerably in a limited and closed sea like the Mediterranean, especially if, as
in the case of Argentina, the attacking planes could operate
from a 'sanctuarised' territory, that is, immune from enemy
air offensives.

Nevertheless, the fact that a major capacity of military
intervention of the riparian countries exists, and that the
whole of the Mediterranean has practically become a 'high
density threat' area, does not suffice to lend credibility to
the preceding questions, nor to give them an unequivocably
affirmative reply.

From a political viewpoint, it is difficult to maintain
that there would be sufficient motivations (except in very
particular cases) to create and impose situations affecting
freedom of navigation, which would be considered by other
Mediterranean countries as a threat to their vital interests;
a threat to which it would be impossible not to reply,
especially on the part of the two superpowers, since they
would certainly not be willing to accept limits on the
freedom of their fleets in the Mediterranean.

A similar argument could also be made concerning the diplomatic use of air and naval forces. It appears hazardous to assert that those naval operations which are commonly defined as 'gunboat diplomacy', or what Edward Luttwak[1] has called 'naval suasion', are no longer possible. But the fact that gunboat diplomacy is still possible does not mean that it has not become more complex, risky and costly.

The political conditioning of the use of military forces at a time of high risk could be stronger than expected. The interests at play could be perceived by the country under pressure as vital and therefore more important than those of the country which has chosen to use military force, thus acting as a dissuasive factor towards the latter.

The small countries might not feel at all inhibited in confronting a more powerful country, or be led to use their international relations - in particular the ties with one or the other of the two superpowers - as a further deterrent element. Thus, those conditions of 'sanctuarisation' which have often facilitated the use of military forces, might be eventually lacking.

In the end, situations might be created in which the naval units, designed as the privileged tools of such a policy, could indeed become 'hostages', given their increased vulnerability. This could augment the danger of **escalation** if such units were to represent - as for example aircraft carriers do - targets of high real and symbolic value. A real or presumed threat to such values might unleash the mechanisms of a reaction stronger than that which is militarily necessary or politically desirable.

Naturally, the degree of applicability of the military tool for political ends (and hence the relative degree of difficulty and risk) depends on the global balance of power between the countries concerned.

Apart from the two superpowers, whose real limit is represented by the dangerous possibility of direct confrontation, the disparities in power among the Mediterranean countries have been reduced in relative terms. This means that there has been an increase in the number of those countries for whom the use of naval forces, as a military or diplomatic instrument, no longer represents an easy and acceptable foreign policy option.

Conclusion

The acquisition by Third World Mediterranean countries of significant military capabilities has resulted in a redistribution of political and military power which it would be naive to ignore or underestimate.

Today they possess, and will possess even more so in the future, a **sea denial** capacity which must be taken into account in any crisis which might arise as the result of controversies over the limits of the EEZs, the limits of sovereignty of the continental shelves, the rights of exploitation of sea resources, the rights of free transit and free navigation, and so on.

Naturally, the possession of military capability does not always mean that it is in any event credible and applicable, or that the political conditions exist for its use.

Although the utilisation of air and naval forces as an instrument of coercion or pressure has become more costly and difficult, it has not become impossible.

Nevertheless, in the Mediterranean the phenomenon of the growing militarisation of the area, and the strengthening of the air and naval forces of all the riparian countries, seems destined to have far-reaching effects.

Reference

1. in E. Luttwak and R.G. Weinland, <u>Sea power in the Mediterranean: political utility and military constraints</u>, (Washington Papers, <u>61</u>, 1979) pp. 7–53.

FROM THE ATLANTIC TO THE GULF AND THE HORN OF
AFRICA : THE SPECTRUM OF CRISIS

William Gutteridge

From Morocco to Pakistan with diversions northwards to Turkey
and Iran and southwards to Somalia and the Horn of Africa
lies a diverse range of countries, a majority of which are in
the Islamic tradition and regard themselves as belonging to
the Arab world[1]. They are not often seen in any real sense
as a unity but they are almost all involved in a series of
tensions or disputes which tend to interlock or overlap one
with another. It is partly this aspect of their relationships
which has caused the extended region to be termed ominously
in official American circles as the 'Arc of Crisis'. Several
of the countries in question also have their own internal
problems which have a potential to burst into flames and
spread.

Today it is unfortunately not so much a matter of the
original Arab nationalists' dream of unifying their countries
into the 'sixth power' of the world but of the international
dangers arising from particular crises and of the potential
for involvement of foreign powers in them, whether at local
request or not. What happens in these connecting regions
extending from the western Mediterranean to the Indian Ocean
relates to the global confrontation and focuses on the proliferation of conventional arms supply, the possibility of
nuclear proliferation and superpower influence and presence.

Areas of Dissension

Over more than twenty years, from northwest Africa to the
exit from the Red Sea there have been clashes of a more or
less prolonged character which have threatened to spill over
into neighbouring areas. Algeria and Morocco, for example,
have been in contention over the activities of Polisario[2]
and over their common borders; Egypt and Libya have been at
odds, and there has been recurrent war between Somalia and
Ethiopia, as well as secessionist wars in Tigre and Eritrea
inside Ethiopia, which was itself originally a Coptic

Christian state.

The areas of dissension as between the different countries have been several. Of central importance has clearly been the reaction on the part of Arab countries in particular to the state of Israel and to the Palestinian problem. Complicating factors have been the dispute about alignment or non-alignment in foreign policy, involvement in Western pacts or treaty organisations, or strengthening of ties with the Soviet Union. Not by any means directly related to this, the differing character of social and political systems has affected relationships: royal kingdoms and popular socialist republics, reactionary or progressive regimes have interacted not in accordance with any consistent pattern. The legitimacy of governments or ruling regimes and the validity of frontiers have all been in dispute. Movements towards Arab unity, as towards African or European unity, have been thwarted over the means of achieving it and because of domination by particular states or groups of states. This has been one factor in causing rapid changes in the temperature of bilateral interstate relations.

The region has not become more stable in the last twenty years partly because the chances of any one power in the locality assuming a firm leadership role, or establishing a continuing relationship within a group of states, have diminished. Contributory elements have been the failure to agree on a common approach even towards the Palestinian issue, the rise of exceptionally rich oil states, ideological differences, the varying character of the leadership and demographic changes. Though the former colonial connections are no longer of great importance in this area, shifts in relationships with the major powers from whom technological advance and investment are triggered and developed are relevant. The result of this complexity is the generation of a competitive, volatile, unstable and potentially violent set of relationships to understand which it is necessary to consider the relative status, mainly in terms of development, of the different countries.

Divergent National Interests

The states of the region, whether belonging to the Arab system or not, have what often seem divergent interests. Egypt, which is the most powerful militarily, stands out because of the size of its population (44 million), its historical pre-eminence in the post-colonial period, and its role in attempting to achieve peace with Israel. The wealthy oil-producing states with small populations and high incomes, especially Saudi Arabia and the Gulf States, have influence

primarily through their capacity for capital investment and
aid. Two countries, Iraq and Algeria, are also oil producers
but have larger populations - about 13 and 19 million
respectively - and have locations, interests in industrialisation, and political stances which tend to leave them on the
fringe of the Arab association. The remaining, non-oil rich
countries, such as Morocco, Lebanon, Tunisia, Jordan and
Syria, are not badly off economically but each of them has
obvious problems internally or on its borders. There is also
a disparate group of very poor countries, such as Somalia,
Mauritania, South Yemen and Sudan, who have little trained
manpower and are in urgent need of economic assistance and
have a chequered history of external relationships.

Mauritania's entry into the Arab league was followed by the
struggle over the Sahara. Turkey, a member of NATO, and
Pakistan have in recent years sought closer relationships
with the Arab states, and even these connections have acquired an additional dimension after the invasion of Afghanistan.

The rise of the Palestinian Liberation Organisation,
progressive acceptance of the possibility of peace with
Israel, and the emergence of the Khomeini regime in Iran have
all contrived to keep the region in a state of flux.
Relations with Iran were a problem even before the fall of
the Shah, mainly because of problems of the Gulf area itself.
Above all, the increasing interest of the rest of the world
in the region's oil resources and consequently for strategic
reasons in bases, or what are euphemistically called
facilities, now make a radically new approach to the security
of the region essential - an approach which must now go
beyond an Israeli and Syrian withdrawal from Lebanon, a
settlement of the Palestinian question, and an end to the
Iran-Iraq war. The need for a comprehensive attempt to
achieve greater security amongst the states of the region is
highlighted by the kind of military contingency planning
which has become progressively a feature of US, and presumably also of Soviet, policy on the basis of a perception of
the interests of industrialised states. Though an improvement in Arab-Israeli relations is unlikely without at least
some external mediation, influence or pressure, machinery and
procedures actually developed within the admittedly diverse
region are essential, if it is not to become recurrently a
theatre for intervention. Intervention need not take normal
military forms, but can consist of arms supply generating
local imbalances and, in particular, the provision of nuclear
technology leading if only to the suspicion of weapons
proliferation. The repeated tension between Libya and the
USA over naval manoeuvres in the Gulf of Sirte is not only
dangerous in itself but clearly indicates the importance of

developing groupings of states at least capable of exercising some kind of moral pressure at times of potential crisis.

Great Power Spheres of Influence?

In other parts of the world there has proved to be some basis for stability residing in a recognition of spheres of influence by the major powers. Some of those who do not see Arab unity as effectively attainable regard the area from the Atlantic through North Africa to the Indian Ocean as so divided. They tend to see future security in terms of increased armaments from, and military 'facilities' for, whatever of the power blocs they favour, thus betraying the aspiration of non-alignment which had many supporters in the post-colonial period. The result of this tendency is to heighten interstate rivalries within the region, because, on the one hand the USA has effectively promised to defend the oil fields, and, on the other, the Soviet Union has signed a treaty with and armed Syria. It would be surprising if there were no attempts on the part of both major powers to try to recruit or promote 'a strategic consensus' in their cause, reinforcing it by the supply of sophisticated weapon systems.

The creation of the American Rapid Deployment Force, insofar as it relates to this 'Arc of Crisis', is symbolic of the dangers, for it assumes a situation in which a state in the region might invite its presence or intervention. It corresponds to Soviet willingness to provide military aid in given circumstances and may be regarded as the product of 'worst case' analysis about the political stability of countries which are either strategically located or have valuable resources, especially oil. The review of military capability which led to this development derived directly from the revolution in Iran and the threat to foreign interests in that country. In one sense it is an attempt to confirm the existence of spheres of interest which have to be respected if peace is to be maintained, but it relates to situations or scenarios which are beyond the direct control of any except the people of a particular territory.

It is, however, not only ultimately the peace of the world which is threatened by the network of tensions and disputes in an area of critical global interest. Order in the region depends on the achievement of change while retaining important elements of continuity. Further civil wars, conflicts between Arab states and each other or other states in the vicinity, another round of violence focusing on Israel and, above all, direct military intervention by outside forces may all be on the cards; certainly the last few years give little ground for hope that they can be avoided. Poverty and wealth side by side are compounded by massive expenditures on arms at a time when a 50 per cent illiteracy rate is typical. The problem of Palestinian rights and peace with Israel has created divisions which in turn affect not only the Islamic Conference but the Organisation of African Unity and the non-aligned movement as a whole.

At a time when the richer Arab countries could, and would probably want to, play a part in improving North-South relations and conditions in the less developed countries, they are distracted by conflicts on their own doorstep which lay them open, willingly or not, to foreign involvement, especially of a military kind.

The complexities of the area under discussion are so great that to tackle its problems is almost as difficult as operating on a global scale. There are, nevertheless, some positive indications. In the first place, there is a degree of cultural and historical unity and continuity: the influence of Arabism and Islam has even now constructive possibilities, and so has increased wealth in some sectors. Moreover, it is likely that both the USSR and the USA recognise the dangers, and in the longer term may appreciate that security is mutual, that access to scarce resources is in the end a common concern and that neither would benefit from chaos. The fluidity of the situation in the area may at present deter them from exercising too firm an influence on their friends or allies, but there is clearly some common ground which could be discovered by the two major powers if an appropriate basis and forum for negotiation were established.

While rounds of talks on the Arab-Israeli dispute must go on, the arc of which the so-called Middle East is the pivot remains the single most dangerous area in international politics.

Conflict of Interests in the Mediterranean

The chain of disastrous and tragic events in the Lebanon in recent years has, however, once again diverted attention from the potential for conflict in the Mediterranean itself which might now arise not because of USA and Soviet naval deployments, but rather as a result of the numerous interstate rivalries.

The recent institution of 'Exclusive Economic Zones' (EEZ) extending up to two hundred miles from the coast and the projection of territorial waters from six to twelve miles have serious implications in themselves[3]. When, as has become inevitable as a result of the negotiations on the Law

of the Sea Treaty, they are associated with the development
of advanced technologies for the exploitation of oil and
minerals from the seabed, real and immediate dangers arise.
Already Libya has taken Tunisia to the International Court of
Justice and secured an advantageous ruling on the interstate
boundary projection out into the Mediterranean across the
continental shelf. A similar case between Libya and Malta is
in progress and, given the geography of the Mediterranean,
other cases of portentous overlaps of economic zones of
special national interest will soon emerge. In the Aegean,
Greece and Turkey, both members of NATO, are seriously at
odds not only over the limits of sovereignty on the continental shelf but on comparable air space. The dangers can
best be illustrated by the example of Turkish military aircraft, which can in certain circumstances barely take off
from airfields on the mainland without, according to the
Greek authorities, infringing Greek sovereignty. Such claims
and counter-claims could quickly affect rights of passage and
freedom of navigation leading to the possibility of armed
clashes.

In practice, over the last decade the military potential,
especially in the air, of most countries on the Mediterranean
shoreline has increased. The acquisition, for example, by
Libya and Egypt of bombers and fighters of a relatively
up-to-date character equipped with air-to-air and air-to-
surface missiles is not an unusual development. In a number
of cases training and logistic support may be inadequate for
prolonged operations but these, no doubt temporary, difficulties do not make the risk of a serious incident less
likely, especially when the speed of possible intervention
and the accuracy and destructive power of the weapons carried
is borne in mind. Corresponding increases in naval prepared-
ness have led to the deployment of more submarines and
frigates by riparian states than ever before and - almost as
dangerous in these situations as the capacity for inter-
ception in the air - the acquisition of large numbers of
small, fast surface craft with effective anti-ship missiles
capable of destroying much larger vessels.

So far the states of the Mediterranean seaboard have had
little success in tackling collectively even environmental
problems such as pollution.

Standing Commissions

Now the Mediterranean faces a degree of militarisation initiated by individual states for which the relevant countries
as a whole are unprepared. This highlights a wide need in
most parts of the region for institutions capable of coping

with incipient crises and to provide platforms on which all states and recognised political groupings of whatever character have a right to present their viewpoints and argue their interests. The possibility of **Standing Commissions** operating at several different levels on a regional or sub-regional basis needs urgent investigation. Such commissions should be representative of interests, comprehensive rather than exclusive, and constituted in a way to provide a forum for discussion both of potential dangers and of possibilities of cooperation. They would not necessarily be committed to reaching definitive decisions leading to action, but they would be expected to encourage cooperation, however limited in scope, at whatever level it seemed feasible. Thus, rela-tively trivial, though in humane terms important, steps to tackle shared medical, agricultural or veterinary problems might pave the way for much more fundamental and large-scale cooperation leading to regional détente.

Balkan Example - A Possible Nuclear Weapon-Free Zone

In some senses, the Balkan states may already be in the pro-cess of setting an example to the rest of the Mediterranean by a piecemeal and pragmatic approach to cooperation. More especially and by definition they could demonstrate the potential for small states to overcome their conventional sense of impotence in the face of global issues[4]. In a region in which historical enmities have in the past led to ferocious conflicts, small scale developments in the handling of specific medical problems, veterinary concerns and even techniques of cheese-making have effectively broken the chain of escalating hostility and begun to reverse the process. Two recent Pugwash Symposia, in Bulgaria in June 1983 and in Romania in October, have concentrated on the role of small states in regional security and the possibility of a nuclear weapon-free zone in the Balkans[5].

Success in encouraging regional cooperation depends on the determination of limited goals in the first place and build-ing agreements on bricks of common interest, as well as resisting the tendency to perfectionism which carries with it the futility of any negotiations. A nuclear weapon-free zone, for example, need not necessarily begin by including all the states of a region or by requiring the elimination of all foreign bases. A gradualist approach, given the good faith of the initial signatories to a treaty, has much to offer. Compatibility with the Non-Proliferation Treaty (NPT) and with the International Atomic Energy Agency (IAEA) require-ments is obviously desirable, but a legalistic approach to the problems of reconciling the different concepts is likely

to result in early stalemate. While in the eastern Mediterranean today a treaty establishing a nuclear weapon-free zone
may seem remote, an informal body to explore the issue might
at least provide a stimulus for the existing nuclear powers
to adopt a more constructive approach to the forthcoming
review of the NPT.

Role of the United Nations and Outside Powers

Apart from such initiatives the apparent intractability of
the problems of this whole region requires a re-appraisal of
some earlier proposals tentatively put forward in this and
other contexts. Experience in the Lebanon, for example,
suggests not the abandonment of multinational peacekeeping
forces as a concept but rather a redefinition of the circumstances in which they can operate effectively. This, along
with attempts to strengthen the role of the UN including that
of the Secretary-General, would be potentially useful also in
other parts of the world such as Namibia. The possibility of
a system of guarantees, whether UN-based or originating with
a small number of outside states, assisting the implementation of regional agreements and the promotion of realistic
non-aggression pacts needs to be explored. The moral imperative in international relations has often been cynically
rejected but could be brought into play, for example, by the
revival of the idea of a UN arms transfer register concerned
with an agreement by both suppliers and users to report, at
least retrospectively, transactions over a given period.

The situation in the 'Arc of Crisis' is such that new conflicts could break out at any time and not only be as destructive as the Iran-Iraq war or the situation in the
Lebanon, but put a premium on superpower intervention, with
the potential for escalation which it always carries. Without
international or regional institutions and procedures, this
is regrettably inevitable. Bodies such as the United Nations
and the OAU are in the end powerless to act unless major
external powers exercise self-restraint and the parties to a
dispute accept responsibility for the resolution of problems
and for crisis management. The lessons of the recent decades
are that there is no miracle cure for the problems of a
series of sub-regions where conflict has become endemic, and
that the role of international organisations and well-
intentioned outside powers is to provide the conditions which
will generate local settlements rather than themselves devise
and attempt to impose them.

References

1. cf. P.J. Vatikiotis, Revolution in the Middle East and Other Case Studies, (London: Allen & Unwin, 1972).
2. J. Damis, Conflict in North West Africa: the Western Sahara Dispute, (Stanford: Hoover Press, 1983).
3. M. Cremasco (Chapter 22 of this book).
4. D. Carlton and C. Schaerf (eds), South-Eastern Europe after Tito, (London: Macmillan, 1983); A. Braun, Small State Security in the Balkans, (London: Macmillan, 1983).
5. N. Behar and I. Nedev (Chapter 16 of this book).

Gothom Arya

Introduction

The South-East Asian countries discussed here are only the ASEAN (Indonesia, Malaysia, Philippines, Singapore and Thailand) and the Indochinese states (Kampuchea, Laos and Vietnam). The security issues involved are mainly related to the conflicts between these two regional groupings, though superpower rivalries and internal problems should also be taken into consideration. These conflicts are dramatic in terms of human sufferings: sporadic fighting is going on inside Kampuchea, and the flow of Indochinese refugees leaving their homeland has been continuing since 1975. The tension due to these conflicts could well escalate, since there is no solution in sight to the present stalemate.

This paper analyses the conflict situation and advances some suggestions about the resolution of conflicts. Factual information about the countries of the region is contained in the Appendix and Tables 1 and 2.

South-East Asia Conflicts

Superpower Rivalries. The period of cold war was marked by a well-defined East-West conflict which reached its peak by the end of the 1960s and was then diffused into a new area of limited cooperation. The post-cold war period was brought about by various factors, such as a mutual desire for a détente, the conflict between the Soviet Union and China, the emergence of Japan as an economic superpower, and so on.

By the mid 1970s, the United States made a global retreat as an aftermath of the Vietnam war. But the interventions by the Soviet Union in Africa and Afghanistan at the end of the 1970s were met with a strong reaction of the USA which reasserted its global presence and re-entered the arms race.

The Soviet Union-China conflict, which was worsening during the 1970s, has evolved into a stalemate, and the relation between them has slightly improved at the beginning of the 1980s, since both sides felt the need to balance the United States' move.

Japan, which prospered under the umbrella of the United States, was asked to assume a greater role in its own defence. Though it did increase the defence expenditure, it seems that Japan prefers to assert its economic rather than military influence in the region.

Regional Groupings. The situation in South-East Asia is influenced by superpower rivalries. In 1954, during the period of the cold war, the SEATO organisation (Australia, France, New Zealand, Pakistan, Philippines, Thailand, UK, USA) was formed in order to contain the 'communist expansion'. The US intervention in Indochina was justified by the 'domino' theory. At the same time, the communist countries were united in their fight against 'imperialism'.

In the post-cold war period SEATO was disbanded in 1977. The need for economic cooperation called for another type of regional grouping, namely the ASEAN. This association became a political success and was able to help the member countries in their strive for economic development.

The Soviet Union-China conflict was reflected in the conflict among Indochinese states in the mid 1970s. This conflict culminated in the Vietnamese invasion of Kampuchea (see Appendix). The Vietnam-China border war was a measure of the extent to which China could carry its conflict with the Soviet Union. By sending its troops into Kampuchea, Vietnam presumably aimed at establishing a 'secure border' and, at the same time, forming a regional grouping in which it could play a 'big brother' role.

Indochina-ASEAN Conflict. There is an atmosphere of mistrust between Indochina and ASEAN countries which is aggravated by the Kampuchean situation. While the ASEAN countries feel the threat of the Vietnamese presence near the Thai border, Vietnam repeatedly speaks about the Chinese threat. Digging into the recent or more remote history, one may find many reasons to explain such perceived threats. But as long as there is no further imbalance among the superpowers, it does not seem probable that this conflict will escalate by itself.

Security Issues

To maintain security, there is a need to understand the causes of conflict in order to minimise them as much as possible. Unfortunately, there are many causes and they are so entangled that it is very difficult to understand, let alone remove them. In general terms, one can describe some

conflicts as being political in nature: conflicts due to differences in ideology, territorial disputes, armament buildup
and so on. Other conflicts may better be described in social
terms, such as tensions caused by population growth, mi-
gration problems, or simply racial or religious animosities.
But many past conflicts came about for economic reasons; many
wars were waged to control trade routes, to fight over scarce
resources, or to weaken a potential trade opponent.

Another dimension is that internal and external security
are not separable. External trouble is sometimes created in
order to lessen internal tension; similarly, a state of internal division and weakness is an open invitation for external intervention.

It is generally believed that only a balance of power can
deter a war. The antithesis is that a balance of power is
usually pursued through military might which in turn
increases the risk of conflicts.

The above-mentioned causes of conflict suggest some ideas
on the improvement of security issues. Internal security is
no doubt better assured by peace and prosperity, but there is
no ready-made formula. It is all very well to hope that
liberal democracy works to create internal peace but one has
to admit that this is rarely adopted in the Third World. On
the other hand, while an oligarchy appears conducive to law
and order, thus ensuring economic prosperity, excessive control of resources by the oligarchy inevitably leads to insurgence. Another point to remember is that economic block-
ades tend to create more problems than to solve. Economic
interdependence and fair economic exchanges are more likely
to dissipate the atmosphere of mistrust and make one think
twice before aggravating a conflict, since it might adversely
affect one's own economy.

In the case of the Indochina-ASEAN conflict, there is no
quick solution, but fortunately the situation is not likely
to worsen quickly. Both sides seem to be waging a rhetorical
peace offensive. But even rhetorics might help, as long as
they are not open expressions of mistrust. With the Soviet
Union and China resuming their talks, things appear to be
going better even though there is no concrete result. The two
regional groupings should agree to talk to each other more.

There is no reason to believe that economic sanctions on
Vietnam have caused any change in the attitude of Vietnam. On
the contrary, it is to be hoped that the opening of trade,
as now tried with Laos, will bring better results.

Since the Indochina-ASEAN conflict is related to the
superpower rivalries, international efforts, especially those
which aim at a new detente, will indirectly also help to
solve this conflict.

Table 1. South-East-Asian Countries: Populations and Trade

	Kampuchea	Vietnam	Laos	Philippines	Indonesia	Malaysia	Singapore	Thailand
1.	0.25b	7.3b	0.25b	38.7a	65.8a	21.4a	10.6	36a
2.	6.7c	51b	3.6b	50b	150b	14b	2.4b	46b
3.	5d	2.8d	2.4d	2.6d	1.7d	2.4d	1.2d	2.1d
4.	n.a.	n.a.	n.a.	43a	55a	114a	153a	56a
5.	n.a.	n.a.	n.a.	23a	43a	23a	14a	14a
6.	n.a.	n.a.	n.a.	25a	17a	16a	14a	14a
7.	15b	15.5b	20b	4b	n.a.	n.a.	n.a.	3.5b

Explanation: 1. GDP (billion dollars)
2. Population (millions)
3. Average annual population growth, 1976-82, (per cent)
4. External trade (per cent of GDP)
5. Trade with Japan (per cent of external trade)
6. Trade with USA (per cent of external trade)
7. External aids (per cent of GDP)

Sources: a. Far Eastern Economic Review (FEER), December 10-16 1982, p. 70 (for 1981)
b. Atlas Economic Mondial 1981
c. Author's estimate
d. FEER, SIAA 1983 Year Book

Table 2. South-East-Asian Countries: Military Indicators

	Kampuchea	Vietnam	Laos	Philippines	Indonesia	Malaysia	Singapore	Thailand
1.	n.a.	n.a.	0.038	0.86	2.39	2.25	0.57	1.28
2.	n.a.	n.a.	14.6	2.4	5.5	11.5	6.1	4.7
3.	n.a.	2599	55.7	347	355	243	92	775
4.	USSR Vietnam	USSR	USSR	USA	UK,France FRG,USA	FRG,Italy USA	USA	USA
5.	Political ideology	Economic difficulty	Political ideology	Authoritarian rule	Social injustice	Racial tension	–	Social injustice
6.	Foreign occupation	Military build-up	Foreign interference	Foreign bases	–	–	–	Border encroachment

Explanation:

1. Defence expenditure (billion dollars)
2. Defence expenditure (per cent of GDP)
3. Armed forces + paramilitary forces (thousands)
4. Primary arms supplier
5. Main cause of internal tension
6. Main cause of external tension

Source: the Military Balance 1981-82; International Institute for Strategic Studies, 1981

Appendix

Tables 1 and 2 summarise relevant information about the individual countries, and the causes of tension as perceived by
the author.

1. Kampuchea

Since the country gained independence on 9 November 1953, it
has been facing political instability culminating in the
takeover by the Khmer Rouge on 17 April 1975. The authoritarian regime of Pol Pot was put to an end by the invasion of
the Vietnamese on 25 December 1978. Immediately (10 January
1979) they created a pro-Vietnamese government, which changed
the name of the country to the People's Republic of Kampuchea
(PRK). At the time it appeared that the strong man of the
regime was Pen Sovan, who served as the President of the
Council of Ministers and Secretary-General of the People's
Revolutionary Party. His removal in December 1981 came as a
surprise. The reason was generally believed to be that Pen
Sovan had become too independent for Vietnamese liking. The
transition to the new era was apparently smooth; Heng Samrin,
thought to be a powerless figure-head, replaced Sovan as
Party chief and Chan Si became President of the Council of
Ministers.

In June 1982, a coalition government of Khmer resistance
groups was announced. This loose coalition of the Khmer
Rouge, the Khmer People's National Liberation Front (KPNLF)
and Prince Sihanouk's forces is called the Coalition Government of Democratic Kampuchea (CGDK). Its formation resulted
in a clear-cut vote at the UN General Assembly of 90 to 29 in
its favour, an increase of 13 votes since 1981.

It is estimated that Vietnam maintains 160 000 soldiers
on Kampuchean soil, while the PRK has only 30 000 men in
armed forces, less than 20 per cent of which are thought to
be operational. On the other hand, the CGDK forces comprise
25 000 to 30 000 Khmer Rouge, 9000 to 14 000 Sihanoukists.

The Khmer Rouge suffered a major military setback in March
1983 when their Phnon Chat stronghold was overrun and their
soldiers were said to flee, giving up fighting. Contrary to
previous years, the Vietnamese offensive continued into the
rainy season. However, a complete military victory by the
Vietnamese is still remote.

According to FAO, Kampuchea's economy is mainly based on
agriculture. Rice production suffered heavily from the
political upheaval, decreasing from 1.8 million tonnes in
1977 to 0.85 million tonnes in 1979. The country is slowly
recovering from the agricultural disaster, though recovery

remains fragile and at the mercy of the weather. In 1980, the per capita GDP was estimated at $35 which is the world lowest. The international aid in 1979 amounted to about 15 per cent of the GDP.

2. Vietnam

Shortly after the defeat at Dien Bien Phu, the Geneva Agreement was signed on 21 July 1954, resulting in the creation of two Vietnams. After a long and painful experience, the USA decided to pull out from Vietnam at the beginning of 1973. On 30 April 1975, the Saigon regime collapsed and the country was reunited under the leadership of the Lao Dong (labour) Party. Pham Van Dong became prime minister and Le Duan party chief. The country moved closer to the Soviet Union. General Giap left the government in January 1980.

For the past 40 years, the Vietnamese have been constantly fighting, most of the time in guerilla warfare; the last major fighting was the border war in February and March 1979 when the Chinese gave them a 'lesson'. The country maintains a most impressive army of one million men, backed with 1.5 million of armed militia. There is no Soviet Union military base as such but the Soviet Union has easy access to the Camranh-Bay and Danang bases.

Seventy per cent of the active population of Vietnam are engaged in agriculture which produces about 40 per cent of the GDP. In 1980, the per capita GDP was estimated at $40 which is ranked 154th out of 169 countries. The international aid, about 15.5 per cent of the GDP, came mainly from the Soviet Union. After the failure of the 1976-80 economic development plan, the economy became more liberal with more incentives introduced.

3. Laos

The country regained independence on 27 October 1953. This landlocked country made a smoother transition towards socialism than the other Indochinese states. The prime minister, Kaysone Phomvihane, is generally considered as a moderate and pragmatic leader.

Laos has a small armed force of 55 000 men. The defence expenditure is about 15 per cent of the GDP. There are about 40-50 000 Vietnamese soldiers, many in the plain of Jars. Many of them are engaged in construction work such as road building; but the reason for their presence may be to fight resistance groups, such as General Vang Pao's group. The support for the resistance is alleged to come from neighbouring countries, though Thailand constantly denies such allegations.

With 75 per cent of active population in agriculture, the country still cannot provide sufficient food for internal consumption. The per capita GDP is among the lowest ($75 in 1980). On 10 December 1979 the regime made a decisive shift from rigorous socialism to a more liberal economy.

4. Philippines

President Marcos holds real power and asserts it in an authoritarian way. After nine years of martial rule, he decided in 1981 to introduce a more democratic form of government. But his Movement for a New Society dominates the political scene while the legal opposition remains weak and divided.

The armed forces comprise 112 800 regular men with a budget of about 2.4 per cent of the GDP. There are also 110 500 men in para-military forces.

The country faces a very serious problem of internal insurgence. The Muslim secessionist movement led by the Moro National Liberation Front (MNLF), is mainly concentrated in the southern island of Mindanao. The movement has several factions along ethnic lines. The Muslims do not consider themselves as 'Filipinos', since the name itself invokes past allegiance to the Spanish rule. The insurgence is localised in the south and is not spreading, but on the other hand, it is not going to be rooted out easily. In the mid-1970s, the MNLF had about 20 000 men, but according to the government there are now only about 8000.

Another serious threat to the Marcos regime is the Communist Party of the Philippines (CPP) which is nationally based and well organised. The military wing of the CPP is called the New People's Army (NPA) and its political front is the National Democratic Front (NDF). The number of NPA fighting guerillas is estimated at 5000.

Recently the USA renewed the agreement which allows them the use of the Clark and Subic Bay bases for five more years in exchange of $900 million.

The civilian industry is progressing regularly (30 per cent of the GDP) while the largest portion of the active population (45 per cent) remains in the agricultural sector. The country receives a considerable amount of external aid (four per cent of the GDP).

5. Indonesia

The country regained independence on 24 December 1949. In the early 1960s, President Sukarno followed a non-aligned policy and allowed the communist party, which had a strong connection with China, to become powerful. An attempt by the communists to take over power in September 1965 was followed by one of the largest repressions in recent times, with about 500 000 people killed. Subsequently, General Suharto became president, adopted a pro-western policy and has constantly shown a mistrust vis-a-vis China. Since then, he dominated the political arena using the Golkar 'party' as a main leverage.

There is no major security problem in Indonesia, except for a small separatist movement in the north-east of Sumatra, the instability in Timor and an agitation by Muslim extremists. The country maintains armed forces of 273 000 men and a small (80 000) para-military force.

With a per capita GDP of about \$280 in 1980, Indonesia is lagging behind other ASEAN countries. This could have been worse had the country not become a main producer of petrol and natural gas (35 per cent of the GDP). The external debt is about \$9.5 billions (25 per cent of the GDP).

6. Malaysia

Malaysia is an Islamic federation and a member of the British Commonwealth. Independent since 31 August 1957, the political system has still similarities with the British system. The ruling party which is in fact a coalition party, commands a large majority leading to a semi-authoritarian regime.

The 14 million population consists of: about 50 per cent Malays, 36 per cent Chinese and 10 per cent Indians. With such a composition there is considerable racial tension. Apart from this the country does not really have a security problem. However, a weakened Communist Party of Malaya (CMP) still operates, mainly in the north near the Thai border. The Malaysian armed forces number 102 000 men. Para-military forces are estimated at 90 000 men. There exists, however, a People's Volunteer Corps of over 350 000. The defence expenditure is rather high, representing about 10 per cent of the GDP.

As the chief exporter of rubber and tin Malaysia has a large surplus in trade balance. The economy is growing steadily with the per capita GDP reaching \$1700 in 1980.

7. Singapore

Singapore separated from Malaysia on 9 August 1965. There is a political stability under the firm leadership of Lee Kuan Yew, so much so that the opposition is rendered marginal and there might be a succession problem. The country was depoliticised, when one generation of politicians was replaced by administrators and technocrats, who might find themselves lacking experience in dealing with the expectation of high life style of the younger generation.

Singapore has about 42 000 soldiers and spends about five per cent of its GDP on defence. This relatively high expenditure for a country at peace could be explained by the perception of the government of the old threat from the communist party, and is the reason for keeping the internal Security Act which gives sweeping powers to the authority.

The majority of the 2.4 million inhabitants are of Chinese origin and many of them are being 'anglicised'. During the past decades, the economy continued to prosper steadily with a growth rate of seven per cent per annum. The per capita GDP in 1980 was about $6050 and the exports represented about 145 per cent of the GDP. However, the present world recession has a significant impact on the Singaporean economy.

8. Thailand

Unlike its neighbours, Thailand has never been colonialised. On 24 June 1932, the absolute monarchy was replaced by a constitutional monarchy. During the past 51 years of semi-democracy, the country has known 13 different constitutions and about 15 coup d'etats. Politics has always been dominated by the military. On 14 October 1973 a student-led demonstration forced the then military government to resign. But the democratic 'ouverture' that followed was short-lived. A massacre of students on 6 October 1976 announced the return of the military regime. General Prem became prime minister on 3 March 1980. Through compromise and moderation, he maintains himself in power despite an abortive coup d'etat and a general election.

The Communist Party of Thailand (CPT) has lost much of its strength due to internal dispute. Its leadership is accused of being too rigid and pro-Chinese.

There are several problems in border areas. In the south, where the majority is Muslim, while the rest of the country is predominantly Buddhist, there is a small separatist movement which fights for an independent state of Pattani. The Thai government gives its support to the Coalition Government of Democratic Kampuchea (CGDK). There are about 60 000 Khmer refugees inside Thailand and about 2-300 000 Khmer displaced persons on the Thai-Khmer border. The possibility that the fighting may spill over the border remains. The Thai-Laos border is open at few points. The Thai-Burmese border is often crossed when the Karen and Shan armies flee the suppression drives of the Rangoon government.

The Thai government suspects that the pro-Chinese Communist Party of Burma lends its support to the CPT guerillas who are active in the border area.

Thailand maintains armed forces of 238 000 men with a defence budget of $1.3 billion.

Though the agricultural trade shows a large surplus, the overall trade deficit, due to export slump, was well over $2 billions in 1983. Despite an anticipated economic recovery, unemployment is rising alarmingly. In 1979, the country received about $0.7 billion in foreign aid.

Relevant Bibliography

Frank Frost, 'The Conflict over Cambodia: Implications of the Khmer Coalition Agreement', Basic Paper 14 (1982) Department of the Parliamentary Library, Australia.

Johan Galtung, 'Violence, Peace and Peace Research', International Peace Research Institute, Oslo.

Far Eastern Economic Review, Asia 1982, 1983 Year Books.

Proceedings of Annual Conference on Displaced Persons in Thailand Committee for Coordination of Services to Displaced persons in Thailand (CCSDPT), 1981-82-83.

Alfonso Garcia-Robles

It seems advisable to point out from the outset that the Latin-American nuclear weapon-free zone has the privilege of being the only one in existence that covers densely inhabited territories. Elsewhere, only in regard to the Antarctic, outer space and the sea bed are similar prohibitions in force, based on treaties concluded in 1959, 1967 and 1971, respectively.

The official title of the treaty which established the Latin American zone and defined its statute is the 'Treaty for the Prohibition of Nuclear Weapons in Latin America', but it is usually referred to as the 'Treaty of Tlatelolco', employing the Aztec name for the district of the Mexican capital where the Ministry of Foreign Affairs of Mexico is located and where the treaty itself was opened to signature on 14 February 1967.

The purpose of this paper is to provide a synoptic view both of the genesis and the provisions of the treaty.

Genesis of the Treaty of Tlatelolco

The first international document in the history of the events directly related to the genesis of the Treaty of Tlatelolco was the Joint Declaration of 29 April 1963. In this declaration the Presidents of Bolivia, Brazil, Chile, Ecuador and Mexico announced that their governments were willing to sign a Latin American multilateral agreement by which they would undertake not 'to manufacture, store, or test nuclear weapons or devices for launching nuclear weapons'.

Seven months later, the United Nations General Assembly, taking as a basis a draft resolution submitted by eleven Latin American countries (the five previously mentioned, plus Costa Rica, El Salvador, Haiti, Honduras, Panama and Uruguay), approved on 27 November 1963 a resultion in which, inter alia, the General Assembly welcomed the initiative of the five Presidents for the military denuclearisation of

Latin America; expressed the hope that the States of the region would initiate studies 'concerning the measures that should be agreed upon with a view to achieving the aims' of the joint declaration; and requested the Secretary-General of the United Nations to extend to the States of Latin America, at their request, 'such technical facilities as they may require in order to achieve the aims set forth in the present resolution.'

Almost one year elapsed between the adoption of this General Assembly resolution and the next step worth mentioning. This interval was not wasted, however. The Mexican government put it to good use with active diplomatic consultations which resulted in the convening of a Latin American conference known as the 'Preliminary Session on the Denuclearisation of Latin America' (or REUPRAL, its Spanish acronym). Meeting in Mexico City from 23 to 27 November 1964, REUPRAL adopted a measure which was later to prove decisive for the success of the Latin American enterprise – the creation of an ad hoc organ, the 'Preparatory Commission for the Denuclearization of Latin America' (known also by its Spanish acronym, COPREDAL). The Preparatory Commission was specifically instructed 'to prepare a preliminary draft of a multilateral treaty for the denuclearization of Latin America, and to this end, to conduct any prior studies and take any prior steps that it deems necessary'.

The Preparatory Commission held a total of four sessions, the last of which took place just under two years after its creation. Contrary to what has generally happened with other disarmament treaties and conventions, the draft articles for the future treaty dealing with verification, inspection, and control were the first to be completed at the second session of the Commission. At that time a full declaration of principles was also drafted to serve as a basis for the Preamble of the draft treaty.

During its third session, COPREDAL received from its Co-ordinating Committee a working paper which contained the complete text of a preliminary draft for the treaty that the Commission had received the mandate to prepare. This draft, together with other proposals submitted by member states, provided the basis for the deliberations of the session. The result was the unanimous approval of a document entitled 'Proposals for the Preparation of the Treaty for the Denuclearization of Latin America' which played as prominent a role in the history of the treaty as that of the Dumbarton Oaks proposals in the history of the United Nations. These 'Proposals' included all provisions which might prove necessary for the treaty as a whole, although in some cases COPREDAL, not having found solutions satisfactory to all, had

been obliged to present to the governments two parallel
alternatives.

Of the few pending questions which the Commission would be
called upon to solve at its fourth session, the most important was the entry into force of the treaty. This issue provoked what was probably the greatest discussion in COPREDAL's
proceedings. Because of this problem and of the positive
precedent established by COPREDAL's solution to the problem,
it is worth examining the proceedings in somewhat greater
detail.

When the Preparatory Commission considered this subject in
April 1966, two distinct views became apparent. According to
the first view, the treaty should come into force between
states that would ratify it, on the date of deposit of their
respective instruments of ratification, in keeping with
standard practice. The representative Latin American body to
be established by the treaty should begin to function as soon
as eleven instruments of ratification were deposited, as this
number constituted a majority of the twenty-one members of
the Preparatory Commission. The states supporting the alternative view argued that the treaty, although signed and
ratified by all Member States of the Preparatory Commission,
should enter into force only upon completion of certain
requirements: the signature and ratification of the Treaty
of Tlatelolco and its Additional Protocols I and II by all
States to which they were opened, and the conclusion of
bilateral or multilateral agreements concerning the application of the Safeguards System of the International Atomic
Energy Agency (IAEA) by each party to the treaty.

As a result of these differing views COPREDAL was obliged
to present, in its proposals, two parallel texts, which
stated respectively the provisions that the treaty would
contain, according to whether one accepted the first or the
second thesis. To solve the problem, the Coordinating
Committee, in its report of 28 December 1966, suggested the
adoption of a conciliatory formula, which could receive the
approval of all Member States of the Commission without
detriment to their respective positions on the alternative
texts. It was this formula, with some modifications, which
was finally adopted and incorporated into article 28 of the
treaty. In keeping with it, the treaty would go into effect
for all States that had ratified it upon completion of the
four requirements specified in paragraph 1 of article 28.
That notwithstanding, the second paragraph of the article
states:

All signatory States shall have the imprescriptible right
to waive, wholly or in part, the requirements laid down in

the preceding paragraph. They may do so by means of a declaration   which shall be annexed to their respective instrument of ratification and which may be formulated at the time of deposit of the instrument or subsequently. For those States which exercise this right, this Treaty shall enter into force upon deposit of the declaration, or as soon as those requirements have been met which have not been expressly waived.

Moreover, the third paragraph of the same article stipulates:

As soon as this Treaty has entered into force in accordance with the provisions of paragraph 2 for eleven states, the Depositary Government shall convene a preliminary meeting of those States in order that the Agency may be set up and commence its work.

As one can see, an eclectic system was adopted, which, while respecting the viewpoints of all signatory states, prevented nonetheless any particular state from precluding the enactment of the treaty for those which would voluntarily wish to accept the statute of military denuclearisation defined therein.

The Treaty of Tlatelolco has thus contributed effectively to dispelling the myth that for the establishment of a nuclear weapon-free zone it would be an essential requirement that all states of the region concerned should become, from the very outset, parties to the treaty establishing the zone. The system adopted in the Latin American instrument proves that, although no state can obligate another to join such a zone, neither can one prevent others wishing to do so from adhering to a regime of total absence of nuclear weapons within their own territories.

Once the question of the entry into force of the treaty had been settled, at the fourth session of COPREDAL, the Preparatory Commission proceeded to settle, without major difficulties, the few other pending problems. On 12 February 1967, the Treaty for the Prohibition of Nuclear Weapons in Latin America was unanimously approved and two days later, at the solemn closing ceremony of the Commission's proceedings, it was opened to signature and subscribed to by the representatives of fourteen of its twenty-one members. In August 1982, fifteen years later, the number of signatory states stood at twenty-five, of which twenty-two were already parties to the treaty.

Additional Protocol I, open to the four states, United Kingdom, Netherlands, United States, and France, which are internationally responsible for territories lying within the limits of the geographical zone established in the treaty, has been signed by all those states and ratified by the United Kingdom, the Netherlands and the United States. With regard to France it seems that the ratification process is at present well advanced.

The five nuclear-weapon states are already parties to Additional Protocol II which is destined for them.

As provided for in paragraph 3 of article 28 previously quoted, as soon as the treaty entered into force for eleven states, the Depositary Government convened a 'preliminary meeting' of those states in order to set up the Agency for the Prohibition of Nuclear Weapons in Latin America known by its Spanish acronym OPANAL. This preliminary meeting (REOPANAL) took place in late June 1969 and carried out successfully all the preparatory work necessary for the first session of the General Conference of OPANAL. The latter was inaugurated on 2 September 1969 in the presence of U Thant, the then Secretary-General of the United Nations, and Sigvard Eklund, the Director General of IAEA. After seven working days the General Conference gave its approval to a series of basic juridical and administrative documents which provided the foundations for the Latin American Agency created by the treaty. To date the General Conference has held seven regular sessions and two special sessions in accordance with the provisions of article 9.

Analytical Summary of the Treaty of Tlatelolco

As a complement to the above brief survey of the preparatory work leading to the conclusion of the Tlatelolco Treaty, the following paragraphs are intended to give a general idea of its contents and to carry out a brief analytical summary of some of its main provisions.

The treaty comprises a preamble, thirty-one articles, one transitional article and two additional protocols.

The preamble defines the fundamental aims pursued by the states which drafted the treaty by stating their conviction that:

The military denuclearization of Latin America - being understood to mean the undertaking entered into internationally in this Treaty to keep their territories forever free from nuclear weapons - will constitute a measure which will spare their peoples from the squandering of their limited resources on nuclear armaments and will protect them against possible nuclear attacks on their territories, and will also constitute a significant contribution towards preventing the proliferation of nuclear weapons and a powerful factor for general and complete disarmament.

It is also worth noting that the Final Document approved by the first special session of the UN General Assembly devoted to disarmament, which met May-June 1978, contains several declaratory statements of a striking similarity to those included in the sixteen-year-old preamble of the Treaty of Tlatelolco:

The Latin American states, for instance, declared themselves convinced:

That the incalculable destructive power of nuclear weapons has made it imperative that the legal prohibition of war should be strictly observed in practice if the survival of civilization and of mankind itself is to be assured.

That nuclear weapons, whose terrible effects are suffered, indiscriminately and inexorably, by military forces and civilian population alike, constitute, through the persistence of the radioactivity they release, an attack on the integrity of the human species and ultimately may even render the whole earth uninhabitable.

The United Nations, for its part, has proclaimed:

Mankind today is confronted with an unprecedented threat of self-extinction arising from the massive and competitive accumulation of the most destructive weapons ever produced. Existing arsenals of nuclear weapons alone are more than sufficient to destroy all life on earth...

Unless its avenues are closed, the continued arms race means a growing threat to international peace and security and even to the very survival of mankind...

Removing the threat of a world war - a nuclear war - is the most acute and urgent task of the present day. Mankind is confronted with a choice: we must halt the arms race and proceed to disarmament or face annihilation.

As to the articles of the treaty, their contents may be described briefly as follows:

Article 1 defines the obligations of the parties. The four following articles (2-5) provide definitions of some terms employed in the treaty: contracting parties, territory, zone of application and nuclear weapons. Article 6 deals with the 'meeting of signatories', while articles 7-11 establish the

structure and procedures of the 'Agency for the Prohibition
of Nuclear Weapons in Latin America' (OPANAL) created by the
treaty, and state the functions and powers of its principal
organs: the General Conference, the Council and the Secretariat. The five succeeding articles (12-16) and paragraphs 2 and 3 of article 18 describe the functioning of the
'control system', also established by the treaty. Article 17
contains general provisions on the peaceful use of nuclear
energy and article 18 deals with peaceful nuclear
explosions.

Article 19 examines the relations of OPANAL with other
international organisations, whereas article 20 outlines the
measures that the General Conference shall take in cases of
serious violations of the treaty, such measures mainly involving simultaneous transmission of reports to the Security
Council and the General Assembly of the United Nations.
Article 21 safeguards the rights and obligations of the
parties under the Charter of the United Nations and, in the
case of state members of the Organisation of American States,
under existing regional treaties. Article 23 makes it binding
for the contracting parties to notify the Secretariat of
OPANAL of any international agreement concluded by any of
them on matters with which the treaty is concerned.

The settlement of controversies concerning the interpretation or application of the treaty is covered by article 24.
Articles 22, 25-27, and 29-31 contain what is generally known
as 'final clauses' dealing with questions such as privileges
and immunities, signature, ratification and deposit, reservations (which the treaty does not admit), amendments, duration and denunciation, and authentic texts and registration.
The transitional article specifies that 'denunciation of the
declaration referred to in article 28, paragraph 2, shall be
subject to the same procedures as the denunciation' of the
treaty, except that it will take effect on the date of delivery of the respective notification and not three months
later as provided in article 30, paragraph 2, for denunciation of the treaty. In paragraph 2 of article 26, the
Government of Mexico is designated the 'Depositary Government' of the treaty, whereas article 7, paragraph 4, stipulates that the headquarters of OPANAL 'shall be in Mexico
City'. Finally, article 28 reflects in its text the compromise formula which, as already explained, overcame the most
serious obstacle which confronted COPREDAL: the entry into
force of the treaty.

The two **Additional Protocols** to the treaty have
identical preambles. Their texts state the conviction that
the treaty 'represents an important step towards ensuring
the non-proliferation of nuclear weapons'. The texts also

point out that the treaty 'is not an end in itself but, rather, a means of achieving general and complete disarmament at a later stage', and finally express the desire to contribute 'towards ending the armaments race'. The operative parts of the protocols are naturally different from one another, although they have identical duration and entry into force for the states which ratify each Protocol.

Under article 1 of **Additional Protocol I**, those extra-continental states which, de jure or de facto, are internationally responsible for territories lying within the limits of the geographical zone established by the treaty would, upon becoming parties to the protocol, agree 'to undertake to apply the statute of denuclearization in respect to warlike purposes as defined in articles 1, 3, 5 and 13 of the Treaty' to such territories.

One aspect which should be borne in mind is that this protocol does not give those states the right to participate in the General Conference or in the Council of the Latin American Agency. But neither does it impose on those states any of the obligations relating to the system of control which provides for semi-annual reports, special reports and special inspections. In addition, the prohibition of reservations included in the treaty's article 27 is not applicable to the protocol. Thus, in the protocol the necessary balance has been preserved between rights and obligations: although the rights are less extensive, the obligations are also fewer.

With regard to **Additional Protocol II** the obligations assumed by the nuclear powers parties to the protocol are stated in its articles 1 to 3 in the following terms:

- Respecting 'in all its express aims and provisions the statute of denuclearization of Latin America in respect of warlike purposes, as defined, delimited and set forth in the Treaty of Tlatelolco'.

- Not contributing 'in any way to the performance of acts involving a violation of the obligations of article 1 of the Treaty in the territories to which the Treaty applies'.

- Not using or threatening to use 'nuclear weapons against the contracting parties of the Treaty'.

Conclusions

The importance of nuclear weapon-free zones has been emphasised several times by the United Nations. The General Assembly in its resolution of 11 December 1975 stated that 'nuclear-weapon-free zones constitute one of the most effective means for preventing the proliferation, both horizontal and vertical, of nuclear weapons and for contributing to the elimination of the danger of a nuclear holocaust'.

Subsequently, on 30 June 1978 the General Assembly, in the Programme of Action adopted by consensus at its first special session devoted to disarmament, stressed the significance of the establishment of nuclear weapon-free zones as a disarmament measure.

The weight which the international community attaches to the Latin American nuclear weapon-free zone was manifest from the very moment the Treaty of Tlatelolco was presented to the General Assembly. In its resolution of 5 December 1967, the General Assembly welcomed it 'with particular satisfaction' and declared that it 'constitutes an event of historic significance in the efforts to prevent the proliferation of nuclear weapons and to promote international peace and security'. Such weight has been once again evidenced when, in the general debate of the first special disarmament Assembly, no less than forty-five states had supportive comments for the treaty.

The Treaty of Tlatelolco has shown the crucial importance of ad hoc preparatory efforts, such as those carried out for two years by COPREDAL, in attaining the desired goal. Furthermore, the Latin American nuclear weapon-free zone which is now nearing completion has become in several respects an example which, notwithstanding the different characteristics of each region, is rich in inspiration. It provides profitable lessons for all states wishing to contribute to the broadening of the areas of the world from which those terrible instruments of mass destruction that are the nuclear weapons would be forever proscribed, a process which, as unanimously declared by the General Assembly in 1978, 'should be encouraged with the ultimate objective of achieving a world entirely free of nuclear weapons'.

Part Five

Security-Related Problems, mainly pertaining to the Third World.

Miguel Wionczek

Economics vs. Econometrics

While the economics of disarmament, that is, the reconversion of military oxpondituro to poacoful ucos, hac attraotod tho attention of many international agencies, political writers and social scientists, the economics of the armaments race itself has been examined much less thoroughly until very recently. This asymmetry probably reflects a combination of various factors:
- widespread belief that the armaments race is inevitable;
- limited knowledge among political and economic experts of the disaggregated information about armaments expenditure of the major arms spenders;
- difficulties in reconstructing and analysing national policy-making processes in the field of military technology decisions and arms procurement;
- limited supply of highly-trained human resources able to treat the subject of economics of the armaments race in a multi-disciplinary fashion;
- general sterility of the economics profession reflected in the ascendancy of econometrics, that is, quantitative theoretical model-building economics, divorced both from political and institutional economics and from real life issues.

Consequently, only a few 'academic' economists dedicate their time and attention to economics (and politics) of the armaments race. At the height of this race hardly any Western **economic** journal of high professional standing publishes relevant contributions on this subject. When such contributions appear in print they consist mostly of fancy econometric models of arms production and trade, as if they were just like any other commodity subject of domestic and international transactions devoid of any political and social implications. Even particularly vicious mass destruction (nuclear and non-nuclear) weapons appear in these mathematical exercises just as if they were consumer goods.

It is symptomatic that the mathematically-oriented theoretical economists want even more rather than less of such 'value-free' and 'neutral' exercises. A participant in the first Conference on Military Expenditures and Economic Growth, in June 1982 - under the auspices of the International Economic Association - proposed in all seriousness that the next generation of researchers in this field focus its efforts on: investigating the relationship between defence and growth in a spirit free of political prejudice; applying quantitative techniques to the issue of interest with rather more common sense than has been customary heretofore; and elucidating how, in the actual circumstances of the individual case, a particular hypothetical change in the scale or pattern of military outlays may plausibly be expected to impinge on the rate of growth of aggregate income and output or on some specific aspect of economic performance[1].

In brief, this proposition amounts to positing less 'political prejudice', a quantification of the impact of arms expenditure on the public budgeting expenditure (as if the expenditure on means of destruction had the same function as that on public health or education), and the effects of armaments on the rate of growth and 'economic performance'.

Once the general sterility of the present day econometrics - condemned publicly in mid-1982 in a letter to 'Science' by one of the fathers of mathematical economics, Nobel Laureate, Wasily Leontieff - is recognised, most of the other reasons given for the underdeveloped state of economics of armaments are simply not valid. The arms race is not inevitable; it is man-made. At no point in modern times has there been so much quantitative and other information publicly available on arms expenditure, arms procurement and arms trade on the one hand, and on the advancement of military R & D and its perverse linkages with the performance of the civilian economy sector both in the industrial and underdeveloped societies, on the other. The difficulties of analysing military policy-making processes and military technology developments are neither larger nor smaller than those of any other subject of social sciences. Finally, the limited supply of highly-trained multi-disciplinary human resources reflecting the shortcomings of the educational system, is a general phenomenon in our times. It is present in the armaments industry itself which somehow proves to be able to cope with it.

The work of such individuals or groups as Seymour Melman, Jacques S. Gansler and Emme Rotschild in the USA, Mary Kaldor and the University of Sussex ADIU group in the UK, and of a few peace research institutes established in western continental Europe, strongly suggests that competent and relevant work on economics of the armaments race can be done fruitfully once intellectual capability finds social motivation[2]. One would expect that intellectuals and social scientists, particularly economists, involved in peace movements would become more active in this important research field, but unfortunately peace organisations look upon the issues of the armaments race almost exclusively from moral, humanitarian and political viewpoints. It is a pity that not enough attention is paid to the economic perversity of the arms race which, contrary to conventional economics wisdom in the past two decades, has stopped acting as a motor of economic growth or as a factor in stimulating the peace-oriented sectors of national economics.

Economic Growth stifled by the Arms Race

Under present technological conditions in advanced industrial economies – both capitalist and socialist – the arms race not only increases the danger of a global holocaust triggered by design or error but represents the most serious impediment to global economic growth and improvement of economic and social welfare anywhere.

This simple but frightening statement can be supported by the following specific observations:

1. The arms race and economic development are in competitive relationship not only in terms of alternative uses of physical, technological and human resources but also in the vital area of policy decisions, social attitudes and perceptions of priorities in the allocation of these resources.

2. Military outlays, by definition and particularly in respect to modern mass-destruction weapons, do not fall into the category of productive investment but into that of 'luxury consumption' goods which differ from 'normal' luxury consumption goods in the sense that they not only diminish general welfare but also that they **cannot** be consumed. In economic and social terms they represent an extreme case of waste.

3. The dynamics of the arms race under present technological conditions involves more than the mere quantitative allocation of human resources for wasteful purposes and an amount of physical resources and financial expenditure 'consumed' for military purposes at national, regional and global levels. The particular characteristic of the dynamics of the arms race is that in every area it draws on relatively scarce resources: scarce raw materials, scarce knowledge and scarce highly-trained personnel.

4. The magnitude of the waste of natural resources is unheard

of historically: on the basis of very incomplete data it is estimated that up to six percent of the world's physical resources - a few infinite, some non-renewable and many scarce - are annually consumed in the arms race by the contending camps led by the respective superpowers. Since almost no data are available from many developing regions in which the arms race continues to accelerate as a part of the global trend, there is reason to believe that the above-mentioned figures represent a gross underestimate.

5. The impact of military expenditure on global employment opportunities is very limited because of the structure of that expenditure. Its greater part is used for capital and technology-intensive activities in societies frequently short of these two factors of production. The composition of military spending also affects perversely the structure and kind of employment opportunities.

6. Military expenditures are highly inflationary because of the characteristics of military procurement and technological military R & D, which together unleashed the unending process of 'luxury consumption goods' differentiation, and replacement of generations of ageing weapons by new ones. The costs of new weapons for the 'consumer' grow at an exponential rate because of the incorporation of new technological gimmicks and of expensive labour at the design, production and deployment level.

7. The very limited spillover of sophisticated military R & D to the peaceful sector of the economy results in a growing gap between the 'dynamic' military sector and the stagnating low-productivity non-military economy.

These seven propositions are supported by a large volume of evidence, scattered in the international press and in specialised journals reporting on military R & D advances (journals edited by technologists for technologists), and/or dedicated to the theoretical analysis of the unlimited number of variants of military strategies (journals edited by the so-called global strategists for consumption of military-industrial establishments).

This sort of specialised literature rarely falls into the hands of economists and other social scientists. If it were otherwise, the economics of the armaments race would have flourished and offered a very useful and relevant contribution to the peace movement. At the present stage one can only say that the deep and growing controversy about the impact of the worldwide accelerated arms expenditure on politicians, military people and technologists directly involved is hardly noted outside these circles in the West. Disappointingly, a similar controversy about the economic burden of armaments is largely absent in the literature originating in the socialist camp, for 'security reasons'.

This controversy has been raging since the early eighties in the USA more than elsewhere when it became clear to many people, including some 'common sense' military, that the tremendous escalation of military expenditure in the forth-coming years, posited by the Reagan administration to 'catch up' with the Soviet Union, will not get the USA out of its present economic depression but may even accelerate it and lead eventually to general bankruptcy. Moreover, it is quite symptomatic that the defenders in the USA of arms race escalation are substituting the earlier outworn slogan 'it is better to be dead than red' with the new one 'it is better to go bankrupt than be dead'. Some more detached and balanced observers go even further in predicting that the global arms race escalation may eventually bankrupt not only both super-powers but their respective allies as well[3].

Production of Useless Equipment without Accountability

Since the USA is still one of the most open societies in respect to access to information on military matters, the publicly available evidence that has been rapidly accumulat-ing in that country in the past few years confirms the seven propositions presented above. It also supports the con-clusions of the studies by Melman, Gansler and Kaldor[2] to the effect that: first, the US military-industrial complex operates without control by the executive and legislative branches of the federal government; and second, that this complex produces 'goods' on which billions of dollars are spent but which often, and with growing frequency, are use-less both for defensive and offensive purposes, from the moment they leave the production line. The first point was brutally made before Congress, in January 1982, by Admiral Hyman G. Rickover[4], the creator of the US nuclear navy, who was forced to retire from office, according to his own state-ment, by the pressure of 'defense' contractors; 'Arms pro-curement programs have become meaningless. Today defense contractors can do anything they want with nothing to hinder them.' Large corporations – he said – through their vast resources and wealth, have become 'another branch of govern-ment' for which there is little or no accountability.

Criticisms of mass production of new weapon systems in the USA – increasingly either technically faulty or burdened with 'baroque technology' and not integrated in any coherent military strategy; whose costs are sky-rocketing, and which are obsolete at the moment of reaching mass production stage

- come with growing frequency from many US government agencies, including ad hoc advisory and consultative expert commissions within the Defense Department itself. A careful reading of the contents of the 'top secret' reports of these bodies, as disclosed by leading US newspapers and mass-circulation weekly journals, reveals the bitter conflicts among the major segments of the US military establishment, accompanied by intensive lobbying activities of many Congress members, aimed at distributing military contracts to those constituencies which suffer from the severe impact of the economic crisis and persistent unemployment.

Among some recent disclosures seriously affecting the credibility of the Administration, the Secretary of Defense and the military-industrial establishment as a whole, the following random samples of the prevailing situation may be mentioned:

1. A report of the General Accounting Office of the US Congress stated that officials in the US Air Force and the Office of the Defense Secretary 'have violated Federal anti-lobbying laws' in a joint campaign with the Lockheed Corporation to push through Congress a programme for purchasing 50 C-5 air cargo planes at a total cost of $10.9 billion[5].

2. A report of two naval aviation squadrons, whose job was to evaluate new planes, advised the Navy not to approve full production of the F-18 as a light bomber - a total of some 1300 planes costing $22.5 billion - because the plane was not operationally suitable, either as a fighter or as a bomber[6]. These findings were overruled, however, by the Defense Systems Acquisition Review Council in mid-December 1982[7].

3. An internal study by Pentagon experts concluded that future costs of arms in the five-year military build-up proposed by the Reagan administration at a cost of 1.6 **trillion** dollars, are seriously underestimated. The report stated that the Defense Department's five-year estimates of weapon costs have been chronically low since 1976, even without the inflation factor. According to the same study, this underestimation continues for many other weapons including M1 tank and Phoenix missile among others[8].

The magnitude of the waste of financial, technological, physical and human resources in the production of deadly junk in the USA and elsewhere can be judged from the following table of cost overruns of the newest generation of mass destruction weapons, elaborated by the first chairman of the Council of Economic Advisers of the Reagan administration,

Murray L. Weidenbaum on the basis of US Congressional Budget Office analysis of 1980[9]:

Major Military Cost Overruns

Weapon Systems	Overruns per cent	Unit Cutbacks per cent
Hellfire missile	322	82
Patriot missile	154	67
SSG-7 ship	79	75
AH64 aircraft	67	43
EA-6B aircraft	52	33
XM-1 tank	49	21
F-18 aircraft	44	40
P-3C aircraft	43	50

The above table clearly demonstrates that major cost overruns on new weapons system in the USA lead to cuts in the eventual size of the systems. The same trends can be detected in all other military establishments of the North Atlantic Treaty Organisation, and perhaps in the Warsaw Pact countries as well. Economic consequences of this phenomenon are clear. Even with the most parsimonious attitudes towards the welfare-oriented segments of public budgets, large overall budget deficits continue to grow, feeding inflation at the national level and increasing the instability of international financial systems.

The basic conflict between the ever-growing 'defence' budgets and the needs of civilian economics will only increase if some overall, however fragile, economic recovery takes place in the industrial countries. According to the analyses, made public in early summer of 1983, of the persistence of this conflict, there is an uneasy suspicion even in some conservative circles in Washington that the military build-up in the USA may be harmful to the US economy, if not at present then in two to four years. Thus, according to a group of six former Cabinet members of the Nixon and Carter administrations[10]:

there is plenty of spare capacity now and briskly rising Defense Department spending is positive (?) for expansion. But in the middle of the decade, the civilian economy presumably will be operating closer to capacity, and an inflation-producing collison - competition for plant capacity and skilled labor - would occur.

A less sanguine evaluation has appeared in a study published in June 1982 by the Council on Economic Priorities, a New York-based public policy organisation. The findings of its study are sobering: a) military spending creates fewer jobs than non-military productive investment, and very few for unskilled workers; b) it channels research into lines that 'have few commercial applications', crowding out non-military research; c) retards productivity growth; and d) inhibits overall economic growth and expansion of social welfare[11].

These are the broad subjects which must be studied by economists and other social scientists both in the advanced and the underdeveloped countries. The arms race is too serious a subject to be left to technologists and global strategists, even if a global conflagration is hopefully avoided.

References

1. D. Greenwood, 'The Impact of Military Expenditure on Economic Growth and Performance', outline/discussion paper for the IEA Conference on Military Expenditure and Economic Growth, Centre for Defence Studies, Aberdeen, (1982).
2. See, in particular, S. Melman, Pentagon Capitalism: The Political Economy of War, (New York: McGraw Hill, 1970); J.S. Gansler, The Defense Industry, (Cambridge, Mass: The IMI Press, 1980); Mary Kaldor, The Baroque Arsenal, (New York: Hill and Wang, 1981).
3. '...the world may witness the spectacle of two superpowers bankrupting themselves to remain superpowers', T.H. White, 'Weinberger on the Ramparts', The New York Times Magazine, (February 6 1983).
4. 'Military-Industrial Complex Assaulted in Rickover Swan Song to Congress', The New York Times, January 29 1982.
5. The New York Times, October 1 1982.
6. ibid, November 15 1982.
7. ibid, December 10 1982.
8. ibid, December 7 1982.
9. M. L. Weidenbaum, 'Reagan Still Can't Hold Spending Down', The New York Times, February 6 1983.
10. E. Cowan, 'Foes Say Defense Budget May Disarm the Economy', The New York Times, May 1 1983.
11. Council on Economic Priorities, Military Expansion, Economic Decline, New York, June 1982.

27   SOCIAL COSTS OF MILITARY PROGRAMMES IN THE
      NORTH AND SOUTH

Klaus Gottstein

The highest social costs are incurred when military programmes lead to war, as has happened more than 120 times
since the end of World War II, almost exclusively in the
Third World[1]. These wars resulted in millions of dead, and
economic ruin and destruction of once flourishing communities
and social systems. Should an all-out nuclear war occur, the
results would, of course, be disastrous to an unimaginable
degree.

But it is not only in the case of war that military
programmes make an impact on many sectors of a society. This
impact is there all the time and it is important to assess it
if we are to weigh the social costs against the expected
benefits.

The Economic Costs and their Social Consequences

During the past four years military spending has shown an
upward trend, faster than in the previous four years, in
spite of the deterioration of the world economy. For 1981
world military spending has been estimated to be $600-650
billion; more than $100 billion of this was spent by Third
World countries[2], which could have used this money for
other vital purposes. Let me quote from an article by
Howard Hiatt[3]:

Over half the world's people do not have safe drinking
water. This accounts for most serious disease and for a
large fraction of the deaths in Third World countries.
Although provision for safe water would require a major
organizational change, access could be provided within the
decade for the majority of people now in need, for an
estimated cost of $30 billion a year - a large sum, but
less than the cost of 17 days of arms production.
  Estimates put at almost 2 million the number of people
who die each year from measles, polio, tuberculosis,

233

diphtheria, tetanus, and other diseases for which effective vaccines are available. Three million children could be immunized with such vaccines for the price of one modern fighter plane ($20 million).

Eight hundred million people are thought to suffer from malaria, and each year 1 million children die of the disease in Africa alone. The diversion of half a day's military expenditures would finance the whole malaria-control program of the WHO. Military expenditures of one hour exceed the total annual budget for all research on malaria and all other tropical diseases.

Between 450 million people and 1 billion people have less food than is necessary for basic survival. The United Nations Children's Fund estimated that in 1978 more than 12 million children under the age of five died of hunger and its effects. The supplementary costs of a 20-year program to provide essential food and to fill health needs in all developing countries have been estimated to be $80 billion. This would be available if all nations were to redirect 12 per cent of this year's military spending.

Within the industrialised countries (ICs) the recent increase in military spending, at a time of economic recession and of efforts at restricting total budgets, coincides with decreases in social spending. Hiatt[3] compares the $4.5 billion allocated for the MX programme, and the $100 million cost for each B-1 bomber, with the reduction of $1.46 billion in the US child nutrition programme, and with the reduction of $914 million in the US Federal Medicaid Program. Similar reductions are noticeable in other countries. Military expenses use up funds badly needed in fields of social welfare, health, education and in support of cultural activities.

Because of the growing sophistication of arms systems the situation is likely to become worse, not better, in the coming years. According to a Pentagon investigation of weapons systems introduced during the last two decades, the costs of a new weapon have risen by a factor of five per decade as compared with the weapon it replaces[4]. Maintenance and repair costs also rise rapidly as well as operational costs. Price increases in the armaments sector are above the general inflation rate.

Excessive military spending is particularly damaging for less developed countries (LDCs) because they have to rely on imports for most of the advanced technical equipment, using up their scarce foreign currency so desperately needed for other purposes. Export of military equipment to the Third World has risen by a factor of seven since 1962, whereas the volume of world trade rose by a factor of only three during the same period[2]. The import of arms by developing countries amounts to more than $15 billion per year, according to some sources[5]. This increases the already enormous burden of debts (more than $520 billion) of the developing countries. Furthermore, it stimulates the ICs to sustain their already over-sized arms industries which otherwise might have been reduced to a more reasonable size. The maintenance of the overcapacity for arms production in East and West necessarily leads to a constant search for new markets, thus having a destabilising effect both politically and economically. There is no natural upper limit, in quantity or quality, to the possession of arms, as long as potential opponents exist and likewise continue to arm. The only limitation is economic.

The Indirect Consequences of Armaments

Even more important than these direct economic considerations, however, are the indirect consequences of armaments for both industrialised and developing countries.

One effect is the expansion of conflicts. Modern arms enable some countries to get involved in internal conflicts of their neighbours; instead of remaining local affairs these conflicts become destructive wars. Libya's intervention in Chad is an example.

Another effect is an increase of **dependence**. Sophisticated technology leads to dependence on the supplier for maintenance and spare parts, and to the necessity for an export-oriented economy to pay for the imports. The requirements of the internal market are thereby neglected.

There is a trend in the LDCs to apply the same principles to military and civilian technologies. Military personnel trained abroad, after returning home, often adopt the behavioural and consumption patterns, and views on industrialisation and economy, existing in the ICs. In the latter, military technology is determined by worst-case scenarios: it is highly complex and operates under extreme conditions almost irrespective of cost. However, the main part of the economy in western ICs is based on quite different criteria: the governing factors are cost-effectiveness, turnover, and coverage of demand. In LDCs, where the civilian market is still underdeveloped by western standards, the preponderance of military technology tends to introduce its very special modus operandi into the civilian sector. This can have the result that for agriculture, trade and industry, equipment is imported without much consideration for cost-effectiveness, output and demand[6].

Some LDCs try to lessen their dependence by the creation of

armament industries of their own. Compared to the civilian sector this requires a relatively higher number of qualified personnel. Arms industries are not well suited for solving the employment problems of LDCs because there is little use in them for the masses of unskilled labour available. Armament industries need an infrastructure which causes even the civilian sector to be more capital-intensive. Furthermore, the element of secrecy inherent in military and armament matters tends to conceal costly blunders and inefficient solutions, apart from being detrimental to the maintenance and promotion of the democratic process.

Another aspect is waste of manpower. Considering the world-wide need for trained experts to tackle the huge problems of LDCs, the comparatively high training costs of military technical personnel are particularly uneconomic. It costs more than $0.5 million to train a jet pilot. For the same cost, many civilian engineers could be trained. According to conservative estimates, about half a million physical and engineering scientists in the East and West are currently employed in military R & D[7]. Many of them could have been committed to solving the urgent problems besetting mankind.

The view has been expressed[8] that armaments have positive economic effects, particularly in LDCs. The military create an infrastructure - it is said - that is often also available for civilian use. In many new countries they play a positive role in education, technical training, health care, supplying food and clothing, civic action, in creating economic demand in a 'Keynesian' situation, and in the homogenisation of nations traditionally divided into tribes of differing cultures and languages. However, the transfer of military installations to civilian use is not always possible. For example, in Thailand, most modern runways or hospitals were too expensive to be maintained after the US withdrawal[9]. Moreover, new infrastructures often destroy the existing ones and change modes of production. Canal systems in India and Vietnam deteriorated after the introduction of railways and roads. Traditional employment opportunities were destroyed when, instead of local means, expensive foreign-made equipment was imported. National homogenisation and introduction of modern civilisation often result in a deplorable destruction of traditionally balanced cultural identities.

Just as expenditures for armaments can contribute to a welcome 'deficit spending' in the Keynesian sense, it can certainly also contribute to the acceleration of inflation in economically inflationary situations. Arms production creates purchasing power without increasing correspondingly the volume of consumable goods. Military bases maintained abroad make the balance of payments of the respective country more negative.

The Economic Effects of Arms Reduction

The fear is often expressed that reduction in armament programmes would result in an increase in unemployment. Such a fear, however, would be unjustified if the funds spent on armaments were devoted to civilian uses. On the contrary, unemployment would be reduced because in the armament industries labour expenditure is particularly expensive. According to US Congressman Les Aspin[10], an expenditure of $1 billion creates:

    35 000 jobs in armaments;
    76 000 jobs in construction work;
    77 000 jobs in health service;
   100 000 jobs in education;
   132 000 jobs in civil service.

Because of the growing sophistication in weapon systems the jobs/dollar ratio in armaments is rapidly decreasing.

Most qualifications needed by the armament industry are applicable in civilian industry. According to an investigation carried out by the Department of Employment of the State of California[11] there were 127 different qualifications in the Californian arms industry. Only six of these were not directly usable in civilian industry, and even in these only six months of vocational re-training would have been required.

The enormous sums spent on armaments (nearly $150 per year for every man, woman and child of the 4.4 billion inhabitants of the earth) support a relatively small number of people. The total personnel of all regular armed forces of the world is estimated[12] to be 26.6 million people (without reservists and paramilitary units who have other paid jobs). Including civilian personnel there may be 55 to 60 million jobs based on military spending, and 20 to 25 million additional jobs in arms production and in special military installations[13]. These are small numbers compared to the world population but they are highly qualified jobs. About 20 per cent of all highly skilled workers are employed in military production[14]. For scientists and engineers the proportion is likely to be even higher. Nevertheless, as shown above, a reduction in arms production need not lead to unemployment.

Psychological Effects

Social tensions are created when large numbers of foreign military experts, technicians and construction workers, for example in the Persian Gulf region, are brought in, often from other LDCs like Pakistan or Egypt. This results in the establishment of enclaves in which the people earn much more than the surrounding population. This leads to social tension, destruction of traditional cultures, and crime. Enclaves of this kind, with the same consequences, are also created by the emergence in LDCs of advanced military and industrial sectors. They intensify the contrast to the traditional sectors and provoke feelings of relative poverty.

This is a psychological effect. Psychological effects are of extreme importance in dealing with armaments. The need to arm is felt because of mistrust of one's neighbour. The neighbour feels the same, and justifies his mistrust by the allegedly defensive - armament efforts he observes across the border. So the spiral continues, and there would be no end to it but for economic reasons. The only alternative would be for politicians to understand and take into account the psychological root of the problem. As Freud has shown, man is governed by two competing instincts: one is directed towards destruction; the other is constructive and, when it prevails, leads to friendly, even altruistic cooperation. The latter instinct is mostly directed towards members of one's own group, the former towards 'enemies' threatening the group from outside. Throughout history, unscrupulous demagogues tried to unite their own followers by convincing them that they were threatened by a common enemy. Hitler was particularly, and diabolically, successful in this. This recipe is still in use world-wide, and is one of the main obstacles to disarmament. The ultimate solution of the problem of war must be universal recognition that in our time **all** of humanity belongs to **our** group, and that there is only one common enemy: our own irrationality which prevents us from tackling jointly the enormous problems facing mankind. The presence of offensive armaments makes it nearly impossible to develop this group-feeling for all humanity. Seen this way, the social cost of those military programmes which can be construed as being based on offensive doctrines is immense. It obstructs the only road which might, in the long run, lead humanity out of the present predicament, out of the constant threat of self-annihilation. This constant threat poisons the marrow of our youth, giving rise to a spreading feeling of 'no future'. Any confidence-building measure indicating the absence of offensive intentions - and, if possible, the absence of offensive capabilities while maintaining the capability for successful defence - should be adopted as a step on the road to a safer and more stable future.

Leaders of the great powers must learn that it is necessary to stop demonising their opponents. They must learn to see them as representatives of political systems which - though different from those in their own part of the world - are the result of historical processes which cannot be changed by force or by external pressure. Conversely, as the above-mentioned psychological effects indicate, external pressure can only result in a hardening of existing postures.

References

1. I. Kende, 'Dynamics of War, of Arms and of Military Expenditures in the "Third World" 1945-1976', in Instant Research on Peace and Violence, 7, (1977) Number 2.
2. World Armaments and Disarmament. SIPRI Yearbook 1982, (London: Taylor & Francis, 1982).
3. H.H. Hiatt, The New England Journal of Medicine, 307, (Oct.28 1982).
4. P.J. Class in Aviation Week and Space Technology, (Nov.19, 1973), quoted by U. Albrecht in Rüstung und Oekonomie, (Frankfurt: Haag & Herchen, 1982).
5. A.J. Pierre, The Global Politics of Arms Sales,(Princeton University Press, 1982).
6. P. Lock, 'The New International Economic Order and Armaments', in Economics, 22, (1980).
7. M. Thee, 'Significance of Military R & D', in Impact of Science on Society, 31, (January-March, 1981).
8. E. Benoit, Defense and Economic Growth in Developing Countries, (London, 1973).
9. P. Lock and H. Wulf, 'Transfer of Military Technology and the Development Process', in Bulletin of Peace Proposals, 2, (1977).
10. Quoted by U. Albrecht op.cit. p. 246.
11. ibid.
12. US ACDA 1980, quoted by J. Rodejohann and C. Wellmann in Rüstung und Oekonomie, op.cit.
13. Ruth Sivard as quoted by Rodejohann, ibid.
14. I. Malecki, in Impact of Science on Society, 31 (Jan. - March 1981).

28 REDUCTION OF MILITARY EXPENDITURE AS A DISARMAMENT CONCEPT

Hans Christian Cars

Background

The conventional approach to disarmament is to seek agreements that forbid or limit the development or use of specific weapons like nuclear, biological, chemical or other weapons with particularly harmful effects. Although some such agreements have been concluded, the arms race still continues. Vast human and industrial resources are devoted to the development and deployment of new and ever more sophisticated weaponry. Funds that might have been saved through the prohibition of certain kinds of weapons seem to be poured instead into other military fields. Such practices may change the course of armament but do not lead to any genuine disarmament that would reduce the threat to mankind and alleviate the economic burden for many countries by releasing real resources for civilian uses.

It is against this background that the idea of negotiating international agreements to reduce military expenditure deserves attention. The purposes of such agreements would be to put a ceiling to the total amount of resources that each contracting party would be allowed to spend on its military build-up.

If properly applied and adhered to, such agreements might prevent resources released through specific disarmament measures from being used elsewhere in the military sector for some other military purposes. Thus it is suggested that what has here been called the conventional approach is not to be **replaced** by another but to be **combined** with such one. This should make it possible eventually to curb the arms race.

National Security - Military Capability - Military Expenditure

Each country participating in a disarmament negotiation is primarily concerned with the question of improving or at

240

least safeguarding its own national security. This security,
which is not easy to define or assess, is usually supposed to
be affected by many different factors. The military capability of a country relative to the military capability of
its most likely adversaries is often regarded as one of the
most important of these factors.

This capability is a result of earlier investments in military training, weapons, installations and other military
equipment and facilities. In other words, it depends largely
on the real resources that have been devoted to the military
sector in the past. In the same way, future capability will
depend on the amounts of military expenditure in the present
year and in the years to come. The military expenditure of
one single year has only a rather limited impact on a
country's military capability and is even less linked with
its concept of national security. This link would, however,
be most carefully analysed by a possible participant in any
future negotiation on an agreement to reduce military expenditure.

Conditions for Negotiations

To arrive at an agreement each party must be convinced that a
mutual and continuous reduction of military expenditure will
be to the advantage or at least be acceptable with regard to
national security, and that this security may not be threatened in the near future by other factors which could provoke
an unforeseen need for increasing military spending instead
of reducing it.

Military expenditure may be not only a factor with important impact on military capability and thus on national security. It may also be one of the few parameters that a country
can itself change in order to affect its national security.
It is, therefore, reasonable to believe that no country will
ever be willing to sign an agreement by which it renounces
the right to use this parameter as it wishes, unless there is
a relatively stable political situation and a good deal of
confidence among countries in the world.

These conditions may seem necessary for successful negotiations on the reduction of military expenditure, but are no
less needed for the accomplishment of many other disarmament
measures as well. The most important and urgent efforts to be
made for the cause of disarmament should, therefore, be to
help establish such conditions.

Subject Matter for Negotiation

Given a propitious international situation and a firm pol-

itical will on all sides to arrive at agreements to reduce
military expenditure, the negotiations may be conducted in
stages dealing with different substantive and technical
issues.

Substantive issues include the rate at which reductions
should be carried out, the duration of the agreement, and
whether certain kinds of expenditure should be subject to
specific limitations. These issues will have to be dealt with
carefully by the negotiators but they cannot possibly be
fruitfully analysed much further before the negotiations take
place. Other issues which may be of a more technical character will also have to be settled by the negotiators themselves, but in these cases some exploratory work may be
carried out in advance. This may prove to be of some help
later on in the context of actual negotiations.

Among such technical issues that will have to be agreed
upon are the problems of definition, valuation, comparison
and verification of military expenditure.

- First of all, the negotiating parties will need to discuss
and agree on the scope and content of the military expenditure that they want to consider, that is, which kinds of
expenditure might be made subject to restrictions in the
event of an agreement. Should, for instance, expenditure on
nuclear weapons and strategic forces be included or should
they be dealt with separately? What about civil defence,
stockpiling of raw materials and other industrial goods of
strategic importance to any war economy? How to draw a line
between military forces, paramilitary forces and regular
police forces? This listing of examples could easily be
continued.

The answers to these and other such questions will undoubtedly have an important impact on the substance itself of an
agreement, but they will also depend upon a number of technical considerations. It would probably be necessary to make
provisions for an exchange of military expenditure data between the negotiating parties, first within the framework of
negotiations and later on for verification purposes when an
agreement has been concluded. Such provisions may take the
form of a reporting system based on agreed definitions of
military expenditure categories and as well adapted as possible to the budgeting and accounting practices of negotiating
states.

- Military expenditure figures represent financial outlays
incurred by the state but they do not always reflect the real
costs for certain goods and services, as their prices may be
influenced by subsidies, taxes and other administrative
measures. Practices in this regard may differ widely between
countries and, in particular, between countries with different

economic systems. It is, therefore, important to assess expenditure data on the basis of an agreed understanding about the problems of valuation in cases where the price of a unit is signficantly different from its real cost of production.
- The problem of comparing military expenditure would probably appear already at the outset of negotiations, because it can be supposed that if each party would compare its own military expenditure with those of the other parties, such comparisons would most likely produce quite different results. In order to arrive at a common and objective basis for their negotiations, which they presumably would want to do, the negotiators would have to agree on a number of methodological issues involved in this kind of international comparisons.

Since an agreement to reduce military expenditure would hardly be concluded for one single year only but have a duration of several years and be concerned with real military expenditure, one would have to deal with the problem posed by the fact that contracting parties may have very different rates of inflation. This means that in order to assess changes in real military spending one has to compare the military expenditure of two different years by taking into consideration the changes that have occurred between these years in the prices of military goods and services.
- It is hard to believe that an international agreement to reduce military expenditure could ever be concluded without carefully elaborated provisions for verifying the compliance of all parties with the stipulations of the agreement. This will call for an exchange of expenditure data but probably also of other information concerning prices, numbers and qualities of military goods and services. The need for information and the methods for obtaining it will largely depend on the scope and nature of the agreement. The means of verification employed in other types of disarmament agreements may in several cases prove to be useful in this context also, but will probably have to be combined with some other means that have not yet been used. The choice of means and methods of verification is of course a highly sensitive political question but involves at the same time a great number of technical aspects.
- Because of the numerous and complex problems referred to above, concerning the definition, valuation and comparison of military expenditure, it would be futile to negotiate an agreement on the assumption that the compliance of the parties could be exhaustively proven on scientific or objective grounds alone. Means and methods of verification together with great openness and confidence between the parties may provide good possibilities for assessing compliance. To some

degree it must, however, always be subject to political judgement by the parties on the basis of the best possible evidence available.

The Work of the United Nations in this Field

Recent history goes back to 1973 when the Soviet Union proposed to the General Assembly that all permanent members of the Security Council should cut down their military expenditure by ten per cent and utilise a part of the funds thus saved to provide assistance to developing countries. This proposal initiated a series of expert groups appointed by the Secretary-General with a view to facilitating future negotiations on agreements to reduce military expenditure. One of the first concrete results that came out of these activities was an instrument for standardised international reporting of military expenditure which was proposed by one of the groups in 1976. The General Assembly decided that this instrument should be tested by a number of voluntarily participating member states. This was done in 1979-80 under the direction of the Secretary-General with the assistance of an ad hoc Panel of experts. This test led to the conclusion that the proposed reporting instrument represented a viable and practical means for international reporting of military expenditure. On that basis the Panel proposed that such reporting should be carried out on a general and regular basis and recommended, therefore, an early implementation of the instrument with a few minor modifications which were suggested in the light of experiences gained during the test.

The General Assembly decided accordingly and adopted in 1980 a system for international reporting based on the tested and recommended instrument. Since that year about 25 countries have participated in the system and reported annually their military expenditure to the Secretary-General. The number of participating countries seems to be growing slowly. The large majority of them are western countries. Only a few developing countries have participated so far, and no country from eastern Europe.

This rather limited participation and, above all, its fairly unrepresentative nature constitute undoubtedly a problem when it comes to maintaining the support for continuous reporting. Several countries feel that there is no point in submitting their expenditure data as long as countries of 'the other side' do not in any way take part in the reporting system. There is even a risk that they may choose to discontinue their reporting unless certain other countries participate as well, at least to some extent.

This situation made the General Assembly decide in 1982 to

invite all member countries to submit their views on practical means of promoting a wider participation of states in the international system of standardised reporting of military expenditures. Eight countries have so far replied, many of them stressing the need for greater openness in military matters as a means of increasing confidence among nations.

The reporting of military expenditure data, however widespread the participation may become, will not in itself result in any reductions of such expenditure. An increasing openness may, however, as mentioned above, lead to an improved international confidence which in turn may help to prevent undesirable decisions based on exaggerated assumptions about military efforts of other countries due to lack of accurate information.

Further, a functioning reporting system like the one presently in operation may in the context of future negotiations – and this is perhaps its main importance – serve as an example of how to define and classify military expenditure. Whether this particular system would prove to be acceptable for the negotiators is difficult to tell, but it should at least be suitable to use as a first basis for discussions on the subject.

At the same time as the General Assembly decided to adopt the reporting system, it also instructed the Secretary-General, with the assistance of a new group of experts, to examine and suggest solutions to the question of comparing military expenditure among different states and between different years, as well as to the problems of verification that will arise in connection with agreements on the reduction of military expenditure.

This study was mainly concentrated on the many theoretical and technical problems involved but also touched upon certain political aspects. In the group's report, which was submitted to the General Assembly's Second Special Session on Disarmament in 1982, the group presented several conclusions and made a few recommendations.

Concerning the problems of comparison the group stated that price changes may occur at different rates in the military and in the civilian sector. In order to estimate military expenditure in real terms it was, therefore, deemed necessary to develop specific price indices for military goods and services. At the same time the group concluded that prevailing exchange rates were not adequate instruments for accurate comparisons of military expenditure of different states. For that reason there would be a similar need for developing a set of parities reflecting the relative purchasing power of different currencies with regard to each state's military sector.

Since both price indices and purchasing power parities can be developed with the use of different statistical methods, there would finally be a need also for a common understanding among the negotiating parties, including a political will and firm determination to arrive at agreed solutions. A point made by the group in this context was that, given such an understanding, it should be possible to resolve the technical problems in a way satisfactory to all parties.

Concerning the question of verification the group stated that provisions for verification would have to be an integral part of any international agreement on the reduction of military expenditure. Because of the rather complex nature of such an agreement no single measure of verification would be sufficient. One would have to use a number of different measures applying both to physical military units and to economic indicators, such as the amounts of expenditure on different military inputs and the prices and qualities of such inputs.

In view of the fact that most states are quite reluctant to provide information on military matters, the group made the rather encouraging remark that a party which intends to comply with an agreement and which is seriously concerned with its survival would not only be interested in obtaining sufficient information from the other parties but would also have a strong incentive itself to provide all the information needed to convince the other parties of its own compliance.

Based on the above conclusions the group stated that successful demonstration of the feasibility of constructing military price indices and purchasing power parities for different states would help to prepare the ground for future negotiations on the reduction of military expenditure.

For this purpose the group recommended that its mainly theoretical study should be followed by a practical exercise in which voluntarily participating states should endeavour to construct appropriate instruments for the comparison of military expenditure. Although it was not explicitly stated, such instruments would of course also serve to facilitate verification.

On this basis the General Assembly decided in 1982 that the Secretary-General should undertake the task of constructing military price indices and purchasing power parities for such countries that may want to take part in this exercise. The group of experts received a new mandate from the Secretary-General to assist him in this task which should encompass a study of the problem as a whole, including:
- assessing the feasibility of such an exercise;
- designing the project and methodology to be employed;
- determining the types of data required, such as product

descriptions, prices and statistical weights;
- constructing military price indices and purchasing power parities.

After the progress reports in 1983 and 1984, a final report is supposed to be submitted in 1985.

The group has held its first two meetings in March and August 1983. By the end of its second meeting ten countries (Australia, Austria, Canada, Finland, FRG, Italy, Norway, Sweden, UK and USA) had communicated to the Secretary-General their willingness to participate in the group's exercise, and links for direct and continuous communication between the group and participating countries are at present being established. It is hoped that the number of participating countries will be increased in the near future so as to include developing countries, as well as countries with planned economies.

In assessing its task the group has agreed that the exercise should have an exploratory character in order to reveal the practical difficulties in constructing military price indices and purchasing power parities, and to demonstrate, if possible, that such indices and parities can be constructed. On that basis the group intends to base its work on the information that will be made available by participating states; it expects this information to include not only disaggregated expenditure data but also data on prices and characteristics for a range of military goods and services. The group is going to proceed on that basis with the selection of an appropriate set of items and to process the submitted data in close cooperation with participating states.

Although the concrete results of this work in terms of the indices and parities constructed may not be of any immediate use for disarmament purposes, we may still hope that if and when negotiations to reduce military expenditure ever take place, experiences gained from this exercise will prove to be useful and help to facilitate the negotiations.

List of References to UN Documents on the Subject

1. Resolutions adopted by the General Assembly
   a) A/RES/3093   (1974)
   b) A/RES/3463   (1976)
   c) A/RES/31/87   (1977)
   d) A/RES/33/67   (1979)
   e) A/RES/35/142B   (1981)
   f) A/RES/37/95B   (1983)
2. Reports prepared by groups of experts
   a) A/9770   (1974)
   b) A/10165   (1975)
   c) A/31/222   (1976)

    d) A/32/194   (1977)
    e) A/35/479   (1980)
    f) A/S-12/7   (1982)
    g) A/38/3541   (1983)
3. Other reports prepared by the UN Secretariat
    a) A/36/353   (1981)
    b) A/37/418   (1982)
    c) A/38/353   (1983)

Canute Khamala

Introduction

The term 'Third World' came into international political par-
lance after World War II to characterise those nations that
refused to be involved in the policy of international conflict and confrontation pursued by the major and mutually
hostile blocs. It is believed that the term had a pre-war
origin, and was identified with those nations which opposed
both private and collectivist capitalism. Defined in this way
'Third World' had the dignified implication of 'third way' -
not a 'third force' of conducting world affairs. With the
passing of time 'Third World' has acquired a different meaning. It is now commonly used to refer to those countries
relegated to abyssmal backwardness and poverty in comparison
with the affluence and technological and industrial superiority of the 'First' and 'Second' Worlds. The phrase 'Third
World' has thus become accepted as international shorthand
for 'under-developed', 'less developed' or 'developing
countries'. It is for all practical purposes synonymous with
'third rate'.

Since this paper is concerned with Third World security, it
is important to understand what is meant by 'security'. Since
World War II 'national security' has assumed a predominantly
military character. It is used to define the ability of a
nation to maintain and defend its integrity through the force
and power of large armies, and the development and manufacture of increasingly sophisticated and destructive armaments. This overwhelmingly military perception of security is
understandable if we recollect that it was the most modern
weapon of mass destruction that helped bring World War II to
an end. Since that time, modern weapon systems (both nuclear
and conventional) with incredibly more destrucive power have
been developed and stockpiled. The possession of such weapons
is regarded by many nations as an assurance of security.
Furthermore, the national scientific and technological capa-

bility to develop and manufacture sophisticated armament systems is currently regarded as a necessary qualification for joining the small but prestigious list of 'world powers'. Earning a place on this list is the envy of many Third World countries, and to a few of them this could be a reality in the long run.

Military superiority is being achieved at the expense of other unsatisfied human needs, and it is becoming increasingly clear that there can be no lasting national security unless certain basic needs of a non-military nature are satisfied. These include adequate food and nutrition, health services, clean water, decent housing, access to energy resources, and sustained national economies that generate productive employment of human resources. Furthermore, the relationship between mankind and his own environment, resulting in adverse and irreversible changes, has future security implications which perhaps only the most far-sighted leaders recognise.

Both aspects of security (or insecurity), that is, military and non-military in the Third World countries, are discussed in this paper. Security in the Third World cannot be isolated from the concept of development and the wide gap that exists between industrialised countries and developing countries in the application of science and technology for development. One of the world's greatest challenges today must be to devise a formula for integrating science and technology into the struggle against human misery, poverty and the misuse of economic and military might. While it would be unrealistic to regard Third World countries as a homogenous group, with similar security and development problems, in comparison with the industrialised countries of the North, there are certain common characteristics which distinguish Third World countries. Practically all of these features have direct or indirect connections with past and present, internal or external, security situations in Third World countries. They will in all probability continue to influence the security and stability of these countries in the absence of a new, globally acceptable direction according to which all the nations and peoples of the world can share in the utilisation of their resources for a better life, now and for future generations, on the basic principle of interdependence and mutual tolerance, rather than by domination and subjugation through force or other unfair means.

Third World Characteristics - Sharing a Common Predicament

It would be misleading to state that the world is sharply divided into three camps, of which the Third World is one.

There are many differences between Third World countries,
both within and between the major world regions. In size they
range from large state nations, such as the Indian sub-
continent, to many small landlocked or island countries.
Scientifically and technologically they range from semi-
industrialised countries, such as Brazil and India, to what
could be referred to as predominantly 'pre-scientific'
communities employing primitive methods to eke out a living
from the land. In terms of wealth, they range from the newly
and fabulously rich oil-producing countries (with a per
capita income sometimes exceeding that of industrialised
countries) to many resource-poor countries with incomes
hardly adequate to satisfy the most basic needs. The Third
World countries have more than two-thirds of the world's
population but they control only about one-fifth of its
wealth. In spite of all these differences and contrasts,
Third World countries share the same predicament of being
poor as a consequence of certain common characteristics. Some
of the more prominent of these are the following:

> inadequate provision of basic needs of modern life, such as
> food, clean water, shelter, education, clothing, and health
> facilities;
> high rates of unemployment and underemployment mostly of
> youth with substantial productive potential;
> comparatively high growth rates of predominantly rural
> populations;
> endowment with natural resources and raw materials but
> lacking indigenous capability to explore and exploit them;
> small size of internal markets and uneven distribution of
> incomes;
> colonial backgrounds to all national systems of develop-
> ment;
> political instability and chauvinism caused by ideological
> disorder.

The last three characteristics deserve special mention,
because many of the problems and tensions in Third World
countries are direct or indirect by-products of their political history and the present economic disorder. Most Third
World countries achieved political independence following
World War II. Some countries, for example in South America,
have come into existence in the last 300-400 years through
settlement. Some have never experienced colonial rule, while
others are still engaged in the struggle for emancipation
from unjust minority regimes. The following discussion
examines the extent to which certain of the common characteristics contribute to Third World insecurity and conflict.

Colonialism and Third World Security

In the modern nuclear and space age, the conflict problems of humanity have become extremely severe. The causes and consequences of these problems have their roots in an inegalitarian form of existence that has virtually become institutionalised. A close examination of these conflicts leads one to the conclusion that some of them are specifically the result of distortions of colonialism with its long record of violence. The Third World countries of Africa, Asia, the Middle East and Latin America were created in accordance with the interests and disputes of colonial powers. Africa, for example, was literally 'carved up' at the Conference of Berlin without regard to such important criteria as the need to create nation states (a body of people marked off by common descent, language, culture or historical tradition). The same is true of the Middle East, South East Asia and Indo-China. The most serious and explosive security situations in some of the world's sub-regions are directly linked to the different forms and motives of political distribution, and the need to influence 'economic' or 'strategic' zones by the colonial powers. One can, therefore, speculate that many of the internal and external conflicts in Third World countries are in fact no more than a manifestation of clandestine motives and aspirations by the big powers to promote their ideologies and protect their economic and military interests.

The partitioning of Africa, for example, has given rise to conflicts and tensions of an ethnocentric nature in many sub-regions of the continent. Peoples with common descent, language, culture, religion and historical background have been distributed between two or more neighbouring state nations. The natural desire of these peoples to form coherent nations has been the cause of secessionist struggles. The potentially explosive situation in the Horn of Africa stems substantially from the ideals of self-determination and territorial integrity at the regional level. Basically, conflict in the Horn of Africa concerns four countries – Ethiopia, Kenya, Djibouti and Somalia – each of which possesses a substantial proportion of the Somali people. The notion of a 'Greater Somalia' formed by the unification of all the Somalis in this region is diametrically opposed to the high value set on the sanctity of territorial borders under the OAU Charter[1]. These basic seeds of conflict have been compounded by the involvement of the two superpowers and their allies to such an extent that security in this region threatens to become a major international issue. In the global context, the conflict relates more to the ideological,

economic, military and strategic motives of the superpowers
than to the ethnocentric nature of the dilemma facing the
people in the region. Indeed, the superpowers are prepared to
exploit the internal social upheavals and even to swap partners in order to promote their own interests. For example,
the Ethiopian revolution of 1974, which overthrew Emperor
Haile Sellassie, was essentially a by-product of internal
social reformation which (at least initially) had little to
do with ideological changes. It was only two years later,
when the Soviet Union moved in, that the ideological element
became evident. The alliance between Somalia and the United
States following the 1974 changes in Ethiopia, and the
resulting exchange of military partners, had little to do
with finding solutions for the real causes of conflicts
between Ethiopia and Somalia.

The Eritrean secessionist movement in Ethiopia, despite its
many years of existence, has not attracted the sympathy of
African states, although many Arab states are known to
support it. To most African states self-determination is
synonymous with territorial integrity, and any movement
intended to undermine the present boundaries, even though
they were artificially created by colonial powers, cannot be
favourably received. There is at least one good reason for
adhering to this principle. The majority of African states,
especially in black Africa (Africa south of Sahara) are
ethnically heterogenous, and claims to nationhood on the
basis of ethnic groupings could plunge the continent into
conflicts of untold proportions as happened in the Congo (now
Zaire) and Nigeria.

Third World countries perceive strong armed forces as an
assurance of their sovereignty and self-determination.
Therefore, on achieving independence, many Third World
countries embarked on expensive programmes of installing and
modernising their military forces. African countries which
have recently been liberated achieved their goal with the
assistance of massive supplies of sophisticated modern
weapons. Between 1969 and 1978 expenditures on arms by
African countries increased markedly, making the continent
the largest arms importing Third World region after the
Middle East[2].

Escalating military expenditure has far-reaching political,
social and economic implications, particularly since the
public dare not question the justification for military
budgets. A major consequence of militarisation has been
political instability evidenced by the all too frequent
toppling of civilian governments in Third World countries. In
many countries the emergence of authoritarian and repressive
regimes dependent on military might has contributed to much

human suffering. In the worst of these regimes extreme human suffering has come close to genocide; there are also millions of displaced refugees who have fled their homeland under the threat of violence. Even in those countries where military-supported regimes cannot be blamed for social disruption and infringement of human rights, excessive expenditure on arms is a serious obstacle to social and economic development. The economic plight of the poor non-oil producing countries during the last decade can at least in part be blamed on the high cost of their military institutions. A significant proportion of their scarce foreign exchange earnings generated from raw material exports is diverted to arms, depriving the people of development-oriented goods and services.

Although there is a recognised need to restrict military expenditures, certain tensions persist, making it unrealistic to expect these countries to demilitarise. In Africa, for instance, as long as the militarily powerful Republic of South Africa with its objectionable apartheid policies is regarded as a threat to the independent states of Southern Africa, and indeed to the rest of Africa, there can be no end to military build-up. The prospect for the future is similar to that in the Middle East where zionism is seen as the main cause of conflict between Israel and the Arab states.

Nuclear Proliferation and Third World Security

Many scores of wars have been fought since World War II and nearly all have taken place in Third World countries. In none of these wars were nuclear weapons used, even though the major nuclear powers were involved in some of the conflicts. Most of the wars have been localised, caused by internal political disputes or disagreements over territorial borders. Technologically more advanced as well as less advanced countries have been involved in these wars. The significant scientific and technological achievements by some Third World countries in the last 20 years have been demonstrated by India's and China's nuclear capability. Some countries, including Israel, Iran, Egypt, Pakistan, South Africa, Brazil and Argentina are believed to have the capability to produce nuclear weapons[3].

The cost of acquiring nuclear weapons is prohibitive to most countries, but possession of these weapons has become a symbol of national power not only in military circles but also in other spheres of international bargaining and influence, such as trade and technology transfer. It is for this reason that nuclearisation is likely to take place in the Third World even if it means massive sacrifices. Moreover, the present economic problems affecting the nuclear reactor

industry in the West, and the high cost of oil imports, are
an incentive to a more aggressive salesmanship and transfer
of nuclear technology. For example, when the FRG agreed to
supply Brazil with eight nuclear reactors and nuclear technology, this transaction was viewed with suspicion by
Argentina, which then declared its intention to go nuclear.
The USA has agreed to help Egypt build a reactor capable of
producing plutonium. France is supplying both South Africa
and Iraq with nuclear reactors. Pakistan, India's rival, will
certainly strive to achieve nuclear equality with the latter.
     A delicate situation exists in Black Africa. None of the
countries in the region has a nuclear capability, yet South
Africa's build-up of arms and superior nuclear technology is
regarded not only as a threat to the decolonisation process
in Southern Africa but as a real security risk to Black
African countries opposed to apartheid. These countries have
neither the economic nor the scientific resources to develop
nuclear weapons to deter South Africa (although Nigeria,
the most powerful, has declared its intention to go nuclear).
Besides, Black African countries face myriad problems of a
non-military nature which, if neglected, would constitute a
security risk; these include inadequate food, unemployment,
under-exploited resources, energy insufficiency and political
instability. The Lagos Plan of Action for the Economic Development of Africa : 1980-2000 lays out some of the problems
and actions to be taken[4]. If African countries are genuinely committed to this plan of action, it is hard to justify the diversion of limited resources to armaments, let
alone nuclear weapons. On the other hand, Black African
states are becoming increasingly aware that sovereignty con-
fers upon nations the responsibility for national security;
that they are morally indebted to fellow Africans under South
Africa's white minority regime; and that military build-up in
that country poses a real threat. The suggestion that African
countries should establish a nuclear consortium to promote a
modest nuclear capability could boost the morale and aspirations of some African states. Consequently, in view of
present realities the arms build-up is unlikely to ease, and
nuclearisation will become an important subject for debate on
the African scene.

Non-Military Aspects of Security in the Third World

The notion that military strength is the backbone of national
security is based on the assumption that other nations are
the greatest source of threat to security. It is, however,
becoming increasingly clear that threats to security may
arise more from man's interaction with nature than from

relationships between sovereign states. The problems of natural resources and international security have attracted the attention of scholars, politicians and military strategists alike. The energy crisis of the last decade has vividly demonstrated the delicate balance between availability of natural resources and international security. National security in its broadest sense cannot, therefore, be maintained unless certain basic human needs are met.

'The elimination of hunger is the most basic of human needs...While hunger rules peace cannot prevail'[5]. 'Global food insecurity and the associated instability in food prices have become a common source of political instability'[6]. Many governments have been threatened and even toppled because of food crises and famines. For example, it is believed that the centuries-old dynasty of Emperor Haile Sellassie in Ethiopia was toppled in 1974 not because of the Eritrean secessionist threat but as a result of many years of famine caused by a long drought. The riots that followed official attempts to raise food prices in Egypt in 1977 are said to have come closer to toppling the government than Israel's military power. Precarious food situations are evident in most Third World countries, especially in Africa and South East Asia, where most of the 450 million people hover between hunger and starvation.

The industrialised countries of the North have built up their wealthy economies on cheap sources of oil, a significant proportion of which is to be found in developing countries, particularly the Middle East. Disruptions and conflicts in major oil-producing countries pose major threats to national security as demonstrated by the Arab oil embargo in 1973. At that time, a western superpower contemplated military intervention in the Middle East to ensure the security of the oil lifeline to the western industrialised countries. Apart from the oil embargo, tension and conflicts between oil-producing countries, such as between Iran and Iraq, that result in senseless destruction of valuable oil resources, constitute a major threat to security both at the regional and international levels. The energy crisis has had traumatic and confusing effects on the economies of nations everywhere during the last decade. Non-oil-producing Third World countries dependent on raw material exports for their earnings have faced the brunt of inflation. Their meagre foreign exchange earnings have all been utilised to import oil, leaving little or nothing for essential goods and services, such as fertilisers, farm machinery and medical supplies badly needed.

There can be no lasting national security in many of the poorer Third World countries in the absence of sustainable economies whose objective should be to lead to self-reliance and creative partnership in the use of national resources. Major adjustments will need to be made at all levels - national, regional and global. At the national level there is a need to re-define 'development' and 'security', and thereby adopt and adapt strategies that can support an appropriate economic development goal. Regionally, Third World countries with common geographical backgrounds and national resources should realise that it is in their best interests to work out a formula of cooperation to explore and exploit their resources for the benefit of their people. Cooperation and interdependence for development can go a long way towards defusing potential conflicts resulting from territorial disputes. At the global level there should be serious rethinking of the relationship between the rich countries of the North and the poor nations of the South. There should be awareness of a growing number of problems which ultimately affect mankind as a whole regardless of where they originate. There can be no meaningful security if Third World countries are denied the opportunity of playing a role in the decision-making processes on such vital issues as food and agriculture, energy, commodity pricing and trade, monetary policies, aid and the transfer of technology.

References

1. S.M. Makinda, 'Conflict and the Superpowers in the Horn of Africa', in Third World Quarterly, 4 No.1, (1982).
2. F.S. Arkhurst, 'Africa: Militarization and the Arms Trade', Proceedings of the thirty-first Pugwash Conference (Banff, 1981) pp.85-87.
3. T. Adeniran, 'Nuclear proliferation and Black Africa: The coming crisis of choice', in Third World Quarterly, 3, No.4, (1981).
4. Lagos Plan of Action for the Economic Development of Africa: 1980-2000, International Institute for Labour Studies, (Geneva, 1981).
5. Willy Brandt, in North-South: A Programme for Survival, The Report of the Independent Commission on International Development Issues, (London: Pan Books, 1980).
6. R. Brown, Redefining National Security, Worldwatch, Paper No.14 (Oct. 1977).

Essam Galal

The strategic causes and implications of Third World conflicts, instabilities and divisions have been documented
almost beyond the point where further analysis can be expected to bring new significant clarifications or understanding
of the patterns.

Take the more dramatic models: Korea, Vietnam, Cuba, the
Middle East, South Africa, the Horn of Africa, Latin America,
Afghanistan and Iran. It is not easy to appreciate the many
circumstances, causes, motivations, mechanisms and forces
that reflected the strategic interests in the various stages
of evolution of the wide spectrum of Third World crises.

Even after allowing for dictates of the irreconcilable
superpower strategic differences, a significant divergence of
views remains in the assessment of the net strategic gains
and losses in almost every instance of interference by one
superpower or the other. Surprisingly, however, there is no
expectation, in the foreseeable future, for a declining
persistence of this pattern of 'non relation' between North
and South.

Areas of Direct Linkage

The direct friction areas reflect the proximity of established spheres of interest as, for example, in Korea and
Berlin. The stabilisation of these direct confrontation
points was a prerequisite for the control of the Cold War, as
well as an outcome of the establishment of nuclear parity. In
that sense, instances of direct friction, for example involving Poland, cannot be visualised under the current strategic
balance. On the other hand, an upset in nuclear parity,
whether real or perceived, if uncontrolled and unresolved may
change the rules of the game in these and other high contention areas. Currently we witness an indication of such a
potential shift, motivated by a perceived loss of parity in
nuclear forces in Europe. The posturing and counter-posturing

in Afghanistan, the Middle East, the Indian Ocean, the Horn of Africa, South Africa and Central America are not un-related.

Regional strategic games, in high contention areas, also have a feedback on percepts of nuclear balance. The Middle East and Afghanistan are obvious examples. But a dramatic deterioration in the Polish situation would be a more striking event, as would be a similar deterioration in Central America. This linkage with crises-prone areas of direct friction certainly necessitates a restrained approach in these areas. It also necessitates their insulation from the ongoing free-wheeling confrontations in the more periph-eral regions of competition.

Areas of High Contention

In areas of entrenched overlapping high-priority strategic interests, for example the Middle East or Central America, a resolution in favour of one opponent is unlikely to be con-ceded by the other opponent as a final solution.

In the light of the basic instabilities and contradictions endogenous in these areas, it is also unlikely to be accepted as a viable solution by significant local political and social forces. Nor can such a final solution be conceived by either side through direct military action.

The alternative process of heating up or cooling down the interactions does not always follow a consistent pattern reflecting an obvious strategic need of either of the stra-tegic opponents. This is characteristic of the complexity of the client relationship in these high contention areas, with overlapping high priority strategic interests, and the socio-political regional environment.

It is not surprising, therefore, to find an exceptional pattern of arms transfer and sales in these areas, recurrent military conflicts, intensive political and economic stresses and the apparent lack of logic or rationality in many moves by all sides. Arms supply, political-economic backing and subversive manoeuvering can hardly be expected to resolve the basic strategic or local contradictions.

The role of the rest of the world is excluded in these areas by the two superpowers. The absence of an inter-national, American or Soviet viable solution thus underlines the negative role the contention is playing for the regional and national security needs of the states in these areas, even if it advances an individual client's immediate goals.

As in the areas of direct linkage, here too there is little scope for trade-offs, either between the strategic contenders or between the conflicting clients, unless such trade-offs

are in the context of a global settlement, or as a way to opt
out of a non-profitable tie.

Regional and national securities of neighbouring states are
unlikely to be safeguarded in the context of a high-
contention clientship, whatever other, immediate advantages
may accrue from such relationships with dependent states. In
reality, the freedom of choice is limited not only for the
dependent client but, as has been repeatedly demonstrated,
also for the strategic sponsor. A sponsor is himself a client
in a certain sense, as for example the UK and France in 1956,
and the USSR in 1967 and 1973. The USA has internationally
demonstrated, if not nationally acknowledged, to be regularly
in this position vis-a-vis Israel.

A number of complicating factors further confuse the issue;
arms supply, economic dependence and political instabilities
are some examples.

The feedback in the strategic confrontation from these
high-contention areas is not often a stabilising influence.
The unpredictability of participants and events is in itself
a destabilising influence in a situation involving staggering
stakes. It is not surprising that the two intentional nuclear
alarms were connected with high contention areas - in Cuba
and the Middle East.

While things can get out of control in direct friction
areas, Berlin for example, the predictability of the forces
involved at least safeguard against miscalculations. In high
contention areas unpredictability and miscalculations are
built-in manifestations of the diversity of participants and
purposes.

Areas of Shifting Strategic Significance

In Afghanistan and Central America we have examples of areas
where one strategic opponent faces a regular challenge in an
'irregular situation'. In a sense both sides are handling the
challenge as a direct friction in a proximal sphere of
interest that justifies claims of exclusiveness and direct
military interference.

In reality these are not isolated instances. A clear pattern of encroaching direct confrontation is spreading from
the original central area in Europe to the periphery. The
race to establish bases in the Horn of Africa, the Gulf area,
the Indian Ocean and East Asia is coupled with forces of
rapid deployment and naval forces. In a sense, the differen-
tial grading of strategic linkage is gradually becoming less
defined.

The connection of this development with the up-grading of
the nuclear arms race is not easy to determine but impossible

to overlook. Witness the changing nuclear strategies, the increasing difficulty of sustaining nuclear technological parity, the disappearing differentiation between offensive and defensive tactical and strategic first-strike and retaliatory weapons. The complication arising from accountable and unaccountable weapon systems, short warning times and non-verifiable nuclear weapons is certainly adding to the declining sense of security and, more importantly, to the declining sense of the 'security' of peripheral interests and goals.

Conclusions

Some basic issues have to be faced before any semblance of order can be re-established:

a) Can nuclear forces achieve anything above central equal security, that is, can they serve any purpose other than mutual assured destruction?

b) Can any nuclear advantages, by either side, regain for nuclear weapons the duality of function that permitted the West to use it in the early phase of superiority to perpetuate or propagate asymmetries in peripheral global interests?

c) Even if technical realities indicate the irrationality of such duality of function, is it feasible to expect nuclear arms race dynamics to adjust to such reality through a commitment to achieve a qualitative and decisive nuclear superiority; through supplementing nuclear parity with decisive peripheral strategic advantages by 'conventional' (non-nuclear) means; through a two-track strategy involving the above, whatever the risks and unpredictability; through mutual agreement on the inevitability of dual arms control as well as peripheral strategic control of contention?

It has been amply demonstrated that arms control motivations do not emanate from the arms race dynamics, they originate from the political pressure of a different and wider constituency.

It must be clear by now that, apart from the overwhelming and alarming nature of the nuclear arms race, it is not the crux of the contentional relationship between the two camps, though it is the most threatening manifestation of this relationship. The crux of the contentional relationship is global interests and advantages in the sense of 'security'. 'Central base' security has been long achieved to the extent it is ever likely to be achieved in the nuclear era, through practical nuclear parity. There is a growing constituency to press for the translation of this reality into arms control.

These efforts are likely to be frustrated in the long run unless they are supplemented by a parallel track constituency that can enforce peripheral control of contentions through detente.

Strategic linkage is as fundamental a manifestation of the nature of the global confrontation as is the nuclear arms race. Only a dual control approach has any realistic chance of being effective.

Such a double track control would involve delinkage of arms sales and military aid; economic and technological co-operation; delinkage of regional conflicts and instabilities from strategic designs and manipulations; and an irreversible commitment to UN conflict-resolution and peace-keeping.

31   INTERNATIONAL COMMONS: SHARING OF
      INTERNATIONAL RESOURCES

Abdus Salam

Introduction

In 1945 Europe was devastated. Soon after, the United States took a remarkable initiative with the launching of the Marshall Plan to finance European recovery. Some $32 billion were generously provided, amounting, in the beginning, to a contribution of around 2.79 per cent of the Gross National Product of the USA. A magnificant act of magnanimity, it was not pure altruism, because the USA knew that by building up Europe, it was contributing to the future prosperity of the United States itself, through trade and commerce. It is un-fashionable nowadays to speak in these terms, but one may have called this act Keynesianism at its best, inspired by the earlier successes of the New Deal in the United States. One of the results of this – all too rare – act of economic wisdom was that during the next decades – the sixties and the seventies – after Western Europe was back on its feet, the prosperity of all countries – including the donor country – increased to levels unmatched in world history before.

The Marshall plan led to similar ideas for US and European aid to be extended to the developing countries. Here, of course, the needs were greater. Perhaps the sheer magnitude of the development tasks meant that the donors felt shy of doing as much as they had done for Western Europe. The aid packages were more meagre, and there was one other limitation. Those were the days of the hottest phases of the 'cold war'. The aid packages extended to the developing countries were not purely economic aid. The cold war had imposed a selectivity; the most generous economic help went hand in hand with military aid. The donors also wanted the sums allotted to help Western interests, including Western exports.

As mentioned earlier, the small quanta of aid funds were inadequate for the needs. Instead of the 2.79 per cent of the GNP of the Marshall Funds, this time the funds (contributed by OECD countries) never went beyond 0.5 per cent, falling to

263

around 0.4 per cent by the 1970s. Even though the Pearson Commission set up in 1969, recommended that the aid quantum be fixed at 0.7 per cent of the GNP of donor countries - a recommendation later endorsed by the Brandt Commission - this target has never been met except by a very few of the donors. Thus, the US share has fallen to less than 0.2 per cent, with a fall also in the shares of the UK, France, FRG, Japan and others. Furthermore, the Eastern bloc never joined the aid consortia; their aid (0.14 per cent of GDP) - is disbursed bilaterally. The OPEC countries started in the early 1970s with 1.18 per cent of their GDP, went up to nearly 3 per cent in 1975 and then declined (with a total of 7.7 billion dollars) to 1.4 per cent of GDP in 1981.

The precise aid percentages are not as important as the way in which the conceptual basis of such transfer of resources is presented. It is my belief, that unless an idea has a sound, generally accepted conceptual currency behind it, it does not win adherence.

Transfer of Resources to the Developing Countries

As emphasised earlier, in the case of the US help to Europe, Keynesian theories which inspired the New Deal, may have been at the back of the Marshall Plan. Involved in this is, firstly, the idea that in order that societies should be economically well-off, one needs a large base of economic activity. Secondly, the securing of this large base needs in its turn the prosperity of all sections of the society, leaving no pockets of poverty within the society. Thus, prosperity for all, an inter-dependence and a perceived mutuality of interests of all sections of the society, is the key idea, with the Marshall Plan extending the scope of the society covered, from the USA alone, to embrace also the continent of Western Europe. The Plan based itself on the view that the prosperity of the USA would increase if Europe became prosperous, and able to exchange goods and services with the USA.

What is needed today is the extension of these ideas to include the developing countries. In the words of Willy Brandt[1]:

The mutuality of interests can be spelled out clearly in the areas of energy, commodities and trade, food and agriculture, monetary solutions, inflation control ... and ground and space communications. The depletion of renewable and non-renewable resources, throughout the planet, the ecological and environmental problems, the exploitation of the oceans, not to forget the unbridled arms race, which

both drains resources and threatens mankind - all of these
also create problems which affect peace and will grow more
serious in the absence of a global vision. ... Whoever
wants a bigger slice of an international economic cake
cannot seriously want it to become smaller ... Most industrialised countries, even during the biggest boom in human
history, have not tried hard enough to get near the minimum
aid target to which most of them had solemnly agreed. That
record is not only disappointing but also reminds us that,
had the target been met, several developing countries would
now be importing more goods and services, thus mitigating
economic difficulties in the North.

To highlight the economic interdependence, particularly in
the context of producing job opportunities in the developed
countries, Brandt continues:

Perhaps one can illustrate part of the problem from the
development of some of the present industrialised countries
in the nineteenth and early twentieth centuries. A long and
assiduous learning process was necessary until it was generally accepted that higher wages for workers increased
purchasing power sufficiently to move the economy as a
whole. Industrialised countries now need to be interested
in the expansion of markets in the developing world. This
will decisively affect job opportunities in the 1980s and
1990s and the prospect of employment.

This sentiment was echoed also by J. Tinbergen[2]:

The second element of a new world employment policy consists of an increase in international income tranfers to
Third World countries in order to increase employment in
these countries. The resulting increase in welfare and purchasing power in these countries will lead to higher
imports from the industrialised countries. This then will
be an important stimulus to higher employment in the industrialised countries too.

The same statement comes from Masaki Nakajima:

In the past, of course, we had the Keynesian approach to
demand development. That, unfortunately, was geared to the
development of a single economy. Today, in order to solve a
massive problem like worldwide unemployment, I think we
have to expand the Keynesian approach so it can be applied
on a global scale. One possible effective area would be
toward a solution of North-South problems.

One may look upon aid as a compensation for the decline in commodity prices. Year after year we have seen that the weakness - economic as well as political - of the developing countries has meant that the commodity prices have not kept up with the increase in prices of industrial goods. As Michael Manley, the Ex-Prime Minister of Jamaica, once explained: 'In the 1950s, ten tons of sugar brought a Jamaican farmer a Ford tractor. In the 1970s, the same tractor costs 25 tons of sugar. Why? Is it that the Jamaican peasant is subsidising by a factor of 100 per cent the social security and welfare of Ford plant workers?' Not only have the commodity prices not kept up with industrial prices, they have also seen such ups and downs that for a developing country there is no possibility of any rational planning of its economic future. These vagaries of price cycles are attributed to the vagaries of stock exchanges. Speaking plainly, is this not a type of organised brigandage, which the rich societies have permitted their stock-market speculators to indulge in?

As is well known, this economic weakness of the developing countries has led them to the brink of bankruptcy. The facts in respect of the economic situation of the developing world are stark. The non-oil producing developing countries have suffered a deterioration in their export earnings of some 100 billion dollars annually between 1980 and 1983. At least 50 billion dollars of this are attributable to lower commodity prices. The pleas of the developing countries to have some consideration given to the commodity prices have consistently fallen on deaf ears. On the testimony of Helmut Schmidt[3] the FRG put forward a proposal for stabilising developing countries exports of raw materials for international discussion as early as 1978, but this proposal was not taken up at the agenda of any international conference. It is time, he says, to raise the proposal again. In the meanwhile the developing countries may be forgiven if they consider aid as part compensation for this decline of commodity prices.

One may look upon aid as part of the compensation for the 19th century exploitation of the riches of the developing countries - a transfer of resources from the ex-colonies, ex-empires which enriched some of the European countries and gave them economic prosperity.

One may also point to the disparity of distribution of world resources and the instability it creates. There is, at present, a tremendous disparity (Table 1) between the rich and the poor in the ultimate criteria of prosperity - the reserves of arable land, forest, coal and iron. Some among those who plough the exhausted soils of Asia and Africa may not for long be able to avert their hungry gaze from the virgin soils of some fortunate and empty corners of this globe. It is hard for them to comprehend that there can exist parts of the world where 15 to 20 per cent of agricultural land has to be 'banked' and the farmers paid not to cultivate it, in order that world prices of grain can be kept up. It is hard for them to believe that open spaces still exist in Canada, Australia, Siberia, and elsewhere, and that material rewards must be paid to those willing to pioneer their colonisation. There is one lesson from history we must not forget: a world as polarised as ours is unstable; it cannot endure this way forever.

Table 1 - The Disparity in Natural Resources
(per capita)

	Asia	North America	USSR	Europe	Oceania	World
Agricultural area (hectares)	0.54	2.63	2.8	0.55	30	1.4
Accessible forest area	0.20	2.07	5.4	0.33	1.6	0.96
Coal reserves (tonnes)	6.3	2000	90	960	812	365
Oil reserves (tonnes)	0.8	27.8	16.9	0.4		12.5
Iron ore reserves (tonnes)	16.4	389.6	502	59.8	25.0	102

(Estimates made by the United Nations in 1950 and quoted in World Population and Production, by W.S. Waytinsky and E.S. Waytinsky).

It was perhaps in recognition of this disparity and the instability which it breeds that Lyndon Johnson expressed himself thus:

Many of our most urgent problems do not spring from the cold war or even from the ambitions of adversaries. They are the ominous obstacles to man's effort to build a great world society, a place where every man can find a life free from hunger and disease. Those who live in the emerging

community of nations will ignore the problems of their
neighbours at the risk of their own prosperity ... There is
no simple solution to these problems. In the past there
would have been no solution at all. Today, the constantly
unfolding conquests of science give man the power over his
world and nature which brings the prospect of success within the purview of hope.

Lyndon Johnson had the courage, pursuing this line of
thinking, to allocate the funds which he saved from the
defence budget of the United States to his programmes against
poverty in that country. One wishes there were more men like
him who could declare that a similar consequence would follow
global disarmament, and that cuts in military expenditure
will mean more funds for global development.

Transfer of Resources

In 1969, the Nobel Laureate Linus Pauling, speaking at the
Nobel Symposium held in Stockholm, on the **Place of Value in
a World of Facts,** made a plea for international taxation
whereby the world distribution of wealth among the nations of
the world would be adjusted by levying a tax on the nations
with a higher GNP and providing the funds to those in the
developing countries. Pauling spoke of the transfer of
resources of the order of $200 billion per year, about 8 per
cent of the world's, then, total income which he thought was
the right figure for an international income tax. I remember
listening to Pauling and thinking to myself: this is a
totally Utopian proposal. No one took it very seriously at
the meeting. Pauling thought it was possible to formulate a
fundamental principle of morality, independent of revelation,
superstition, dogma and creed and acceptable by all human
beings in a scientific, rational way by analysing the facts
presented to us by the evidence of our senses. He believed
that a major fact of our lives was that there is so much
suffering in the world, much of it unnecessary and avoidable.
To minimise this suffering we must provide every person not
only with adequate food and shelter but also with education.
To produce the funds required, Pauling identified militarism as one of the major causes of human suffering. At that
time militarism cost the world over $250 billion per year; it
costs three times that much today. This amount of wealth
wasted on military conflicts each year is greater than the
total annual personal income per year of two-thirds of mankind. An elimination of these conflicts would enable these
funds to be spent on minimising the suffering from depri-
vation of the majority of mankind. Pauling suggested that

scientists and scholars should begin to formulate a practical
schedule of progress towards the goal of such transfers. Only
the intellectuals and scientists of the world could analyse
this problem in a sufficiently thorough way; they should take
political actions as individuals, as science advisers, as
educators, and by applying pressure on governments and
voters.

Since that time there was a formulation of what is called
the New International Economic Order which was adopted in
1974 by the 6th Special Session of the UN General Assembly.
Unfortunately, just after these proclamations were made, came
the increase in oil prices and rise of the monetary economics. Few people today remember the work which was done on
the international economic order. But, to my knowledge, not
much thinking went into emphasising Pauling's ideas of world
taxation. I have now come to believe that Pauling's idea was
one of the most important to emerge in the last decade. It
seems a great pity that it was not given a proper economic
formulation by the economists of the world either from the
rich or the poor nations, and that the concept of world
international taxation has not become common currency   to
replace aid commonly thought of as charity dependent on the
vagaries of national governments.

One of the few who have discussed this issue in recent
times is again Willy Brandt who said in 1980:

It is our conviction that we will have to face more
seriously the need for a transfer of funds ... with a certain degree of automaticity and predictability disconnected
from the uncertainties of national budgets and their underlying constraints. What is at stake are various possible
forms of international levies.

Why should it be unrealistic to entertain the idea of
imposing a suitable form of taxation on a sliding scale
according to countries' ability? There could be even a
small levy on international trade, or a heavier tax on arms
exports. Additional revenues could be raised on the international commons, such as sea-bed minerals[4].

International Commons

Brandt advanced the idea of **international commons** as a
prelude to full-fledged taxation. That certain resources of
the seas should be declared as belonging to mankind as a
whole is an idea which the developing countries have espoused
since 1968. A convention to regularise this has now been
embodied in a draft for a 'Law of the Sea' which the UN

Conference has recommended all UN states to adopt. This was at Montego Bay, after nine years of patient negotiations marked by a willingness to compromise as a necessary part of the search for a larger solution. One hundred and nineteen nations have so far found it possible to overcome their individual reservations and marginal disappointments and sign the instruments which make the Law of the Sea a new international fact of life, giving substance to a 'Sea Bed Authority' which will be sited in Jamaica.

The US government, however, has decided to stand out and vote against adoption of the recommendation. This decision was taken by the Republican administration in 1981, repudiating the skilful negotiations by the Carter administration to arrive at a compromise formula for the draft convention. After the USA had decided to renege on the Carter administration's pledges, Britain, too, has decided to stand out. Since these two nations represent a substantial slice of the world's economic power and technological capabilities, their decision to stand out against the recommendation can be a very serious wrecking manoeuvre.

In this context, the remarks by Jean Kirkpatrick, the US Ambassador to the UN, on 3 March 1983, are significant. Writing in a journal on Regulation published by the American Enterprise Institute, she complains: 'The UN regulatory initiatives extend quite literally from the depths of the oceans to the heavens, from the Law of the Sea Convention to an Agreement Covering the Activities of State on the Moon and other Celestial Bodies.' According to her, the USA balked at signing the Law of the Sea Convention which required that mining companies and other undersea ventures be licensed by a new international authority, pay what would amount to royalties to it and be bound by its decision on production and the like. In Mrs Kirkpatrick's view, the big push within the UN stems from a sort of class warfare, poor nations versus rich with regulation as a weapon for the redistribution of wealth. According to her, this type of thinking guides many of the participants in a UN political process:

There is a good deal of vote-trading, arm twisting, demagoguery, playing to the galleries and the result is that proposed agreements which are supposed to benefit all nations often turn out to be, above all, instruments for global redistribution of wealth and a new global paternalism. In a world body of 157 nations, the USA and the capitalist West are an outnumbered automatic minority. The UN agencies then are the scene of a struggle that we seem doomed to lose. The international bureaucracy functions as the new class to which power is to be transferred. Global socialism is expected and, from the point of view of many, is the desired result.

As her remarks clearly show, there is an urgent task for us, particularly the intellectuals from developing countries, to invest the idea of **international commons** with a theoretical basis so that it comes to be accepted by the populations of the developed countries.

Applications of Science and Technology

One way to make these ideas more acceptable may be to declare that these commons will be used only for global tasks. Among these urgent global tasks are the applications of science and technology to global problems. If, for example, these **international commons** were used for building up research and development capabilities, now sadly neglected, in the sphere of energy and the environment, there may be less oppostion than there has been.

To take the case of environmental tasks, everyone speaks of the degradation of the biosphere, of the disappearing rain forests and the imminent disappearance of large numbers of animal and plant species. The Report 'Year 2000' commissioned by President Carter states that in the next 17 years a quarter of a million plant and animal species will disappear because the developing countries will be forced to cut their forest wealth in order to make up for scarce fuel and to grow more food. One may ask in this context if it is not the concern of the environmental groups in the developed countries also to help to preserve this global heritage? Should they not come to the rescue of the developing countries? Should this type of global assistance not be a first charge on the **international commons**?

As a scientist, I would like the **international commons** used for research on global scientific problems. This was one of the suggestions made at the Vienna Conference on Science and Technology in 1979. The global problems suggested were research on: diseases of the developing countries; greening of deserts; weather modification, particularly for developing countries; alternative energy; productivity of marginal soils; earthquake predictions, and the like.

I should mention Masaki Nakajima's 'Dream for Mankind'. The following is his list of global super-infrastructure projects which may constitute elements of a 'Global New Deal'.

Outline of Projects for a Global New Deal

1. **Greening of deserts** (North African nations and Arab
                                states)
   Greening of the deserts in the Sinai and the Arabian peninsula.

2. **Collection station for solar heat**

   Erect a large-scale installation for the collection of
   solar energy in a remote part of the world. Total investment in land, pipelines, and accessory equipment would
   reach $20 to $50 trillion. Its total annual output would
   be equivalent to 200 billion barrels of oil.

3. **Electric power generation using sea currents**

   There are 12 promising areas along undeveloped ocean
   shores extending from the equator to the temperate zones.
   Maximum generating potential of one area, 35 million kW.
   Total for 12 areas about 200 million kW.

4. **Himalayan hydro-electric project** (India, China,
                                Bangladesh)

   Damming of the Sanpo River on the upper reaches of the
   Brahmaputra in the frontier area between China and the
   Indian province of Assam to make it flow into India
   through a tunnel across the Himalayas. Potential generating capacity 50 million kW maximum, 37 million kW on
   average. Annual generating capacity 240 billion to 330
   billion kWh.

5. **African central lake** (Central African nations)

   Control the flow of the Congo River by building a dam to
   create a vast lake in Congo and Chad regions of Central
   Africa to improve natural conditions in the area.

   The implementation by the richer nations of the super-
projects would lead to stimulation of constructive demand in
manufacturing industries, as well as technological incentives, in lieu of arms production. Hopefully, this would be
accompanied by an increase in GNP and employment opportunity
both in developed and developing countries. According to
Nakajima 'Now is the time for mankind to exert a bold, new
and brave, long-range vision, a vision which transcends

narrow short-term national interests ... As the prophet-King
Solomon said in the Bible: "Where there is no vision mankind
perishes".'
   It is the grand vision behind these projects which is so
commendatory and it is this global vision which alone will
solve our problems of the future.

Conclusions

I would like to see the ideas of world taxation brought into
the sphere of fundamental economic thinking. As a prelude to
this, I would like to see the ideas of **international
commons** and the sharing of global resources (for example,
the riches of the seas and of the Antarctic) taken up
vigorously on a theoretical, as well as at a political level
- for example, at the Summit Conference.
   Personally, I would like to see these **commons** expended
on scientific research on global problems in the first
instance. I would like to see much greater emphasis given to
global programmes like International Geophysical or Bio-
spherical Programmes which, at the moment, organisations like
ICSU undertake on a meagre budget with contributions from the
not too affluent UN bodies like UNESCO. As an example of
joint scientific projects, there are the programmes of col-
laborative research for European nations like the fusion
research programme and laboratory at Culham in the UK or the
European Molecular Biology programme and laboratory at
Heidelberg. On the other hand, there are very few global
laboratories for global problems research. These should be
the first charge on the **international commons**.

References

1. Willy Brandt, 'North-South: A Programme for Survival'
   Report of the Independent Commission on International
   Development Issues, (London: Pan Books, 1980).
2. J. Tinbergen et al, 'A new world employment plan',
   Development and Peace, 2, (Spring 1981) pp. 10-20.
3. Helmut Schmidt, The Economist, 26 February 1983.
4. Willy Brandt, op. cit.

APPENDIX A

Statement from the Pugwash Council on the 33rd Pugwash Conference

'AVOIDING NUCLEAR AND OTHER WARS AND REVERSING THE ARMS RACE'

The 33rd Pugwash Conference on Science and World Affairs met in Venice, Italy, on 26-31 August 1983. It was attended by 152 scientists and scholars from 34 countries and seven international organisations.

The Conference was organised by the Italian Pugwash Group with the generous support of the City of Venice, to whom we express our thanks and appreciation. A warm message of greetings was received from President Sandro Pertini.

The meeting took place in a period of exceptional peril in international affairs. Superpower relations are strained, regional armed conflicts are ripping the fabric of human society in several parts of the Third World, and both conventional and nuclear arms races threaten to career completely out of control. Not since the Pugwash Conferences began in 1957 has the world been more in need of a renewed commitment to international cooperation in the pursuit of peace.

The following statement on the topics treated at the Conference was prepared by the Pugwash Council and should not be interpreted as a consensus of all the Conference participants, among whom a wide range of views was represented.

Strategic and Intermediate-Range Nuclear Forces

The lack of progress in both sets of USA-USSR arms-control negotiations in Geneva - the Strategic Arms Reduction Talks (START) and the Intermediate Range/European Nuclear Forces (INF/ENF) talks - is deplorable. It is especially urgent that the deadlock in the INF/ENF talks be broken before December, when otherwise a new set of NATO missile deployments is scheduled to begin. These deployments and the likely responses by the Soviet Union would increase tensions and reduce crisis stability, and they might well lead to the complete collapse of nuclear arms-control negotiations covering intercontinental as well as intermediate-range systems.

275

Neither side needs more nuclear missiles militarily; it is rather political factors that make the continuing action-reaction syndrome in nuclear deployments so difficult to stop. The pursuit of 'parity' in nuclear forces – a seductive concept politically – is in fact part of the problem, not of the solution. 'Sufficiency' of nuclear deterrent capability is the correct criterion, and in these terms the forces of both the USA and the USSR are already much more than enough.

This being the case, both sides can afford to try **restraint** as a means of avoiding further needless competition in nuclear forces. If no INF/ENF agreement is reached by December, NATO could and should defer its deployments to allow more time both for negotiations and for national initiatives. And the Soviet Union could increase the chance of such NATO restraint (as well as increasing the chance of an early agreement) by **beginning** before December to reduce the number of SS-20s within range of Western Europe.

President Andropov's clarification in August 1983 that the Soviet Union is prepared, in the context of an INF/ENF agreement, to dismantle (rather than merely move) a number of SS-20 missiles now within range of Western Europe is a step towards a solution. A successful prescription for a formal agreement will also have to account somehow – at least implicitly – for the French and British nuclear systems (which the USA has so far opposed); and many of us think reaching an agreement by December will also require separating out at least temporarily the complex matter of nuclear-capable aircraft (which the USSR has so far opposed) while negotiating an interim ceiling on missiles. For purposes of reaching a **lasting** agreement, it seems clear that intermediate-range nuclear forces – missiles and aircraft alike – eventually will have to be considered in the same overall negotiating framework with intercontinental nuclear forces.

Effort is urgently required to deflect some other dangerous trends in strategic forces. Various characteristics of strategic cruise missiles, which make verification very difficult, suggest that large-scale deployments in different basing modes of such systems would seriously jeopardise future prospects to limit nuclear armaments. Therefore, it is important and urgent to limit by agreement the development and deployment of such systems.

Concerns about the feasibility of a first strike by either side are contributing to interest in 'pre-programmed response' and 'launch-on-warning', which is troubling. Such strategies significantly increase the chance of accidental war, and they are completely unnecessary as long as a first strike remains as implausible as is the case today. Preserving the implausibility of a first strike is crucial, and doing so requires restraint on deploying systems with characteristics that could facilitate a first strike capability.

Both anti-ballistic missile (ABM) and anti-satellite (ASAT) technologies could be dangerous in this respect, although the 'leakproof' ABM system advocated by President Reagan is simply unrealistic. The existing ABM Treaty should not be weakened, and a treaty should be sought banning the use of force in and from space. The Soviet   proposal of 22 August 1983 is a useful step towards the latter goal. Complementing efforts to prevent the weaponisation of space, work should continue on both sides towards   a mutual and verifiable freeze on nuclear forces of all kinds – which of course would be a logical first step towards reductions.

European Security

European security is imperilled not only by prospective deployments of additional intermediate-range nuclear forces in and around that region but also by the large number of nuclear weapons already there. A start should be made on reducing the existing dangers by agreeing to remove all nuclear weapons from a strip extending 150 kilometres or more on each side of the NATO/WTO boundary. Nuclear-free zones embracing the entirety of various combinations of countries in northern, central and southern Europe raise more complex issues but very much deserve further study.

NATO should give the most serious consideration to joining the Soviet Union in its pledge of no-first-use of nuclear weapons. This and other 'denuclearisation' proposals naturally direct attention to the question of whether the balance of conventional forces alone can be relied upon to prevent armed conflict in the region. A positive conclusion would be made easier by adjustments to the conventional forces on each side, increasing their defensive capabilities while minimising their offensive ones. It may be hoped that a favourable climate for changes of this nature would be among the benefits of reaching an agreement soon in the Mutual Force Reduction (MFR) negotiations in Vienna.

Security in the Mediterranean and Middle East

A nuclear weapon-free zone in the Middle East would be difficult to establish, but negotiations to that end combined with a drive to secure the full implementation of the Non-Proliferation Treaty (NPT) regime in the region and the application of the relevant safeguards would help to halt the still mounting distrust.

The stability and peace of the whole Mediterranean is now threatened by a combination of inter-state rivalries, local arms races, great-power naval deployments, environmental problems, and potential competition for the resources of the sea bed. For the time being there is a real opportunity to anticipate acute crises by instituting bilateral and multi-lateral discussions between the states of the region on these matters; successes with the simpler issues could provide a basis for tackling the more intractable regional security problems and prevent the compartmentalisation of the Mediter-ranean into conflicting zones of interest. Small commissions, set up to assist negotiations, might help in finding solu-tions for some of the most serious present conflicts in the area.

Arms Race, Arms Transfers and Disarmament

The sheer magnitude of armaments and the arms race consti-tutes a global problem. During the past four years military spending has shown an upward trend, faster than in the pre-vious four years, in spite of the deterioration of the world economy. Military outlays, by definition, and particularly with respect to modern mass-destruction weapons, represent in economic and social terms the extreme case of waste.

Excessive military spending is particularly damaging for less developed countries because they have to rely on imports of their advanced military equipment, and thereby waste their scarce domestic resources so desperately needed for other purposes. Ample data exist to show that military expenditures contribute to inflation, do not lead to productive invest-ment, draw on scarce human and natural resources, hinder economic development and international economic cooperation, contribute to unemployment and have very little spin-off to the civilian sector.

Most of the harmful consequences of military expenditure also apply to arms transfers. Many economic and political benefits are commonly ascribed to selling arms, such as lowering per unit costs, improving balance of payments and reducing unemployment as well as gaining political leverage. In fact, on closer observation they simply do not hold up.

The psychological effects of the arms race are of extreme importance. The need to arm is felt because of mistrust in one's neighbour. The neighbour feels the same and feels jus-tified in his mistrust by the (although allegedly defensive) armament efforts he observes across the border. At all times demagogues have tried to unite their own followers by con-vincing them that they were threatened by a common enemy. The ultimate solution of the problem of war must be that humanity recognises that in our time **all** of humanity belongs to **one** group, and that there is only one common enemy: our own irrationality which prevents us from tackling jointly the truly global problems which mankind faces, and first among them the prevention of nuclear war.

Common security is based on mutual trust and openness rather than on fear and instilling fear. Towards this end the concept of confidence-building measures needs to be expanded from the narrow military measures to which they have been confined, so that it includes anything which contributes to cooperation and collaboration. International attention should be turned to political measures of building confidence - mutual information, openness, as well as increased scientific, cultural and trade exchanges. Ongoing efforts such as the UN approved system for voluntary reporting on military expenditures and general international cooperation should be supported and encouraged.

Third World Security

Since, historically, conflicts have always been a dominant feature of the process of development, it is essential to work towards the establishment of an environment supportive of development with a minimum of violence, and free of externally induced security problems and oppressive and repressive internal systems. The perception of Third World countries of what their own security is and what is threatening it should always be taken into account.

A number of conflicts, armed and violent, have taken and are taking place in the Third World. Even if at the beginning many have an essentially internal nature, they tend often to acquire an international dimension. Superpowers and other external powers tend to get involved directly or indirectly through allies and proxies. This involvement usually results in the escalation of such conflicts, and might complicate their solutions. Superpowers do not look at Third World conflicts per se, but essentially from the angle of their bilateral global strategic balance of power.

There is thus a need to insulate and isolate local conflicts from outside interferences. International arrangements might be needed for this purpose; for example, guidelines to restrict the deployment of troops beyond the NATO and WTO areas, to prevent the dispatch of military advisers, and to control arms sales and transfers.

Such guidelines could be linked with other international instruments attempting to better regulate international relations. Compliance with the guidelines could be monitored by an independent agency which could also analyse ongoing or latent armed conflicts, with a view to finding non-violent equitable solutions.

Although several Third World countries still maintain bilateral strategic military linkages with major powers, there has been a growing tendency among Third World countries to band themselves together in a non-aligned movement both on global and regional levels. A strong non-aligned Third World could exercise effective influence in global issues, also act as a bridge between the superpower blocs, and finally contribute to the emergence of a new international security system.

The current trend for regional cooperation within the general framework of non-alignment is one of the most encouraging developments and holds great promise for the resolution of conflicts among neighbours and enhancing the security of concerned states. This cooperation should be further encouraged, perhaps through the establishment of regional security commissions.

Several non-nuclear weapon states have acquired special status. Amongst an increasing number of threshold states, one has conducted a 'peaceful' nuclear explosion and two more states may be in possession of nuclear weapons. These countries seem to have crossed the threshold and may be considered as 'undeclared' nuclear weapon states. The emergence of these states in Africa, the Middle East and South Asia has made the issue of proliferation far more complex. Disguised proliferation has occurred in the most sensitive regions of the South and with the acquiescence of certain countries of the North. The disguised nature of proliferation and the acquiescence of some of the nuclear-weapon states are ill-concealed secrets. These developments are likely to make the resolution of local conflicts much more difficult.

The nuclear-free zone concept is an attractive complement to the NPT. Countries participating in such zones undertake neither to manufacture nuclear weapons nor to allow stationing of nuclear weapons of others on their territories. Latin America is the only region where such a zone has so far been partially implemented apart from Antarctica, outer space and the sea bed. Emergence of such zones in other sensitive areas would be desirable.

*   *   *   *

The United Nations has an important part to play in many of the problems discussed above, and their efforts should receive maximum support. The International Year of Peace declared by the United Nations for 1986 and the World Disarmament Campaign are noteworthy examples.

APPENDIX B

The Pugwash Conferences on Science and World Affairs

Martin Kaplan

The Pugwash Conferences on Science and World Affairs resulted from the Bertrand Russell - Albert Einstein Manifesto of 1955 calling upon scientists of all political persuasions to gather in conference and devise ways to avoid the danger of nuclear war. Other signatories of the Manifesto were Max Born of the Federal Republic of Germany; Frederic Joliot-Curie of France; Hideki Yukawa of Japan; Leopold Infeld of Poland; Cecil Powell and Joseph Rotblat of the United Kingdom; Percy Bridgman, Herman Muller and Linus Pauling of the United States of America. These Conferences - named from the place in Nova Scotia where the first Conference was held in 1957 - have attracted the most respected representatives of the scientific communities, mainly from the East and the West but also from the North and South, and have created an important bridge between scientists of divergent political viewpoints.

Since 1957 more than 100 Pugwash Conferences, Symposia and Workshops, with the participation of nearly two thousand natural scientists, scholars and experts in various fields from all over the world, have been held in closed meetings in an atmosphere of free and informal discussions, without publicity and official responsibilities. The major findings have been transmitted to high levels of governments, the United Nations, and leaders of the world scientific community, as well as to the public.

The Pugwash meetings have also made important contributions towards establishing cooperative links between scientists from the industrialised and developing countries, aimed at removing the threats to peace which are a consequence of the growing gap between the affluent and the needy portions of the world, and the arms trade and militarism which affect many of these countries.

Discussions in Pugwash meetings have often had an important influence on the negotiation of arms control agreements, such as the Nuclear Test Ban Treaty of 1963; the Nuclear Non-

Proliferation Treaty of 1970; the Convention on the Prohibition of the Development, Production and Stockpiling of Bacteriological (Biological) and Toxin Weapons and on their Destruction of 1972; and the Anti-Ballistic Missile (ABM) Agreement of 1972. Pugwash exchanges have also helped to lay the groundwork for the Strategic Arms Limitation Talks (SALT), the Conference on Security and Cooperation in Europe (CSCE), and the Mutual Force Reduction (MFR) negotiations.

By convening private meetings of influential scientists from opposing sides to discuss contentious issues and possible means for their peaceful resolution, Pugwash has exercised an influence on the prevention of armed conflicts, or on bringing them to an end, during the Cuban missile crisis, the civil war in Nigeria, and the Vietnam War. It has tried to maintain channels of direct communication between scientists from Israel and Arab countries.

Recent meetings have been particularly concerned with the problem of nuclear forces in Europe and their relation to general strategic forces and with obstacles in arriving at a convention banning chemical weapons. A series of workshops on European nuclear forces, which started in January 1980, has had an impact on official policies with regard to these weapons, but the extent of this influence is hard to measure. Also, it has helped to create a better informed public on the various issues. This has involved, for example, the implications of and arguments for a no-first-use policy, unilateral steps for a moratorium on deployment and deep cuts with respect to intermediate range nuclear weapons, and the removal of battlefield nuclear weapons. In the chemical weapons field particular attention has been given to problems of verification of destruction of stockpiles and of non-production of weapons, and to the investigation of allegations of use.

Although the main thrust of the effort is aimed at avoiding nuclear war, by influencing favourably the formulation of nuclear and other military policy in the upper echelons of governments and alliances, Pugwash also recognises the need to reach other population groups in seeking support for its goals. An example of this is the 1982 Pugwash Declaration on the Dangers of Nuclear War issued in Warsaw on the occasion of the 25th anniversary of Pugwash. It was signed by 111 Nobel Laureates in the natural sciences. It outlines specific steps and calls upon all members of the world's scientific community, all governments and all peoples to help remove the threat of nuclear war. This Declaration was one of the first public statements by a large group of influential scientists calling for a 'stand-still freeze' on nuclear arsenals and a stop to the development of new weapon technologies. Pugwash has long stood for 'no use' of nuclear weapons in conflicts under any circumstances, and for large cuts in existing nuclear arsenals leading to comprehensive nuclear disarmament.

* * *

The governing body of Pugwash is the Council with the following composition: Chairman: Professor Maciej Nalecz (Poland). Members: Academician Angel Balevski (Bulgaria), Mr Etienne Bauer (France), Professor Francesco Calogero (Italy), Professor Bernard Feld (USA), Mr Shalheveth Freier (Israel), Professor Jacques Freymond (Switzerland), Dr Essam Galal (Egypt), Professor Hellmut Glubrecht (FRG), Professor Lameck Goma (Zambia), Professor John Holdren (USA), Professor Eberhard Leibnitz (GDR), Professor Patricia Lindop (UK), Academician Moisei Markov (USSR), Professor Goku Menon (India), Professor Jorma Miettinen (Finland), Academician Oleg Reutov (USSR), Dr Marcel Roche (Venezuela), Professor Joseph Rotblat (UK), Professor Jack Ruina (USA), Dr Herbert Scoville, Jr (USA), Professor Toshiyuki Toyoda (Japan), Professor Vladimir Trukhanovsky (USSR), Dr Miguel Wionczek (Mexico).

Professor Dorothy Hodgkin is President of Pugwash and Dr Martin Kaplan is Secretary-General.

INDEX